FRONTIER LIVING

The end of General Forbes's road on the bank of the Monongahela
opposite Pittsburgh about 1800, an early "Gateway to the West."
Here travelers to the town crossed the river on a flatboat ferry.
Those going on west, down the Ohio, paused to build or buy a loopholed
ark for the hazardous journey, or to seek passage as payment for
their labor on the craft of a prosperous family.

EDWIN
TUNIS

FRONTIER LIVING

WRITTEN AND ILLUSTRATED BY EDWIN TUNIS

Thomas Y. Crowell Company
NEW YORK

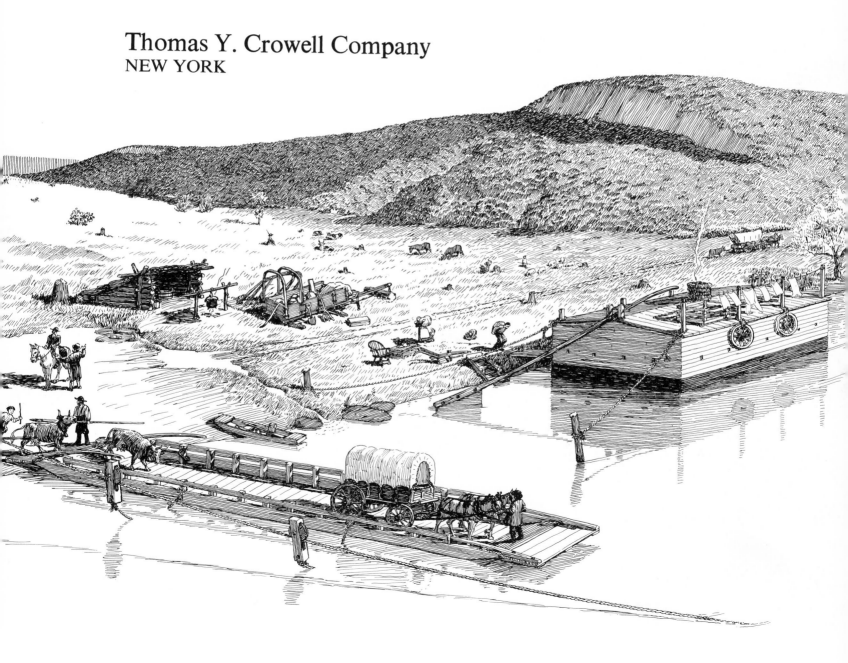

Books by Edwin Tunis

CHIPMUNKS ON THE DOORSTEP

COLONIAL CRAFTSMEN

COLONIAL LIVING

FRONTIER LIVING

INDIANS

OARS, SAILS AND STEAM

SHAW'S FORTUNE

THE TAVERN AT THE FERRY

WEAPONS

WHEELS

THE YOUNG UNITED STATES

 Published in Canada by Fitzhenry & Whiteside Limited, Toronto.

Manufactured in the United States of America

L.C. Card 75-29639
ISBN 0-690-01064-8

The first McCormick reaper, 1831

ACKNOWLEDGMENTS

I AM GRATEFUL to many who know more about phases of this subject than I know and who have provided access to information I couldn't otherwise have reached. Listing them is but a lame return for their kindnesses: Miss Elizabeth Baer, Librarian, Evergreen House Foundation; Mr. Milton Bayne; Mr. John G. Brown; Mrs. Elmer Clusman; Miss Ida M. Cohen, The New York State Library; Miss Judith Cousins, The Index of American Design; Mr. John Cummings, formerly curator of The Bucks County Historical Society Museum; Dr. David Ennis, Regional Vice President, The Canal Society of New York State; Mr. Perry W. Fuller; Mr. W. Edwin Gledhill, Museum Director of The Santa Barbara Historical Society; Mr. George E. Hardy, III; Mr. Joseph Kindig, III; Miss Lillie Kissac, Museum of the City of New York; Dr. John Smylie Morrell; Mrs. Blanche Reigle, Curator, Pennsylvania Farm Museum; Dr. Frank M. Setzler, Head Curator of Anthropology, The Smithsonian Institution; Mr. Robert P. Turner, The Historical Society of York County, Pennsylvania; Mr. Arthur Woodward, formerly of The Los Angeles County Museum.

To Abelard-Schuman Limited, for their kind permission to quote on pages 45 and 58 from *Pioneer Life in Kentucky* by Dr. Daniel Drake, copyright, 1948.

To Robert M. McBride Company, for their kind permission to quote the verse on page 74 from *Early American Inns and Taverns* by Elise Lathrop.

To Dr. R. L. Cassell, for his interest and his detailed replies to a barrage of questions, special thanks and an apology for moving his ancestral home across the Ohio River.

As always, I thank Lib, my wife, for her constructively critical eye and her patience and ingenuity in reducing a raddled manuscript to intelligibility.

Long Last   E.T.
December 26, 1960

CONTENTS

Acknowledgments   6

Foreword   10

1. THE DEEPWATER FRONTIER   13

North America in 1725   14

2. THE PIEDMONT   15

The Flintlock Rifle   16

People in the Woods   17

Invasion   18

The Log Cabin   20

Household Articles   24

Food   25

Clothes   28

Hunting   30

Indians   32

Forts   32

Medicine and Witchcraft   33

Justice   34

Childhood and Sports   34

Pack Trains   35

3. THE SOUTHERN VALLEYS   39

The Seven Years' War   41

4. THE GREAT SALIENT   42

The Revolutionary War   44

The Garden of Eden   44

The People   44

Daily Life in the Clearings   46

Linen   46

Wool   47

Weaving, Dyeing, and Fulling   47

Housekeeping   48

Sweet'nin'   50

Outdoor Work   51

Beef Cattle   52

Farming   52

Villages and Trades   54

Saturday   56

Sunday   57

School   57

Parties   58

The Land Ordinances, 1785–1790   60

5. ROAD AND RIVER   61

The Travelers   62

The Floating Forts 62

Navigation 63

Trade on the Rivers 64

Pirates 65

Keelboats 65

Upstream Navigation 66

The Rivermen 67

Other Boats 67

Indian Treaties and Louisiana, 1795–1803 68

The Louisiana Purchase 68

6. THE OLD NORTHWEST 69

Public Land 69

The National Road 70

The Freight Wagons 71

The Coach Lines 72

Inns 73

Farms 74

The Barn 76

Corn 77

Scythe and Cradle 77

Water 78

Housekeeping 79

Clothes 81

People 82

Religion 83

Towns 84

Money 85

Utopias 86

The "Permanent" Indian Frontier 87

7. THE COTTON FRONTIER 88

8. SHRINKING DISTANCES 90

Steam Navigation 90

The Erie Canal 91

The Pennsylvania System 93

Early Railroads 94

Southwestern Boundaries 96

9. BEYOND THE MISSISSIPPI 97

Missouri 97

Texas 98

The Black Hawk War 99

The Iowa Squatters 100

Buck and Bright 100

The Claims Clubs 101

10. CARAVANS TO SANTA FE 103

The Jump-Off 103

Guns 104

The Trail 105

Santa Fe and the Ranchos 105

Trading 107

11. THE FUR TRADE AND THE
MOUNTAIN MEN 109

The Beaver and the "Company" 110

The Company Posts 111

The Rendezvous 112

12. THE BITTER ROAD TO
 OREGON 114

   The Missionaries 114

   Organization of the Wagon Train 115

   The Oregon Trail 116

   The Order of the Day 118

   The Buffalo 119

   On the Trail 120

   The Pathfinder of the West 120

13. THE HARRIED SAINTS 121

   The Prophet 121

   Exodus 122

   The Promised Land 123

14. ALTA CALIFORNIA 124

   Missions, Presidios, and Pueblos 124

   Gay Prosperity 125

   The Ranchos and Trade 127

   Gringo Settlers 128

   Boundaries and "Manifest Destiny" 129

15. EL DORADO 131

   The Rush of the Argonauts 131

   The Diggings 133

   The Roaring Camps 134

   Washoe and Pike's Peak 135

16. TWO THOUSAND MILES 137

   Stages in California 137

   Freight and Mail 138

   The Overland Mail 139

   The Concord Coach 140

   The Pony Express 141

   The Civil War and the West 142

   Thirty Miles an Hour 142

   Laying the Rails 142

   The Golden Spike 143

   The Clearing of the Plains 144

17. THE COW HUNT AND THE
 COWHAND 145

   The Longhorns 145

   The Cow Hunt 146

   Horses 147

   Cowhands 148

   Saddles and Equipment 150

   "Bleeding Kansas" and Homesteading 153

18. THE SODBUSTERS AND THE
 CATTLE DRIVES 154

   Soddies 154

   Water 155

   The Cattle Trails 157

   The Long Drive 157

   Sheep 159

   Barbed Wire 159

19. THE RUN 161

   Index 163

FOREWORD

AT FIRST GLANCE it would appear that the way to write this account would be territory by territory, state by state, but we haven't enough book for that and it would be repetitive; so it seems better to let time, section, and circumstance point the way. We shall talk about the conditions of daily living, changing materially as men and women moved the frontier westward, met new conditions, and at the same time, settled new bases behind it and gradually improved communication with them and with the old ones. In a sense there were two frontiers: the harsh edge that moved ahead of law, and the still primitive consolidation behind that edge, where men set about apportioning land and forcing it to yield.

Circumstance is an integral part of this account. The other two factors, time and section, also get into the text, but there is an effort to keep them sorted by inserting maps, along with scraps of history, between some of the chapters and even within some of them. Those who are wholly familiar with American history may pass these by or merely glance at them critically.

We all know that the hardy cowhand, presented in colors that would have astonished him, that have in fact *colored* his modern successor, is the world-wide symbol of the American frontier. Accepting his pre-eminence, many of us tacitly assume that that frontier began at Dodge City, Kansas. It actually started quite a long way east of the cow country, and there was a lot more to frontier living than running gun fights ending in necktie parties. This book tries to restore proportions, but the author confesses to presenting conditions east of the Mississippi River in rather more detail than those west of it. This may be excused, he hopes, by the fact that nearly every phase of the far West has been dealt with in popular literature, sometimes with honesty and accuracy, while the forest frontier, with a very few notable exceptions, has been bypassed since James Fenimore Cooper stopped romancing about it.

FRONTIER LIVING

1

THE DEEPWATER FRONTIER

IN 1607 THE WHOLE of the English frontier in North America was Jamestown Island in Virginia. Its colonists had pushed eighty miles up the James River by 1620 and in so doing created a pattern that persisted along the coast through the eighteenth century: The base colony was always on or near a river mouth and its inland extensions stuck close to navigable water. Wide spaces between rivers remained uninhabited for years.

Human curiosity to see what is beyond the next hill sent some individuals over the Appalachians in the seventeenth century, but the mountains long remained the great barrier; in fact, that's what the coastal colonists called them. The Indians on their western slopes felt no pressure from the white men before 1700, so the few explorers and traders went among them in reasonable safety, and a number of trading posts operated in the Ohio valley. The traders brought in wonders in the way of mirrors and beads and, alas, rum, for which the natives gladly exchanged valuable furs.

The coast settlements remained isolated pockets until the middle of the eighteenth century. Separately, they looked to England, not to one another. Such communication as existed between them was by water; there were no roads longer than a few miles. Each colony thought of itself as English and made a reasonably successful stab at reproducing English life in the new country, just as Englishmen were doing elsewhere around the world. While some colonies sought immigrants in the mother country, only William Penn invited all comers of any nation. The land ownership and religious freedom he offered were bait enough for the Palatine Germans and the Scotch-Irish. They poured in, unfettered by any sentimental attachment to England. Wherever they landed they tended to head inland, the first trickle of the tide of white men that ran inexorably across the continent for two centuries, flowing through gaps and around obstacles, seeping always westward wherever resistance weakened a little.

Labels on map:
Duluth • Lake Superior • Quebec
St. Esprit • Sault St. Marie
N E W   F R A N C E
Michilimackinac • Montreal
Fort Macinac • Lake Huron
St. Francis Xavier • Lake Michigan
Fort des Miamis • Detroit • Lake Ontario • Iroquois • New York • Albany • Massachusetts • N.H. • Boston • Salem
Lake Erie • Pennsylvania • Hartford • Conn. • Providence
Fort Miami • Lancaster • Philadelphia • New Jersey • New York
Fort St. Louis • (F R E N C H) • Ohio River • THE GREAT BARRIER • Maryland • Del.
Crevecoeur • Annapolis
Missouri River • Cahokia • Virginia • Williamsburg • Norfolk
L O U I S I A N A • Kaskaskia • Mississippi River • North Carolina • Edenton
U N E X P L O R E D • Cherokee • New Bern
(F R E N C H) • South Carolina
TEXAS • (SPAIN) • Sabine R. • Natchez • Charleston
New Orleans • Mobile • Biloxi • Pensacola • F L O R I D A (S P A N I S H) • St. Augustine

NORTH AMERICA IN 1725

The English colonies occupied only a small part of the continent. Their boundaries were vague and many of them overlapped. The Appalachian Range was a barrier to settlement, but most of the colonies presumed indefinite extension of their boundaries beyond it. The English claims extended from Newfoundland to some unmarked line between the Carolinas and Florida. The spread of inland settlement was stopped north of Albany by the grim Iroquois Indians, and the presence of the Cherokees in the western Carolinas discouraged expansion to the south.

France controlled the major part of known and habitable North America in two great tracts: New France (Canada) included the Great Lakes and extended to Labrador; Louisiana was the entire Mississippi Basin, a vast inverted triangle with its apex at New Orleans and its base north of the headwaters of the Missouri River. The east side of the triangle was the ridge of the Appalachian Mountains; its west side was the Rockies. There were not more than enough French settlers in both areas together to populate one respectable colony. The French weren't interested in settlement; they wanted space for trapping.

Mexico, or New Spain, as it was called, reached eastward almost to New Orleans. From there its edge ran northwest approximately to the Grand Canyon, then west in a vague arc to the dent in the California coast where Los Angeles is now. There were Spanish missions and military posts north of the Rio Grande, but the population was sparse. The same was true of Spanish Florida

Between the eastern edge of the Great Plains and the Pacific, a huge area was completely unexplored.

A clearing in the "fur back"

2

THE PIEDMONT

T HE FIRST shipload of Palatine Germans reached Philadelphia in 1710 and they continued to arrive even after the Revolutionary War. We wrongly and confusingly call these people "Pennsylvania Dutch." They preferred to cling to their own language and ways; to run their own affairs and to remain aloof from those of the colony. They bought cheap land beyond the ring of Quaker farms, and with encouragement from the English, pushed westward into unsettled country. From the colony's viewpoint the Germans made a good buffer against the Indians; nobody noticed until too late that they had the best farm land in Pennsylvania. By 1720 German farms and villages almost reached the Susquehanna River. This was the heart of the Piedmont, the great plateau between the Appalachians and the Atlantic Ocean.

The earlier Swedish settlers along the Delaware built the first log dwellings on this side of the water. The Germans certainly saw those houses

and noted how perfectly they suited a country that was all trees, but whether the idea was new to them or whether they remembered such homes in the Black Forest is uncertain. Either way, they built neat log cabins for themselves and passed the method on to others who built them less carefully as far west in America as trees grew.

For neighbors the Germans around Lancaster had the people usually called Scotch-Irish, which isn't a very accurate name. They were not Irish; they had visited in Ireland only a hundred years. They were Scots and fighters. When James I confiscated most of Ulster in 1607, these people had moved over from the Scottish Border and run the native Irish into the hills. But after a century things were bad in Ulster; so, bringing their cross-grained independence along, thousands of them came to America where, it was said, land could be had for the taking. They came to nearly all of the Colonies, but most of them came to Pennsylvania. Their influx started in 1710 and they at once set

15

about acquiring the "free" land. They had no money, and they had no patience with such nonsense as recorded titles. The land was there; only heathen Indians were using it. So the white men took it and some of them were able to keep it. Many later arrivals, forewarned, skipped the official nosiness of Philadelphia and came in the back door by way of the Chesapeake Bay and the Susquehanna River. Ten thousand landed in a single year and there came a time when one sixth of the colonial population were Scots.

They were bad farmers. Many of them had been spinners and weavers in Ireland, and of those who settled permanently some may have continued these trades around Lancaster, but most of them became hunters and trappers. They followed the game west as it thinned out locally, drawing with them a few young Germans, who lost touch with their church groups and whose children, like those of the Scots, grew up illiterate but self-reliant in the wilderness.

THE FLINTLOCK RIFLE

Hunting required firearms. The guns the Scots brought with them were smoothbore muskets, wildly inaccurate. The Germans had the Jaeger rifle, but it was very heavy and its bullet fitted its bore so tightly that the ball had to be forced down the barrel by hammering on the ramrod with a mallet! Such a gun wasn't much good in the American wilderness. The hunters persuaded the gunsmiths of Lancaster to make them a lighter rifle with a longer barrel and a much smaller bore. The forerunners of such guns appeared as early as 1719. The final design came about 1727. The bullets used in it were smaller than the bore, and to make them tight enough to shoot they were loaded with greased leather patches wrapped around them.

Clever men among the hunters soon copied the new guns at little forges in the woods. The pattern moved with the frontier. In time Daniel Boone carried such a rifle into Kentucky and so did others who followed him, and because the whole civilized world was then agog over the new Promised Land, the gun became known as the Kentucky rifle.

Most of these guns were a couple of inches under five feet long. The outside of the barrel was octagonal and was usually browned with acid. The stock extended the full length of the barrel and was generally made of hard maple, darkened with soot and polished until it looked almost like tortoise shell. Kentucky rifles had more "personality" than any guns ever made; they were loved by the men who used them and were given feminine pet names.

A long recess in the underside of the stock held the indispensable hickory ramrod, scorched with dark bands for ornament. The butt of the stock was protected by a nicely fitted brass plate; and on the right side, just against the butt plate, the wood was hollowed out and fitted with a hinged brass cover. This was the patch box for bullet patches and a lump of patch grease.

Also on the right side was the flintlock that caused the gun to shoot when the trigger was squeezed. Though it wasn't absolutely sure-fire, this was the most practical gunlock used in the eighteenth century. It was also used for muskets, blunderbusses, and pistols. It allowed a gun to be held ready for immediate use and provided a means of conveying fire from flint and steel to the powder charge in the barrel. To load, the hunter measured a charge from his powder horn and funnelled it from his hand into the muzzle of his gun; then he placed the patch, with a bullet on it, over the gun muzzle and shoved the two together to the bottom of the bore, using both hands on his ramrod to do it. He primed the lock with a little powder and closed the pan cover over it; then, as soon as he cocked the lock, it was ready to fire. The loading operation took about a minute.

PEOPLE IN THE WOODS

With a rifle, a good ax, and the skill to use them, the pioneer had the essentials of survival in the woods. He could defend himself and get food and clothing with the gun, and with the ax he could build himself a shelter and clear away the trees for planting crops.

Not all of the pioneers were Scots or Germans; there were Englishmen among them and even some Irishmen. Some were the younger sons of large families in the coast colonies. Their only opportunities at home were work as hired farm hands or a long apprenticeship in a craft; the woods looked good to them. Large families were the rule on the frontier, too, and younger children usually moved a few miles deeper into the wilderness to try to make a place for themselves. They lived a rough life that tended to produce rough men and women. The strong and resourceful might survive; the others retreated or died.

American fiction writers, and some who were not supposed to be writing fiction, have usually idealized the frontiersmen. Beyond doubt there were gentle, God-fearing, and even educated folk among the early woods dwellers, but not enough of them to set the tone of living. One suspects it was often they who found the life too hard and retreated. The successful frontiersmen had many of the attributes the novelists give them: they were fearless and keen-eyed marksmen, strong of body, self-reliant, and well-grounded in the things they had to know. But an examination of old documents reveals that more than a third of them couldn't write their names. They were unwashed and infested with fleas, bedbugs, and body lice. In justice it must be said that no one who slept under a bearskin on a cold night could very well avoid these companions. But bearskins didn't make people superstitious, foulmouthed, and belligerent, as the majority of these were.

Dr. Benjamin Rush, the great Philadelphia physician, a signer of the Declaration of Independence, described three successive types of frontiersmen, admitting that an individual might progress from one class to the next. First there was the hunter, the true pioneer, the breaker of the

A Pennsylvania, or Kentucky, rifle and the mold for its bullets

woods. He was a shiftless drunkard "with the manners of an Indian," who threw up a rough shelter and cleared enough space for a little patch of corn. He might own two scrawny nags and a single cow.

The second man was primarily a farmer but not a good one. He, too, was a loafer and a drunk, but he had a better cabin, he grew some wheat and rye in addition to corn, and he planted some fruit trees. He put up weak fences, and wild animals broke into his fields. His horses had too little food to enable them to work properly, and his cattle sometimes starved to death in the spring waiting for the grass to grow. He added some acres to the total of cleared land, but he finally had to sell out or was sold out to pay his debts.

The third man, who might be the buyer of the second man's farm, had enough capital to provide himself with good animals and proper farm tools. Perhaps he built no better house, but he did build

a good barn, because warm animals need less food. His fences were strong and his orchard was well-pruned. He added oats, buckwheat, and forage peas to his crops and planted a vegetable garden to supply his table. His descendants may still be living on his land.

Something like this succession repeated itself time after time as the frontier moved west. In the long view, it's evident that the first two men, unattractive though they may have been, were as necessary to the settlement of the country as was the third man. He built on their crude foundation. The first two fought Indians, killed off "varmints," and made a beginning at clearing away the forest to make agriculture possible. Such men and their hard-bitten, long-suffering women were the cutting edge of civilization. They were almost savages; but their improvidence and their lack of graces should be balanced against the hardships of the lives they had to lead.

INVASION

We, who never saw it, rhapsodize about the magnificence of the untouched natural forest. But the unanimous reports of the white people who first invaded it are of gloom, oppressive silence, and unrelieved loneliness. It seemed empty. There were woodpeckers, but almost none of our familiar songbirds; the grass seeds and weed seed they feed on didn't grow in the woods. For the same reason, deer, which prefer grass to leaves for grazing, were not as plentiful as has been imagined.

Probably preceded by a questing dog, a young couple venturing into this limitless green cave made a small caravan led by the husband on foot, his long rifle, loaded and primed, lying in the crook of his arm. Two horses followed him. The first was ridden by his wife, wedged between as much additional freight as the animal could carry. The second horse, on a lead rein, wore a pack-saddle on which were lashed the minimum necessities of a new establishment: an ax, a hoe, a sack or two of corn for food and seed, an iron pot and perhaps a long-handled skillet, a pottery jug or two, and possibly a pewter mug and a wooden noggin. A few more tools and some extra cloth-

ing were tied on somewhere. If a cow brought up the rear, she probably carried a small burden, too.

This was a slow procession, making long stops to allow the animals to browse on leaves and shrubs, since it wasn't possible to carry enough grain to feed them. At night they were hobbled. The travelers made a fire if the weather were dry enough to allow anything to be ignited with flint and steel and found what shelter they could beside an overhanging rock or a big log, sleeping "with one eye open" for trouble. The trace they followed, if there was any whatever, was no more than a footpath. On either side of it stood trees that quite commonly had trunks up to five and six feet thick, towering more than a hundred feet high, with foliage so dense that almost no sunlight reached the ground.

In most cases the journey was a short one and our couple were in surroundings such as they were accustomed to see. This was what their parents had done before them. These youngsters had been raised in the woods, and moving fifty miles west of their home farms put them in pristine country. They looked for land in a valley that was reasonably flat and fertile. They tried to judge its fertility by the kinds of trees they found. The next matter of importance was a spring, an easy thing to find in an all-wooded country. They would locate their shelter close to it. Nearness to neighbors, if there were any, would also be considered; people needed to consolidate for defense when Indian trouble started.

The first urge was to let in some sunlight. The husband felled young trees and used their trunks to throw up a "half-faced camp." Two forked posts, set about ten feet apart, supported a pole against one side of which light logs were leaned. More logs, stacked horizontally, closed the ends. A covering of bark was added to keep out most of the rain. One whole side was entirely open, with a fire burning in front of it. When the camp was

Half-faced camp

finished, the large trees near-by were girdled and killed by cutting through the bark all the way around the trunks.

Some corn had to be raised the first season and they planted a crop at once between the dying trees in holes made, hither and yon, with a hoe or even with an ax. With luck, there might be a little grain for the winter. Meanwhile, the man ranged the woods to get game for food. It was probably the thing he did best. The great lack was bread. When the corn brought from home ran out, the settlers ate lean venison and the breasts of wild turkeys and, rather pathetically, called them bread; when they said "meat" they meant bear meat.

THE LOG CABIN

The half-faced camp wouldn't do for winter weather, so the man used all his spare time cutting trees for a real cabin. He selected trees about ten inches thick. When seventy or eighty had been cut down he asked the neighbors to a log raisin', and they came from miles around, bringing their axes and probably their own food. The hosts provided at least a gallon of whisky and whatever game they could. Despite their crudities, the frontier people seldom failed to give help to one another. A log raisin' was treated as a frolic, as was any event that brought people together and gave them an excuse for socializing. Enthusiasm was kept up by frequent application to the jug, but the work went forward. The festivities didn't end

until the morning of the fourth day, and families who had traveled as far as thirty miles either camped in the woods or strained the capacity of near-by cabins.

The first day's work was cutting logs from the felled trees, snaking them to the site with horses or oxen, and laying the foundation of the house. The finished cabin would be about twenty feet long by sixteen feet wide. Two big logs, laid parallel the length of the house, served as a foundation. If there was to be a wood floor, it was made with half-logs, called puncheons, laid flat side up with their ends resting on the foundation logs; but few early cabins had any better floor than packed earth. While one group settled the foundation and another snaked logs a third rived clapboards for the roof. The roof men cut logs three feet long, propped them on end, and split slabs from them with a froe. This tool was a long stout blade with a socket at one end from which a wooden handle projected upward at a right angle to the back of the blade. The blade had to be long enough to reach across a log and beyond it a few inches, because the needed force was applied by banging with a wooden club on the back of the projecting blade. In order to stand such treatment, and also because this was a splitting and not a cutting operation, the blade was nearly an inch thick at its back and was distinctly wedge-shaped in section. The rived planks were about an inch thick and varied in width.

The main "do" was on the second day when the neighbors gathered again to "roll up" the cabin walls. Four experts acted as corner men. The rest of the men supplied the ample muscle needed to roll twenty-two-foot logs up inclined poles to the top of the wall. The corner men used their axes to cut saddle-shaped notches in both sides of each end of each log, leaving a little less than a third of the original thickness of wood between opposed notches. A length of grapevine or a strip of hide measured the distance between notches.

The cabin grew by pairs of logs: two on the sides, followed by two on the ends, and so on, with the lower notches of each new log resting on the upper ones of the preceding pair. The notches locked the logs in place and at the same time reduced the spaces between them. The logs extended irregularly beyond the corners. The log crib was built about seven feet high with no openings in it except the gaps between logs. At the seven-foot level, eight or nine six-inch logs were laid the short way across the crib as joists for the floor of the loft. Their ends were notched halfway through, and they lay notch-side down on the walls. Loft floors were sometimes made with puncheons, which needed no joists since they were supported by their own ends. A course of wall logs or as many as three courses were run above the loft joists. Three gave a little extra head room in the loft and held the joists in place.

Riving clapboards

Saddle-notched logs

The last two end logs below the roof projected farther beyond the side walls than the rest. Long logs, resting on these a little beyond the walls, made a kind of plate-cornice for the roof. Six-foot-high forked posts were set up at each end of the cabin to support the ridgepole. They stood inside the gable ends on the projecting logs mentioned above.

The builders made the gables of progressively shorter logs and beveled the ends of them to the roof angle. These logs were simply stacked, with no others interlocking to keep them in place; once the roof was on, their ends were held by it. The roof had no sloping rafters. Instead, stout poles were spaced horizontally as purlins from end to end, and the roof clapboards were laid directly on them. Some very primitive cabins had bark roofs. These were even leakier than the clapboard ones under which dry spots were scarce in a wind-driven rain. A steep pitch would have helped a lot, but most cabin roofs seem to have been pitched little more than thirty degrees from the horizontal. As a rule the clapboards overlapped like shingles, but long ones reaching from ridgepole to eaves were not unknown. Nails couldn't be spared for them, so they were held down by poles laid over them that ran the full length of the roof and were pinned or lashed to the projecting ends of the purlins.

The earliest cabins are said to have had no chimneys and no constructed fireplaces. The fire burned on the dirt floor, and the smoke escaped through a hole in the roof as it did from an Indian

Rolling up the walls

wigwam. Nobody can have been happy with such an arrangement. The cabins that have survived or were drawn while they survived show fireplaces built outside their walls.

The builders cut an opening in one end, after the walls were up, and built a smaller crib against it to contain the fireplace, interlocking the logs of the little one with those of the main cabin. They may have notched the cabin logs for this purpose before they put them in place, since it would have been difficult to do afterward. They lined three sides of the fireplace crib with stones bedded in mud and added a hearth of flat stones. The fireplace was made large enough to handle at least a four-foot backlog, and some of them burned six-foot logs.

The chimney was again a crib laid up with small logs or sticks and thickly plastered with mud. To reduce the risk of fire, they usually built it as an independent structure standing a foot or so from the house wall.

The openings for the fireplace and door were cut with a saw. Blocks inserted between the logs on either side of the openings kept them from sagging where they were cut.

A small group of specialists finished the cabin on the third day. They rived and hewed planks to frame the doorway, pinning them to the cut ends of the logs with wooden treenails driven into auger holes. With similar planks they built an Indian-proof batten door and hung it on wooden hinges. They added a strong wooden latch and

A "block cheer," a bedstead,
and a puncheon bench and table

an extra bar for use in time of attack. Such doors are scarce now. The one illustrated is a guess; its hinges were made for an eighteenth-century barn. It was wise to peer down through a crack from the loft every morning just to be sure no Indian was standing against the door, waiting to rush it when it was opened. The builders made a small hole in the door for the thong that lifted the latch from the outside. The latchstring was pulled inside at night, of course.

Windows were risky; few early cabins had any at all. When they did have them, there was no glass in them; they were merely holes covered at night and in bad weather with heavy sliding shut-

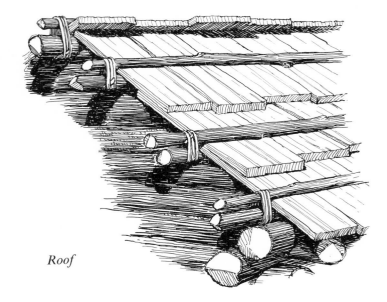

Roof

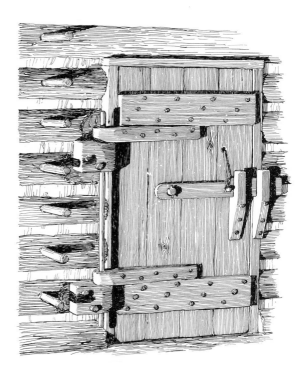

The inside of a cabin door

ters. The carpenters floored the attic with rough rived boards, leaving an opening over the cabin door. Behind the door they bored a vertical row of holes and drove pegs into them to make a ladder so the boys, who slept in the loft, could get to bed. A row of pegs near the ceiling served to hang up clothes. A plank across two pegs made a shelf

23

for the family's meager "table furniture." Two more pegs over the fireplace were the resting place of the owner's rifle, powder horn, and shot bag.

The only furniture was what could be made on the spot. A sixteen-inch-long section of a hickory log, stood on end, made an enormously heavy "block cheer." The settlers bored holes into puncheons and drove the whittled-down ends of sticks into them as legs to make stools and benches. Three puncheons, side by side, made the top of a two-legged table. It rested on two billets thrust between the logs of a wall, each supported with a leg under its outer end.

A bed went into a corner at the end of the cabin opposite the fireplace. For it the carpenter selected a post with a branch a couple of feet from its thicker end. He made a hole in the floor for its butt; the upper end he fastened to the ceiling. This post was set about four feet from the end wall and six feet from the side wall. The carpenter thrust one end of a pole between two side-wall logs and rested the other on the branch of his post. Split planks, running crosswise with their outer ends resting on the pole and their inner ends in a wall crack, completed the bedstead and made a "spring" that only fatigue could endure; the padding, made of corn husks or dry leaves covered with a couple of deerhides, did little to soften it.

Outside, other men chinked the spaces between

the logs. There were a couple of ways of doing this, but the Reverend Joseph Doddridge, who was born in a western Pennsylvania cabin in 1769, wrote that chinking billets were rived from logs. These went lengthwise into the openings between the logs, and the cracks around them were stuffed with a mud-and-moss mixture.

The cabin was complete; there remained only the housewarming. Everybody who had been connected with the job and all of their children attended. A fiddler scraped jigs and reels. The dancing and drinking and potpie-eating went on until sunrise. Since seating space was scarce, the women rested on the men's laps between "square sets." Behavior wasn't always seemly and the party was likely to be enlivened now and then by a rough-and-tumble fight which was watched by all with interest and shouts of enthusiasm. It would never have occurred to anyone to stop a fight. They all went home eventually, leaving the new settlers to distribute their scant possessions in the cabin.

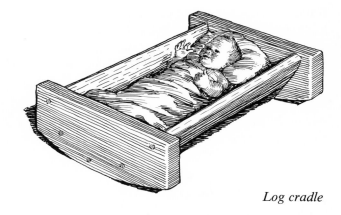

Log cradle

HOUSEHOLD ARTICLES

If a cradle wasn't needed at once, it would be shortly, and seldom for years was it empty. Father made it by hollowing out half of a fair-sized log of soft wood. Since such a cradle would rock a little too freely and perhaps spill the baby, he pegged

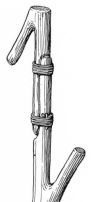

Wooden pothook

Dugout gum and pail

on flat end pieces. He accomplished the hollowing-out by burning, and then chipping and scraping with a knife, just as the Indians made dugout canoes. The same method served for making other articles: With a lot of time and effort, the settler could convert a log section three or four feet thick into an excellent storage barrel for corn or dried meat. This kind of barrel was called a gum because many were made from gum logs. He made a pail the same way from a smaller log. Bowls, too, he burned out: large ones for stirring up corn-bread batter and smaller ones for eating mush-and-milk.

Pottery dishes were so rare that they may be considered absent; the frontiersman scorned them because, he said, they dulled his knife. Here and there a little pewter was cherished as a symbol of elegance, rather than as an article for daily use as it served in towns. Square wooden trenchers served as plates. Wooden spoons, brought along on that overburdened pack horse or whittled out on the spot, were the only table utensils except the hunter's ever handy knife which, by the way, he usually called a scalping knife and not without reason.

His wife cooked in the fireplace as did everyone everywhere, even in the most pretentious mansions in the coastal towns, but the frontier woman did it with a minimum of equipment. Her andirons were a couple of flat stones, no fancy iron ones with hooks to hold a roasting spit—and no spit. When meat was to be roasted, she hung it in front of the fire on a rawhide thong and gave it a spin now and then to keep it turning. She

24

hung her stewpot over the fire on a wooden pot-hook (a duplicate of the Indian one) from a lug pole set across the inside of the chimney. This pole was put in green so it wouldn't burn readily, and her husband had to renew it at intervals, as it dried out in the heat. In addition to the indispensable pot, a bake kettle, an iron skillet with three legs and a long handle, a gridiron for broil-

the top, was pounded with a pestle ten feet long and six inches thick. The pestle was so heavy that help was needed to lift it, so he hung it at the end of a limber pole called a sweep. Using the handle that passed through the pestle a couple of feet from its bottom, two people could work together, banging the pestle down and letting it spring up again.

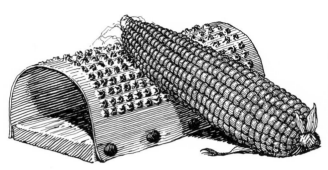

Sheet-iron corn grater

A trencher and a wooden spoon

ing, a long iron fork, a ladle, and perhaps a strainer would complete the utensils list of the best equipped kitchen in the woods.

FOOD

Neighborliness may have extended to lending a little corn to new settlers, but there wasn't always enough surplus to permit it. The newcomers watched their own first crop anxiously for the "roast'n' years." Fresh green corn is good even to the well-fed, but these starch-starved folk ate it in a kind of ecstasy. They still ate it when it reached that half-hard state that is neither green corn nor grain; then they crumbled the kernels by rubbing the ears on a homemade grater.

When the corn grew too hard for the grater, the settler broke it up in the hominy block. This was a mortar, given its name because its prime use was for crushing fully hardened kernels that had been hulled by soaking in lye. The settler made his hominy block by burning a round-bottomed cavity into one end of a three-foot log. The log stood on end and the corn, placed in the hole at

Bake kettle

Stewpot, skillet, and gridiron

25

Really hard corn that hadn't been processed required the use of a hand mill, or quern. Its essential parts were two flat circular stones, as much as fifteen inches across and perhaps four inches thick, placed one upon another like layers of cake. The bedder, or lower stone, was fixed in the center of an open box that served to catch the ground meal. The box stood on some kind of firm support. The upper stone, called the runner, had two holes in it. One, passing clear through its center, was about three inches across at its top and was tapered like a funnel. A smaller hole, only a couple of inches deep, was near the stone's outer edge; it was the socket for a wooden handle by which, with a lot of effort, the millers rotated the runner on the bedder.

The bedder had no holes in it, but now and then an old one shows a mound, or boss, in its center to serve as a kind of "axle" for centering the runner. Shelled corn, fed into the center hole, emerged as meal from between the stones at their edges. This meal wasn't all of suitable fineness. It had to be sifted, and the coarser parts were reground. The sifter was hardened rawhide stretched on a wide hoop and punctured all over with a red-hot wire.

One person could grind with a small hand mill, using a stout peg as a handle, but it took two people working together to operate a standard mill. To make this easier, the handle was made three feet long or more, and its upper end was inserted in a fixed, horizontal beam directly over the center of the runner. It was hard work for a couple of youngsters to operate such a mill. Not every family owned one, nor a hominy block, for that matter. It was common practice to send two of the older children to a neighbor's to grind a sack of corn.

There were a number of ways to cook corn, nearly all of them originating with the Indians. The idea that hominy was (and is) eaten after being treated with anything as violent as lye is a little startling; but after the lye had softened and loosened the hard outer shell of the corn, the frontier wife washed it thoroughly in clear water. She washed it again after she removed the hulls. The hominy softened and swelled and became snowy white when it was boiled. It was good with bear or pork gravy; "hog-and-hominy" was the basic food on the farms that followed the first clearings.

The simplest way to cook corn meal was to boil it as mush. Throughout English America, six or

Hominy block

seven nights a week supper was mush-and-milk or, when the cow was dry, mush with maple syrup or molasses. Johnnycake and corn pone were for breakfast and midday dinner, in that order. Both were made as quite thin batters with sour milk or buttermilk—or in a pinch, water—and soda, salt, and whatever kind of shortening was available. If there was an egg on the place, it could go into the pone but not properly into the johnnycake, which was supposed to be quite dry so that it would keep well as the ration of a traveler; its formal name was *journey cake*. The skillet made a good pan for cooking johnnycake slowly, next to the fire but not over it. If a pan was lacking, a flat stone would serve. The finished article was crisp and not much more than half an inch thick. The same batter could be thinned a little and fried in the skillet as "cawn dodgers."

The pioneer woman baked her pone in a lidded iron kettle, leaving it overnight in the hot ashes on the hearth. If she was fortunate enough to possess a real bake kettle, she used that. It was a pot designed for this kind of baking. It had three legs and instead of covering the rim of the pot, its lid was inside, resting on a ledge an inch or so below the rim. With such a kettle the cook could make a better job of browning her pone on top by covering the lid with hot coals. Corn pone so cooked was soft and succulent in its center, but it had a thick crust not quite so hard as the pot it was cooked in.

Pigs had to be driven through the woods on foot to get them to the frontier, so the outermost settlers did without pork for a while, but not for long. Swine were the most successful domestic animals in the forest. They ran loose and foraged for themselves, living on acorns, beechnuts, and various roots. Wolves and panthers killed some, but the layer of fat under a pig's skin made him almost immune to rattlesnake bite. A pig usually killed and ate any snake that bit him, as well as a great many snakes that were merely passing by. The porkers became a little wild in the woods; when they were wanted for ham and bacon, it was often necessary to bring them home with the aid of a rifle.

Hand mill, or quern

Long after every household had domestic animals, the gun still contributed heavily to the larder. In addition to bear, deer, wild turkey, and an occasional elk or buffalo, hungry people sometimes ate panther, which is said to taste much like veal, or rattlesnake. Small game was plentiful. In the fall every nut tree had dozens of squirrels cutting in it. The proper way to shoot a squirrel with a rifle was to "bark" him by hitting the tree immediately beside him, so that the concussion killed the animal without tearing him up. Porcupines, beavers, and possums were less plentiful than squirrels but were valued for the pot.

Twice a year the migrations brought duck, geese, and swan to rivers and ponds, and incredible numbers of passenger pigeons to the woods. These big pigeons are now extinct, but once their flocks darkened the daytime sky and their nightly roosting broke the branches of big trees. They were so easy to kill that a boy with a stick could get enough for dinner in a few minutes. That's why they are extinct.

Almost any kind of meat was likely to be cooked as potpie. This wasn't pie in our sense at all; we would call it "stew with dumplings." Its preparation was simple, and its cooking did not call for close attention from the cook. Potpie was "spoon meat," needing no dissection at the table, and its leftovers could be stretched with added ingredients and reheated to be just as good, or better, on the second day.

These people knew how to preserve meat by soaking it in brine; the difficulty was to get enough salt for the purpose. Meat was also heavily smoked, without salt, to preserve it, and so was some fish, but not much. They cured most of their meat by cutting it into strips and drying it before a fire as what they called jerky, or jerk. They dried squash, too, as the Indians did.

Even the earliest settlers had cows. They belled them and turned them loose to get most of their living in the woods. The cow was brought to the cabin door twice a day so the housewife could milk her while the children struggled to restrain the calf which, in view of the cow's slim diet, was being robbed. Frontier people preferred sour milk to sweet, which was just as well, since there was no way to refrigerate it. Tea and coffee were not only scarce, they were also despised as "slops that don't stick to your ribs."

Crude distilling apparatus served to make whisky almost as soon as there was any grain to make it from. After the Revolutionary War, when it was proposed to tax whisky, these frontier people started a rebellion that faded before the threat of an army of fifteen thousand men led by the President of the United States! The descendants of the Scots still make a little private whisky in the mountains. On the frontier everybody drank whisky-and-water as an ordinary beverage. It was also drunk without water and was a constant source of trouble when it relaxed the inhibitions of people who had all too few of them to start with.

CLOTHES

The rugged pioneer hero almost invariably appears in modern illustrations clad from neck to toes in fringed buckskin. He did find leather the best covering for his legs, but unless nothing else was to be had, he never used it for his hunting shirt; there is no colder and clammier garment than a wet leather one. The favored material was

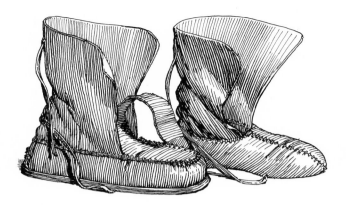

Shoepack and moccasin

Shot pouch and powder horn

linsey, also called linsey-woolsey, woven with a woolen weft on a linen warp; it was warm and durable. A summer hunting shirt was made entirely of tow linen, that is, linen of coarse second grade to which some impurities still clung. Very scratchy.

The hunting shirt was often the only upper garment worn, though there is mention of a man wearing one over a "shirt and jacket of the common fashion." The hunting shirt was a loose garment without buttons, reaching halfway down the thighs and lapping over the full width of the body in front. Its sleeves were generously wide. There was no collar, but there was always a shoulder cape, fringed by preference with bright-colored cloth. The shirt was confined at the waist by a hand-woven belt that had no buckle but was tied in back with strings. The overlap of the shirt in front served as a pocket in which a man carried some johnnycake, a bit of jerky, a twist of tobacco, and some unspun tow to clean his rifle. The belt had other uses than merely surrounding the hunting shirt: Its wearer tucked his mittens under the front of it, he slung his tomahawk from its right side or at its back, and to its left side he attached the leather sheath of his scalping knife.

"Britches," or "trowsers," were buckskin and were often fringed along the outer seams, like an Indian's leggings. Some young bucks adopted thigh-high Indian "leggins" unchanged, suspending them from a waist band, and wearing a breechclout with them like any aboriginal warrior. Hunters customarily wore one-piece Indian moc-

casins with extra long cuffs that they tied to their legs with rawhide thongs at the ankle and calf. Moccasins left much to be desired as footgear and were described as "a decent way of going barefooted." They were miserably uncomfortable when wet and they had to be stuffed with deer hair or dry leaves to be even bearably warm in winter. Not the least complaint against them was the need to mend them at the end of every day. In a hunter's shot pouch there was always a roll of buckskin for patching and an awl. Before he turned in, he did his chore of sewing, using strips

of buckskin (he called them whangs) for thread.

There were plenty of hides to make leather, and oaks and hemlocks to supply tanbark for curing them grew within a few yards of the cabin. The bark was prepared by pounding it on a stump with a club. Probably it wasn't reduced to the wheat-grain size a professional tanner would have demanded, but it was made fine enough to serve. Hair was removed from the skins by soaking them in wood ashes and water. They were then washed and put, with layers of ground tanbark between them, into a trough sunk in the ground. The trough was kept full of water, and the hides had a long soaking in the tannic acid that was leached from the bark. Eastern tanners soaked them six months. When they were removed, they had to be washed, oiled with bear oil, and curried to softness by being worked with the turned-over edge of an old knife.

Some men and, in winter, almost all women wore shoepacks. The tops were quite high—eight or ten inches—but the foot part, adopted from the two-piece moccasin, was much like a modern loafer. Most shoepacks had soles and were sturdier than moccasins. Anyone could make them at home, while a pair of civilized boots required the work of a professional craftsman.

As with the leather hunting shirt, a frontiersman is never shown now without a coonskin cap. Not that he didn't wear a fur hat in the wintertime (not all of them were coonskin), but he did have the good sense to wear a straw hat in summer. His wife plaited it for him. If she had no straw, she used cornhusks or rushes.

An essential item of the backwoodsman's equip-

ment was the leather shot pouch that hung at his right side from a strap over his left shoulder. In it he carried a chunk of lead for bullets, his brass mold for casting them, the flint-and-steel that was his only means of starting a fire, and some cast-lead rifle balls unless he carried these in a separate pouch attached to the front of his belt. His powder horn, which had grown originally on the head of a cow or a buffalo, hung just above his shot pouch on the strap that carried it.

At times a frontier woman was reduced to making deerskin clothes for herself and her children; but she hated them and was ashamed to be seen in them, though she didn't seem to mind being seen barefoot, as she nearly always was in warm weather. The costume she preferred was a linsey petticoat (by which she meant an outer skirt, not an undergarment); a linen "bed gown," which was a smock, open at the back of the neck and belted at the waist; a linen neckcloth; and a sunbonnet "made without pasteboard," that is, with a limp brim. For cold weather she had a shapeless fur hat and a large linsey shawl which she folded to a triangle and draped around her shoulders.

If she could get wool, she knitted stockings to wear under her shoepacks in winter. As flax came to be grown and sheep to be raised just behind the "front lines," spinning wheels appeared in most cabins and, it is estimated, about one house in five had a homemade loom that the local women kept busy the year around. Some men also wove and no one thought it odd; but a boy who learned to help with spinning wool was careful to keep the fact concealed from all but his family. It was considered sissified, or "galish," as the woodland word had it. No boy had enough free time to learn the much more difficult operation of spinning flax. The girls spent long hours learning it and doing it. In the earliest times, clothing was so scarce that when strangers appeared children were hastily hidden so that their nakedness would not be seen.

HUNTING

There were, of course, no game laws or seasons except those made by nature and the one made by man that held it bad luck to hunt on Sunday.

Frontiersmen loved to hunt and it was sport to them, but they didn't hunt as sportsmen in the sense of giving the game a fair chance. They hunted for food and they used every means of getting it; neither the doe nor her fawn was spared. They tracked animals in snow. Salting the ground to make artificial licks at which deer would congregate, they then shot the deer from blinds. On lakes or streams they hunted drinking deer at night from dugout canoes with pine-knot flares set in their bows. A boy poled the boat as silently as possible while the hunter sat amidships behind a bark screen that kept the light out of his eyes. The deer were hypnotized by the light and the "hunting" was slaughter, restrained only by the absence of a repeating rifle.

Neither buckshot nor bird shot was used in muskets or rifles. Small shot will harm the bore of a rifle, and a man couldn't very well carry two guns. So what he couldn't get with a single lead slug, he missed; but it wasn't much.

The few settlers who didn't bring dogs with them acquired dogs after they arrived, sometimes sharp-nosed, droop-tailed Indian dogs. It wasn't long before the canine over-population began to kill sheep and calves and to make strife between neighbors.

Wolves were a constant menace to pigs and lambs and even a danger to small children. Though they sometimes made pets of wolf cubs, the frontiersmen waged constant war on the full-grown animals, arranging elaborate stratagems to lure them into some pocket where one or two could be destroyed. The most successful wolf traps were pitfalls. They required a lot of hard labor to make and, incidentally, they could break the leg of an unsuspecting cow, horse, or man. These pits were eight feet deep and were larger at the bottom than at the top. Once in, it was impossible for a wolf to jump out, but if he were left too long in a trap, he could sometimes tunnel his way out. The wooden cover of the pit was a little smaller than the opening at the top and was secured along its center line to the underside of a pole, the ends of which rested on the edges of the pit. The two ends were kept in place by stakes but were not fastened to anything. Bait was lashed onto the cover. The weight of a wolf on either leaf of the cover would cause it to rotate a quarter turn and

Wolf trap

drop him into the pit. The trap reset itself with the aid of a stone suspended by a bridle from the edges of the cover. Curiously, though they weren't hurt by the experience, being trapped took all the fight out of wolves. A man could safely lower himself into a pit with several of them and dispatch them with his knife.

As the frontier moved, what had been outpost clearings became farms. The people on them raised most of their meat, and hunting, though still fun, was no longer a necessity. Then there seemed to be too much game; it raided fields and flocks, so the people staged game drives. All the men and boys from miles around distributed themselves in a huge circle and started moving slowly toward its center. Not realizing they were encircled, the animals moved ahead, and presently most of the game in the area was concentrated in some small valley under the guns of men who methodically slaughtered it all. One western Pennsylvania drive killed 724 animals larger than beaver, and an estimated 500 small ones. Among the larger beasts were panthers, bears, wolves, wild cats, deer, elk, and (the number is surprising) 111 buffalo. The Indians saw game drives, perhaps not inaccurately, as malice against them; without game they could not survive.

INDIANS

The Delawares and the Shawnees were the tribes in the path of the white men pushing west. They were both Algonquians. The Shawnees were from the south, or at least most recently from the south; they were people who never stayed long anywhere. The Delawares, or the Lenapes (as they called themselves), were traditionally the "grand-fathers" of the Algonquians. They had long lived near the Atlantic coast between the Delaware River and the Hudson. They had trouble not only with the white settlers but also with the powerful Iroquois in northern New York who overcame them. Forced slowly westward, on the upper Ohio River they came into contact with the French, who incited them to resist the encroaching English frontier. This took practically no persuasion. The French always treated Indians like members of the human race and since their interest was the fur trade, they showed little inclination to destroy the forests or to displace the tribes.

The frontier settlers found themselves increasingly harassed especially during the Seven Years' War which we usually call the French and Indian War. Had the Indians had any notion of organization or strategy, they would have been even more formidable. They were fighting for survival, using the tactics of frightfulness and stealth. Stealth was natural to them; frightfulness seemed justified by desperation. When they were fighting among themselves, few Indians except the Iroquois mur-

dered women and children, and torture for its own sake was a custom of but few tribes.

The frontiersmen, however, found their estimate of Indians as heathen savages fully confirmed. They fought back with the same ghastly tactics and with better weapons. They had rifles; the Indians had all but abandoned bows, but usually they had only muskets to replace them. The Indians scalped the white men, and the white men retaliated, scalp for scalp. In justice it must be said that though the white men killed defenseless captives, they never burned a captive at the stake.

FORTS

The lone settler had little chance of defending his family against an Indian attack, so in every neighborhood there was a fort where all could gather for mutual defense. Newcomers often lived in the fort until they could establish themselves. At the first rumor of trouble messengers warned every cabin, and its occupants went at once to the stronghold, leaving their possessions to be brought in later. Often the alarm came at night. The fort was seldom more than a mile away and the people walked to it in silence. For all but the smallest children, the word "Indian" was enough to keep them perfectly quiet.

The alarms usually came in spring and summer, and the people had to live in the forts for

weeks at the very time when they most needed to be in their corn patches. The men partially solved this problem by going in groups to each cabin in turn and hoeing, with sentries posted to watch for trouble. Hating the restraint and discomfort of the fort, a few families were stubbornly foolhardy. They returned to their cabins when the first scare produced no Indians. A good many didn't get back to the fort again, and those who did endangered their neighbors, who had to rescue them. In winter the Indians holed up in their wigwams and the settlers usually had peace, but the thaw that often occurs in November might bring with it a sudden attack. The Reverend Mr. Doddridge claims that the term "Indian summer" had its origin in this circumstance.

The first forts were merely stockades made of close-set posts, ten or twelve feet high. Save that they had hinged and barred gates instead of narrow barricaded passages, the forts were exactly like the "castles" the Indians built for themselves. After a time the forts acquired projecting bastions at their corners to enable defenders to shoot along the sides and deal with attackers who were so close under the walls they couldn't otherwise be hit. Probably few of these neighborhood forts had blockhouses connected with them before the beginning of the French and Indian War in 1754; some certainly did not have them. Cleared land around a fort left the Indians nothing more than stumps to hide behind. It was safest to build a fort on the top of a knoll so that all its approaches were uphill, but this had a disadvantage, too. Few hilltops have springs, and so there was usually no water inside the stockade. The best that could be done was to put the gate in the side that faced a spring.

Cabins stood against the inside of one or more of the fort's walls. They were ordinary log cabins, but a little smaller than usual and differing also in the fact that each shared its end walls with its neighbors, like the rooms of a modern motel. The roofs, too, were special. Instead of pitching two ways to a ridgepole, they sloped one way only, reaching from low eaves in front almost to the top of the stockade. Because of the fire hazard of a chimney that touched a roof, fireplaces were built against the walls that faced the court.

33

Every man and every boy over thirteen was a soldier. A man who shirked his duty was summarily driven from the community. Officers were appointed to achieve some sort of organization, but they were without real authority. In the older frontier states military titles are still conferred casually on prominent civilians. There was no artillery, but the rifles were deadly up to two hundred yards. A stockade with alert guards was practically impervious to Indian attack. The natives seldom attacked a fort at all, and there seems to be no evidence that they ever took one.

MEDICINE AND WITCHCRAFT

People were often injured, wounded, or sick and the treatment given them was usually as bad as the complaint, if not worse. The remedies were certainly imaginative. A decoction of white walnut bark was believed to act as a purgative if the bark were peeled downward from the tree; upward peeling of the same bark produced an emetic! A favored remedy for snakebite was the application to the wound of short sections of the offending reptile; these were cremated afterward. On the same homeopathic theory, "the hair of the dog" was literally applied to a dogbite. Snakes, by the way, were a constant menace. A man hoeing a small patch in the spring often killed a dozen rattlesnakes or copperheads in a morning.

Charms and incantations were frequently called upon as treatments. Black cats were almost always shy part of an ear or an inch or so of tail because their blood was necessary for the treatment of erysipelas. Bleeding the patient was in high repute as a remedy for almost any affliction, but there was seldom anyone around who knew how to perform the operation. Any unusual or incurable disease was ascribed to the malice of a witch, and appropriate measures were taken to nullify her spell. Witches were always women and always evil, but there were men of good will (and sharp commercial instincts) who were witch masters, able to cast counter spells. It isn't clear how the master's spell affected the witch but, once cast, the only way the witch could rid herself of it was by borrowing something from the family of her

"Hating out"

victim. Decent, kindly old women were often horrified at being refused a perfectly innocent and reasonable request.

Witches turned men into horses and rode them. They could also put a hex on a rifle that spectacles on the hunter might have removed. A witch could milk a cow *in absentia* by performing the milking operation on a rag, no doubt muttering weird incantations the while. Witches also shot cattle with balls of hair! However, a witch could be killed by shooting a bullet with a little silver in it at a picture of her drawn with charcoal on a board. And good riddance, too.

JUSTICE

Where there are no official police, any group of people will make shift to police itself. The pioneers were beyond the reach of law, but they managed to restrict misbehavior within certain limits. They were especially severe with anyone who injured the group. Minor offenders, like petty thieves or those who shirked their share of community work, were "hated out." They cut the culprit out of all social activities, but they by no means ignored him. On the contrary, they conferred unpleasant nicknames on him that were not merely whispered behind his back. One and all told him loudly what they thought of him any time they met him.

A thief who stole something of consequence, like a horse, received more forceful treatment. (Horse thieves were a frontier problem from Pennsylvania to California.) Here, they stripped such a one to the waist, forced him to hug a tree, and then tied his wrists together on the far side of it. His bare back took a Biblical thirty-nine strokes with a hickory stick. A first offender got off with only this much because his muscles and his rifle were needed in the community, but a confirmed thief was exiled. There were no formal trials, but the rod was often used to extract a confession.

CHILDHOOD AND SPORTS

A boy growing up in the woods was quite untroubled by any thought of the three R's, but he learned from babyhood the things he had to know for coping with a forest life. It would seem to him that no one taught him to identify trees; he just knew their names and the qualities and uses of each, as he knew the family dog, horse, and cow. The ways of wild animals he learned not as "nature study" but as practical preparation for the life of a hunter. He learned early to make snares and deadfalls and to catch small animals with them. He acquired a woodsman's eyes and ears, automatically alert at all times and instantly conscious of the least item that was not just as it should be—a slight motion, an odd sound, or the faint trail left by the passing of an animal or a man. He learned, too, the woodsman's self-control, copied from the Indian's, that would not show surprise or chagrin by the slightest change of expression. This vigilant guard over the muscles resulted in a "dead pan" that showed no emotion at all.

34

Though the bow wasn't used by his elders, it was a good weapon to teach a boy marksmanship while he was still too small for a gun. Before he was ten, a frontier boy could impale an occasional squirrel with an arrow. He also practiced daily at throwing a tomahawk, not because he was told to do it, but because it was fun. Presently he could judge distance so well that he could be sure of sinking the blade in a tree trunk every time.

There were chores to do also. A boy worked with his father in the corn patch when it was safe to do it, and he helped with clearing and fencing. His was the job of keeping the fireplace supplied with wood and bringing in the cow for milking. The bell on her neck removed finding her from the realm of the impossible. A wise boy broke a twig here and there as he hunted the cow, so as to find his way home if he missed her. Once he found her, there was nothing to worry about. He had only to start her off; she could always lead him home.

A boy lived for the day when he would own a rifle, and since his ability to use a gun was valuable, he was ordinarily given one when he was twelve or thirteen. Once he had it, it was seldom out of his hands and he practiced with it as constantly as his allowance of powder and shot would permit. This was no toy; it was the indispensable equipment of a man. In a year or so the boy was assigned his post at the fort and from then on he *was* a man. He would probably be married by the time he was sixteen to a girl his own age or a year or two younger. While he was learning to shoot she had learned to grind meal, to cook, to spin and sew and, perhaps, to weave, to make soap, to milk a cow—all the things her mother did. The only dolls she had ever had were made at home

35

out of cornhusks, but she would have had plenty of baby practice handling her steadily arriving brothers and sisters.

Marksmanship practice didn't end with the attainment of manhood. Shooting matches were important features of weddings and other social gatherings. The shooting was often for a prize: a fat turkey, a jug of whisky, or on special occasions, a rifle. The target was usually the fairly large head of a handmade nail, and the range was about sixty yards. There are tales of men who could hit the nailhead squarely with two bullets out of three, but for such shooting, the gun was fired from a rest. To "hit the nail on the head" didn't refer to a man with a hammer. Every one of the 130 woodsmen who went to Boston with Captain Michael Cresap in 1776 could put nineteen of twenty bullets within an inch of a nail.

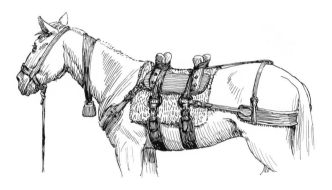

Double-girthed, hickory-crotch packsaddle with breast strap and breeching

One-piece wooden stirrup, Pennsylvania

PACK TRAINS

The Piedmont settler wasn't wholly independent of civilization and of "store-boughten" goods. He had to have gunpowder, and he had to have lead from which to mold his bullets. Around 1740 a pound of powder cost two dollars and a half and a pound of lead sixteen cents in the nearest towns. Of other desirable items he could buy in towns, the chief ones were salt and iron. But he could get none of these things without something to give in exchange, and there was also the matter of transportation.

Land clearing had as a by-product an abundance of wood. It was burned to get rid of it, and the burning made ashes. These could be converted into potash, called alum salt, that was in demand on the coast by soapmakers, tanners, wool carders, dyers, glassmakers, and papermakers; and the process of conversion wasn't beyond the primitive means of the frontier. Some sort of hopper was needed; a gum would do, or a box hopper was built of rived slabs. A small outlet was made near its bottom. Some grass or pine needles were thrown in to act as a strainer, and the rest of the space was filled with fresh wood ashes; these were wet down thoroughly and kept wet. Lye leached out of the ashes, and trickled from the outlet of the hopper. The lye was then boiled outdoors in an iron pot, preferably one with an extra-thick round bottom. More lye was added as water evaporated. The inside of the pot acquired a thick hard crust of potash, quite dark from the carbon that was mixed with it, and known as black salt. It was chipped off the pot with some difficulty. A bushel of black salt would buy a cow and a calf in the wilderness or a small stock of powder and lead in a town.

There were other frontier products that had a market in the East: furs, of course, and deer hides; nearly all men in the Colonies who worked with their hands wore leather "britches." Bear grease was salable; it was made into soap or burned in grease lamps. Ginseng root, snake root, and a number of herbs that grew wild in the woods were in demand for medicines.

Every fall each neighborhood pooled its horses to make up a community pack train and sent it east or, more often perhaps, southeast, since the valleys ran that way and the going was easier. No doubt a group of people went along sometimes, but only two men were actually needed to handle the twelve or fourteen horses. The master driver rode at the head of the line, and his assistant brought up the rear to keep an eye on the packs. The train moved in single file, with each horse's lead rein fastened to the packsaddle of the animal ahead.

Every horse wore a bell hanging from a wide strap on his neck. The bells were silent on the trail, with their clappers tied, except when entering the town of their destination; then the clappers were "opened" to create a flourish and "get there with the bells on." The real purpose of the bells was the same as with the cow, to find the horses when they had been turned out to forage overnight. Their feet were hobbled then so that they could not go far or fast, but they could still hide.

Small, nimble horses were preferred, though they couldn't carry more than two hundred pounds lashed to a wooden packsaddle. Two bushels, weighing eighty-four pounds each, made a load of black salt, but the horse had also to carry his own ration of grain, enough for the round trip, because it would be a waste to buy feed for the re-

turn journey. Bags of it were cached along the trail on the way down to be picked up on the way back. This grain was corn, peas, or beans; seldom, if ever, was it oats. Food for the men was carried in the saddlebags of the horses they rode. It was johnnycake, jerky, and perhaps ham, bacon, or cheese.

The trading points moved westward with time and the frontier. In Pennsylvania they were successively Lancaster, Harrisburg (there was a ferry there), Carlisle, Shippensburg, and Fort Loudon; in Maryland, Baltimore Town, Frederick Town, Hagerstown, Oldtown, and Fort Cumberland. The pack train put up at an "ordinary" that had a paddock for the horses and provided plain food on an eat-what's-put-before-you basis. The men slept on the floor of the common room with their feet to the fire. The bill was paid in black salt or with a deer hide or two. Purchases were accounted in terms of money, but little or none changed hands. The towns didn't use much of it; early frontiersmen had no use whatever for it at home.

Most frontier families had relatives in the towns, so the pack trains carried messages both ways and, in addition, they brought home a light but valuable commodity in the form of news. Settlers moving west joined a returning pack train, if they could, and children sometimes rode in the panniers—woven of thin splints of wood—packed in with blankets and clothing, with only their heads showing. The burdens on the return journey, in addition to the inevitable ammunition, were simple but various. Iron bars for making guns and for a hundred other uses were bent into an open U-shape by town blacksmiths so that they could readily be hung over a horse's back. Many an up-country smith could make a gunlock, forging and filing each part and making springs from old saw blades, but it was easier to buy locks ready-made from the Lancaster gunsmiths who were specialists. Salt was a kind of necessary luxury; so were cast-iron cooking pots and skillets. Sometimes a little pewter traveled west, or—as a present for the "old woman"—a yard of fancy printed calico or a loaf of cane sugar.

In time, as the tote roads grew longer and the western population increased, community pack trains gave way to contract drovers who owned many horses and employed men to handle them. The growing town of Pittsburgh had no other way to obtain goods from the East until after 1783. It was expensive transportation and as a result iron sold there for twenty-five cents a pound, with salt at ten dollars a bushel.

As clearings in the forest enlarged, grain and fruit in some quantity began to be grown in the back country. These products were too bulky to be carried on pack horses, so they were reduced to their essences, so to speak; they were turned into whisky or peach brandy or applejack. A horse could carry two eight-gallon "kags" of these liquids, worth a dollar a gallon in town but only half that at home. By then there were a few professional coopers in the hills to make the kegs.

3

THE SOUTHERN VALLEYS

THE HIGH SLOPES of mountains don't recommend themselves for settlement. Although the valleys were by no means densely populated, by 1725 settlers occupied the best locations east of the Appalachian ridges. Mountains and Indians together discouraged further westward expansion, so most new settlers and a lot of restless old ones drifted south into Virginia and North Carolina. They seldom knew which colony they were in, since the boundaries, even if described on paper, weren't marked on the land and the settlers had no maps. But they hoped they were in Virginia, where the law provided for "cabin right": A man who put up a cabin and planted an acre of corn could claim four hundred acres of land.

The Virginians themselves pushed west, urged on by Lord Fairfax, who had vast reaches of wilderness for sale at sixpence an acre. Thus the colony was sparsely but continuously settled from the coast to the Barrier. North Carolina, however, was settled near the sea, and after the first quarter of the eighteenth century it acquired some independent-minded settlers in its western valleys; but the whole middle section of the colony was cabinless, with only a trail to connect the ends.

South of the new settlers lived the strong and stubborn Cherokees; on the west stood those mountains, here higher than ever. The only way to move seemed to be eastward and many did that, but in the main they dug in where they were and became organized communities by about 1740. Such a community wasn't a town; it was fifty or sixty cabins strung along both sides of a "crick" for ten miles or so, with a fort at a convenient point. This was a much larger population than surrounded one of the neighborhood forts up north, and the stronghold was correspondingly larger and more elaborate. It almost always had at least one blockhouse.

Some blockhouses stood alone, but usually they were built into a corner of a stockade; there might be more than one attached to a very large fort. The blockhouse was a two-story log structure

much more carefully built than most cabins. The logs for it were hewn flat on their upper and lower sides and were painstakingly notched to lie with no wide cracks between them. Sometimes the logs were reduced to square timbers, making the walls flat and difficult to climb. The logs of military blockhouses were cut to the exact dimensions of the building and the corners were neat and square, but even when the logs projected beyond the walls, as those of the settlers' blockhouses usually did, they were all cut to the same length. Lying so closely on one another, they offered slight foothold for an attacker.

The first floor of a good-sized blockhouse measured twenty by thirty feet on its outside. Its ceiling was about twelve feet high. The second-floor ceiling was lower—eight feet—but the second floor was larger in area than the ground floor; it overhung the lower walls by thirty inches on all four sides. The clapboard roof was hipped, and sometimes it had an open watchtower built into its peak.

The one entrance door faced the quadrangle of the fort. Solid puncheons floored the lower level, and the thick plank floor upstairs was perforated all over with holes through which to fire rifles at invaders below. The only access to the upper floor was through a trap door reached by a ladder that could be drawn up by last-ditch defenders. Loopholes, cut in all four walls of both floors, were two feet apart. Each was about three inches wide and as high as the thickness of a log.

A good blockhouse had a stone chimney within its walls and fireplaces on both floors; a very good one had a dug well under the ground-floor puncheons, but this was exceptional. As long as their ammunition held out, a few men could defend a blockhouse—if the attackers didn't succeed in igniting the roof with fire arrows. These were ordinary arrows with bundles of grass burning on their tips. Those that hit the roof could seldom heat it enough to make it catch; but sometimes it did catch, and then the situation called for heroism.

People lived in the southern valleys much as people lived in the North, and they were no less rough and earthy. But there was a new sense of permanence about them. Men set about farming as if they intended to farm in that place for life, and the enterprising ones built little gristmills. Most of these were tub mills which, though they demanded a swift stream, required no milldam.

The tub mill was a crude turbine. Its small rotor, some three-and-a-half feet in diameter, lay horizontal in a shallow tub through which the water poured either from a wooden flume or directly from a natural waterfall. The upper end of the vertical wooden shaft passed through the bedder stone without touching it and turned the runner by means of an iron rynd, fixed across the shaft, with its ends in recesses chipped out of the stone. There was no gearing. By raising one end of the horizontal, underwater timber that carried the lower bearing of the mill, the miller could lift the whole moving mechanism enough to separate the stones and save them from wear when there was no grain between them.

The father of the tub mill was the "Norse" mill of the Scottish burns; very early American tub mills were probably exactly like their parent. The mill in the larger illustration is from North Carolina. No one knows its actual age, but its iron rotor blades, its hopper, chutes, and bin suggest that it didn't belong to the first settlements.

Religion, which got scant attention on the Pennsylvania frontier, began to be an important part of life. Log churches were built. Local men took turns leading prayer meetings, and any itinerant preacher attracted not only a whole community but all the people of near-by communities as well. The more loudly he inveighed against sin and the more vehemently he urged sinners to repentance, the more he was admired.

Into this area in 1753 came Daniel Boone at the age of nineteen. He and his parents and his ten brothers and sisters moved from Berks County, in eastern Pennsylvania, to the bank of the South Yadkin River in one long, slow trip. Daniel married a North Carolina girl and they bred nine children.

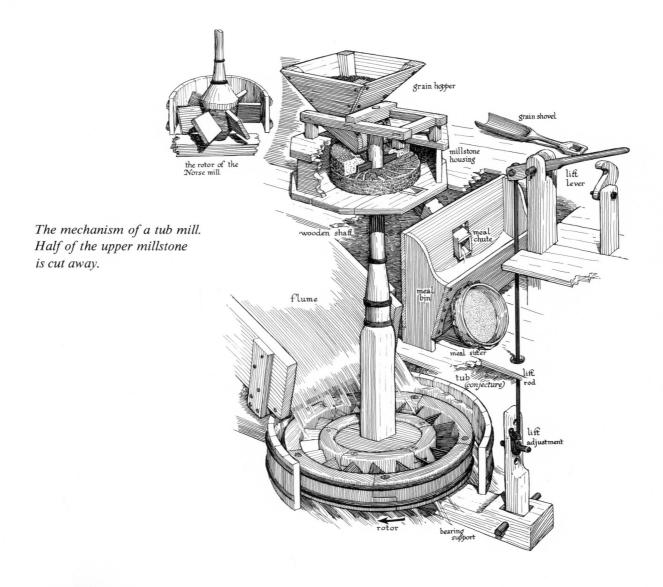

The mechanism of a tub mill. Half of the upper millstone is cut away.

the rotor of the Norse mill

grain hopper

grain shovel

millstone housing

lift lever

wooden shaft

meal chute

flume

meal bin

meal sifter

tub (conjecture)

lift rod

lift adjustment

rotor

bearing support

Cumberland Gap

THE SEVEN YEARS' WAR

The French watched the westward drift of the pioneers and didn't like it. In 1749 they sent Céloron de Blainville to post their border along the Ohio and Allegheny rivers. Céloron actually nailed signs to trees and buried, here and there, engraved lead plates proclaiming the domain of Louis XV, King of France, in stately language. The French put teeth in their claims by building a line of strongholds southward from Presque Isle on Lake Erie, Forts LeBoeuf and Venango in the woods, and Fort Duquesne at the Forks of the Ohio. Governor Dinwiddie of Virginia sent Major George Washington to LeBoeuf and Venango to protest that they were on British soil. The French, with cool politeness, disagreed. The next year, 1754, the French began the French and Indian War, by dispossessing Washington from Fort Necessity near the Monongahela River. Eventually, most of the nations of Europe were drawn into that scrap.

In 1755, General Braddock failed spectacularly to take Fort Duquesne and lost his life in the attempt, but he cut a wagon trail from Fort Cumberland in Maryland almost to the Ohio River. Three years later John Forbes cut another trail from Harris's Ferry (Harrisburg) through southern Pennsylvania. The French destroyed Fort Duquesne before he reached it. Fort Pitt (later Pittsburgh) was built to replace it. When Quebec fell in 1759, the French signed the Treaty of Paris (1763)

and abandoned the North American continent entirely, except for two little codfish-salting islands off Newfoundland. Spanish Florida was also ceded to Great Britain by this treaty.

Americans looked at once with greedy eyes beyond the mountains, but with the ink still damp on the treaty, King George III forbade all settlement west of the Fall Line—a line drawn well east of the mountains through the lowest rapids of major streams. It was a futile ban, for already many settlers were beyond the line; 150 had grouped themselves around Fort Pitt two years after it was built. The frontiersmen paid the king no mind, but Easterners still thought of themselves as loyal subjects, and to them the edict seemed to cancel the Colonies' claims to land beyond the Appalachians.

Both frontiersmen and eastern colonials had marched with Braddock and with Forbes. Legend makes it a man from the Maryland seacoast who shot General Braddock in the back. Many tidewater men had spotted settlement sites in the hills and headed back to them as soon as the war was over. The land they coveted was beyond the mountains but east of Fort Pitt. These were third- and fourth-generation colonials. They had done something to win the war and they felt, resentfully, that England, not America, had profited by their fighting. The Scotch-Irish were born independent; now these Englishmen began to think as Americans.

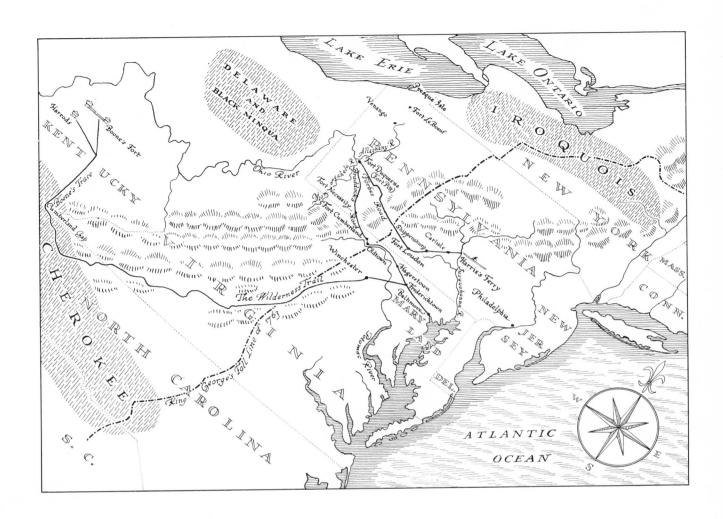

4

THE GREAT SALIENT

CAINTUCK

SETTLERS PENETRATED the southern Appalachians in 1769 and grouped around the Watauga River, in what is now Tennessee. They hadn't crossed the ranges completely, but they were over the divide; the Watauga drains eventually into the Mississippi. They were beyond all semblance of law. However, the settlement became home to three remarkable men: James Robertson, John Sevier, and Daniel Boone. Led by them the scattered colony organized its own government, set up a constitution, and voted itself authority to exercise all civil functions. After five years, North Carolina took over Watauga,

but from it all western settlers caught the idea of acting for themselves. John Sevier drew on his Watauga experience when he organized the short-lived State of Franklin.

Watauga was the jumping-off place for Kentucky. Judge Richard Henderson came there in 1775 with his illegal Transylvania Company in his pocket. With the help of Daniel Boone he negotiated an equally illegal treaty with the Cherokees by which, for "ten wagonloads of cheap goods and whisky," the company bought most of the present State of Kentucky and part of Tennessee. The judge dispatched Boone with forty men to mark the best way into the territory. Boone passed through Cumberland Gap, at the extreme southwest corner of Virginia, and struck north on an

Indian trail called the Warriors' Path, blazing trees on Boone's Trace as he went. Then he turned northwest, still blazing. For this second part of the trace the party followed a "buffalo street." Hundreds of woodland buffalo lived in Caintuck and for centuries netted the place with their wide trails, always following the easiest route. Dan'l and his men completed a fort with four blockhouses at Boonesboro, just south of where Lexington is now, in June of 1775.

Long before anybody settled in it, Caintuck had the reputation of being an earthly paradise. The legend flourished in Europe where it picked up bits from Jean Jacques Rousseau's popular rhapsodies about the Natural Man which extolled the primitive way of life. These notions infected even the hard-bitten early settlers of Caintuck; life there was to be "all git and no give." To the Indians, too, Kentucky was a happy hunting ground. By mutual agreement, no tribe lived there—it was too good for that—but the Shawnees and the Delawares from the north and the Cherokees from the south made forays into it for game and, not infrequently, for war.

Caintuck was officially a western extension of Virginia, remaining so until it became a state in 1792. Boonesboro wasn't the first settlement; James Harrod had built a blockhouse some miles farther west in 1774. Judge Henderson and his first settlers reached Boone's fort before it was finished. The rumor that the way was open spread through the eastern Colonies like fire on spilled oil. Settlers poured in. The diary of William Calk survives. He and a friend took off from tidewater Virginia, down the Wilderness Trail, which followed the Appalachian valleys, in time to catch up with Henderson on Boone's Trace and *"git Down to Caintuck to Boons foart about 12 o'clock where we stop and they come out to meet us and welcome us in with a voley of guns."*

Some settlers built cabins near the fort, but the judge's store "sold dear" and a good many moved over to join Harrod. Others went off into the woods to set up groups of their own and, for many, it was a fatal mistake. On the way in, Calk had met returning settlers who were fleeing rumors of Indian trouble. In 1777 "the year of the bloody sevens"—it broke, encouraged and aided by the British, who were having trouble with their colonies. Harrod's and Boone's forts survived attacks; everything else in Kentucky was leveled, and many people were killed. Caintuck fully earned the somber name that Chief Dragging Canoe gave it, "the dark and bloody ground." Pleas for Eastern assistance got nowhere, so Boone, Harrod, and young George Rogers Clark, who believed in aggressive tactics, organized a local militia; and in a year the worst was over.

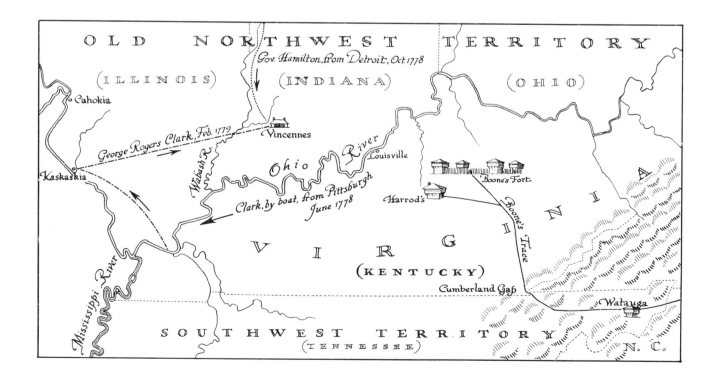

THE REVOLUTIONARY WAR

The frontier was grimly and unanimously for independence, and backwoodsmen did yeoman service with their rifles in the fighting. In 1778 George Rogers Clark struck at the British support of the Indians. He floated 350 men down the Ohio, took Kaskaskia, on the Mississippi, and then, incredibly, crossed the "Drown'ded Lands" of southern Illinois in midwinter, his men often wading in icy water up to their necks. When they suddenly menaced the British at Vincennes, its flabbergasted commander, Governor Henry Hamilton, surrendered not only the town (it was originally French, as was Kaskaskia) but also the whole of the Old Northwest Territory north of the Ohio River, which was confirmed to the United States in 1783. This was land still strongly held by Indians, but by Indians now sufficiently impressed by Clark to be hesitant about raiding Kentucky.

THE GARDEN OF EDEN

Kentucky was in fact a kind of paradise. Its soil was rich, much of it lying over limestone. Its forests were magnificent, with some trees of preposterous size—like a sycamore twelve feet thick—reliably reported. There were natural openings in the woods here, too. Lowland was often covered by canebrakes which were good pasture but were almost impenetrable when the cane was tall

in late summer except along the buffalo streets. There were also open glades, called ranges, covered with buffalo grass and "peavine," which was prairie vetchling (*Lathyrus polymorphus*). The now-famed Kentucky bluegrass is of European origin.

Many varieties of mineral springs, including salt licks, occur throughout central Kentucky. No vegetation at all grew around some of these due to the salt in the soil and the constant trampling of animals. The licks, coupled with the ample forage, and plenty of sweet "freestone" water made a perfect combination for grazing animals. The deer and buffalo population was denser here than anywhere east of the Mississippi, and that meant a corresponding number of predatory animals. The "painter," or cougar, was a menace to domestic herds. The hunters were in their glory; it took them only twenty-five uninhibited years to reduce the game to scarcity.

THE PEOPLE

Once the Indian menace drew back, settlers poured over Boone's Trace in an almost continuous stream. They took what land they wanted and marked their boundaries by blazing the bark of "witness trees"; tomahawk claims, these were called. Far too few registered their claims when offices for the purpose were established, so latecomers with money in their saddlebags were able to take the land away from them. Daniel Boone lost all of his, and he was but one of hundreds.

This was a population more mixed than that of pioneer Pennsylvania. Many were bad farmers who had exhausted their eastern land, and their practices in Kentucky were no better. Many had had nothing in the East and were no worse off here. They were in a narrow salient extending four hundred miles into the wilderness between the Ohio River on the north and the lands of the Cherokee Indians on the south and based only on the settlements near Cumberland Gap that were themselves outposts. There was no communication with Pittsburgh by way of the Ohio; the Indians along the north shore of the river made water travel dangerous until 1794 and suicidal before 1785.

We are ashamed of the way our forebears treated the Indians, but they themselves had few qualms about it. They hated the sight and thought of an Indian. There were men in Kentucky who would, and did, shoot down any Indian they met, anywhere. Notable fighters of Indians were local heroes, and since every man was an Indian fighter of sorts, most of them swaggered as heroes. The tradition of the Ring-tailed Roarer was born. Whoop! Half horse, half alligator! He could whip his weight in wildcats and was ready to do so at a hat's drop. He was equally ready to make public proclamation of his prowess, clarioning his defiance as did the Greek heroes before Troy.

No young man could refuse a challenge to fight and stay in a community. Some fights were "fa'r"; but the usual order was rough-and-tumble—kick, bite, scratch, throttle, and gouge. Many an ear was torn off and many an eye deliberately and slowly gouged out by a victor's thumb. This last abomination was subject to agreement before a fight started, but like the challenge itself, a gladiator dared not refuse it. These braves made their own law for some years and when a soberer law threatened to restrain them, they moved out and took their ideas west. They were notorious outside Kentucky, and their excesses of liquor, language, and behavior put a mark on the whole country.

Only a few were criminals; most were merely boisterous beyond reason. They felt they had constantly to reassert their virility, but that done, most of them were generous, good-natured, humorous—and lazy. While the game lasted, getting a living was easy for a loafer who wasn't trying to wrench a farm from the woods. It's said that Simon Kenton, the greatest wildcat-whipper of them all, never worked a day in his life.

The Ring-tailed Roarers were ever present, but they weren't the whole of Caintuck. Life was crude everywhere and many cabins sheltered what Dr. Daniel Drake described as "dirty hearths, ragged boys, trollopy girls, and crying babies," but most families were trying hard and hoping for improvement. In such households there was little leisure; all of its members worked and the group was self-sufficient (it had to be, or quit). No individual stood above another socially. Here men were literally "free and equal" in a way quite different from the theoretical equality our founders had in mind when they wrote the Declaration of Independence. Land was for the taking, they thought. Few had any money and having it conferred no advantage. This complete leveling of social classes was new in the world. It has had an enormous effect on social ideas in the United States, and it has reached across the oceans.

The frontier was hard on women; they lived lives of almost unrelieved drudgery. They bore too many children, of whom scarcely half lived to grow up. Women wore out; men, as may be imagined, often died violent deaths. The widowed remarried as soon as possible with no sentimental mourning period. Single blessedness was impractical; both man and woman needed the help of a mate.

Flax brake; scutching block and blade

DAILY LIFE IN THE CLEARINGS

The first Kentucky cabins and the life in them were much like those of the Piedmont, but once the Indian menace lessened, a crudely simple farm life developed in Kentucky, as it did in North Carolina and Watauga. For a while in Kentucky, however, people were thrown even more on their own and each other's resources because they were so far from any base of supplies. Never again, not even in Oregon, was any sizable group so nearly cut off. They made their own salt by boiling down the water of the salt springs. When they found caves of saltpeter, they ground up the stuff in hominy blocks and made their own gunpowder. But the settlers who had been raised near the coast spread the knowledge of a more civilized way of life and a wish for better things that hadn't bothered the earlier woodsmen.

broken up on a flax brake. The plants were laid across the edges of a set of fixed parallel planks, called knives; a second set of knives, which meshed with the first set and was hinged to it at one end, was brought down forcibly on the stalks. Broken flax had still to be scutched, or swingled, to knock the bits of stalk out of the fibers. The swingler slashed downward at the flax as it lay over a swingling block, which was the end of an upright plank. Flax swingling was one of the chores for which neighbors gathered to help.

The little wheel

LINEN

"Hetchel"

People had to make their own clothes from scratch, so they planted flax as soon as enough land was cleared to permit it. Only a little cotton was grown anywhere in America until after 1793 when Eli Whitney invented his gin for getting the seeds out. The flax plants were pulled in midsummer and rotted in frequently wetted piles on the ground to weaken the hard core and the sheath between which the useful fibers lay. After two or three weeks, the stalks were dried over pits with slow fires in them and then stored to await further processing in winter when there was time to do it.

Preparing flax for spinning was laborious work. The woody parts of the stalks had first to be

Impurities still remained and to get the last of them the fibers were pulled through progressively finer "hetchels." These were wooden slabs studded uniformly with iron spikes about three inches long. The linen that the coarsest hetchel caught could be used to make sacking and canvas. The next grade was the scratchy tow linen for men's work clothes. Last of all was the pure fiber—long, strong, and glossy—for the women's and children's clothes and the men's Sunday shirts. The women spun all three kinds on "the little wheel," as they called the flax wheel.

Spinning wheels were often made in the cabin where they were to be used. The linen spinner sat at her work with her right foot operating a treadle that turned the wheel. Two grooves in the edge of the wheel guided two belts, one turning the spindle, the other the bobbin that ran on the spindle, which because it had a slightly smaller pulley, turned just a little faster than its axle. This extra speed kept a tension on the spun yarn that reduced tangles. The whole purpose of spinning was to twist the yarn. The skill lay in feeding new fiber by hand to the spindle smoothly so there would be neither slubs (lumps) on the yarn nor thin, weak places in it.

WOOL

Men drove sheep early along Boone's Trace and bred them in Kentucky. Dr. Drake wrote, from his experience as a twelve-year-old boy in the 1780's, that though he couldn't hold a sheep, he could shear one if it had its feet tied together and was lying on the ground. Back East they sheared a sheep and then washed the wool, but in Caintuck they washed the unhappy animal in a pond and then sheared him. In both places there was an endless job to be done of picking out burrs and matted "feltings." The women carded the wool into slivers, so it could be spun, by dragging bits of it between two flat wooden cards studded with short wire teeth. The finished slivers were eight or ten inches long, light and fluffy, and tapered toward both ends. They were spun into yarn on "the big wheel" that the spinner turned by hand. She stood at her work, walking backward and feeding slivers to the yarn as the spindle twisted it;

then she came forward again to allow the yarn to wind up on the spindle. The big wheel had no bobbin. When the spindle was full, she wound the yarn onto a reel, either a "niddy noddy" held in her hand or a clock reel with rotating arms, like a windmill, that clicked as it counted its own revolutions. The yarn was tied into hanks before it was removed from the reel.

WEAVING, DYEING, AND FULLING

At least as early as 1788 there must have been some professional weavers in Kentucky (we read of linen and wool being sent out to be woven), but most weaving was done at home on a barn-frame loom built by the householder. It was a clumsy thing, but the weaver could raise and lower the alternate threads of her warp and pass a weft-filled shuttle between them. She swung the heavy batten toward her and bumped its comb-like reed against each new weft to pack it into

Wool cards

The big wheel

47

place. When the fabric grew so much that it was hard to reach, she stopped and reeled off more warp from the yarn beam at the back of the loom. Then she came around to the front again and took up the slack on the cloth beam, which was a roller that held the finished fabric.

Little if any all-wool cloth was woven on the frontier; linsey made the wool go further, and it probably wore longer because of the strong linen warp. Butternut was the common color for dyeing; it was a permanent brown-yellow made by boiling the inner bark of the white walnut tree. Black walnut hulls produced a rusty black. Oak bark and copperas (ferrous sulfate) made a better black, which also served as ink. Blue could be obtained from the bark of the blue ash tree, but the preferred blue was indigo. When it was obtainable at all, it cost eighteen pence a pound (that was officially thirty-six cents), but you wouldn't relish the amount of work it took to earn that much.

Unless their cloth was fulled first, woolen garments shrank. Fulling also thickened the material, so the settlers held fulling parties. The new cloth was saturated with hot soapsuds and thrown on the puncheon floor of a cabin. The guests, sitting in a circle on stools, stomped on the fabric with their bare feet. They passed the time with songs and stories and jokes. After the party, the cloth was rinsed and hung on a fence to dry in the shade. Later, water-powered fulling mills took over the job.

Linen was hard to dye and was usually bleached instead. Its natural color is a tannish gray, but after days of being spread in the sun and being given frequent sprinklings and turnings it became snow-white. No one took all this trouble with tow linen; only the best was bleached.

HOUSEKEEPING

The Kentuckians made themselves brooms. Armed with his London-made Barlow knife, Pap whittled a broom out of a small hickory log as he sat a while by the fire after supper. He stripped the wood back from one end in thin splints a foot or more long, working round and round and leaving the upper ends of the splints attached, until he got down to the heart of the log, which he cut out entirely. Then he shaved more splints, downward, leaving their lower ends attached just above

48

the tops of the first lot. He didn't go clear to the heart with these but stopped when he reached a core the right thickness for a handle. He bent the upper splints down over the lower ones and lashed them there. When the rest of the upper end of the log had been reduced to handle-size, the broom was finished. Smaller "scrubs," with short handles and short splints, were made the same way.

While Pap was whittling his broom Maw, with her pipe going well, spun or knitted. The older children shelled corn, and the babies played with the cobs. Anyone who wished might help himself to a turnip. Fruit trees took time to grow and the settlers, particularly those from the East, missed their apples and substituted turnips. The light of the fire on this group was supplemented by "taller dips" made on the place, or by a "boat lamp," a shallow dish with a lip, that burned grease by means of a tow wick—and gave off as much foul-smelling smoke as light.

Cows were brought into the woods here, as they were farther east. They ate corn husks and stalks in winter. Dr. Drake mentions that when his mother had to milk a wild cow, the children drove the cow into a fence corner and menaced her with sticks until the operation was completed. With no loss of masculine dignity, a boy might operate

the tall dasher churn to make butter. A good housewife made cheese with excess milk, using a press, homemade from a small gum, and equipped with a long lever for the needed squeeze.

A good housewife also made her own soap, or went without it. It was an unattractive, smelly job and it wasn't uniformly successful. She saved and rendered any kind of fat and boiled it with wood-ash lye, strong enough to float an egg, stirring the mess constantly and always in one direction. The one-direction idea was a little mumbo jumbo to assure that the soap would "come." The end product was harsh and slimy. It could be hardened with salt, but few bothered to harden it.

There were no easy ways to live on the frontier. Grind sausage? No grinder. Chop the meat up into bits with an ax. Two-handed knives for chopping meat and simple hand-operated sausage stuffers were common near the coast, but in Kentucky a woman stuffed her sausage into cleaned pig intestines with her fingers. Wash clothes? First catch some rainwater in a log trough under the cabin eaves, or in dry weather haul water in pails from the spring and "break" it with wood ashes so that soap would make suds in it. Heat the water in a pot over an outdoor fire. Beat the wet clothes on a stump with a club to get the

Splint broom

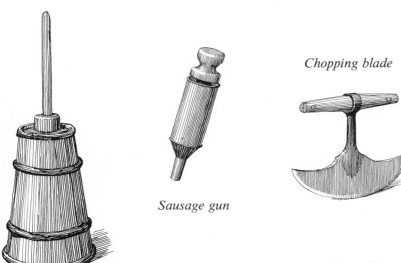

Coopered churn

Sausage gun

Chopping blade

doughnuts, for supper. Wheat flour appeared as soon as the woodland soil lost enough of its richness to grow the plant. People longed for it, but dogs raised on corn meal wouldn't touch wheat bread.

SWEET'NIN'

Communication was established with New Orleans by river about 1790. Until then true molasses wasn't to be had at any price. The backwoodsmen gave the name *molasses* to maple syrup and to a sweet liquid they managed to extract from pumpkins. No report can be given on the quality of this because it has been some time since anybody tasted it. Maple syrup, maple sugar, and honey were the common "sweet'nin's." Every family had a maple grove, and sugaring was an early spring job of men and boys. They tapped the trees crudely and wastefully with an ax and drove homemade buckeye (horse chestnut) spiles into the cuts. The sap dripped into pails hung on the spiles all through the day while the sun was on the trees and stopped at night. It was collected at dusk in a barrel lashed to the kind of simple sled known as a pung and dragged to the fire.

dirt out; then dry them on the fence. Few did any ironing; those who did heated a sadiron on the hearth, with its bottom to the fire, and used a puncheon bench for an ironing board.

These were a different breed from the earlier pioneers. In Kentucky many people ate their mush-and-milk from pewter bowls with pewter spoons, and here tea was not considered slops. There was little of it to be had before the Ohio River was open, but tea was in general use in the late 1780's. Most people drank cheap black bohea on weekdays and green "hyson skin"—that wasn't much better—on Sundays. That night there might be pumpkin pie or "wonders," which were

the curious symbol—a long-tailed four with a cross-cornered lozenge at its bottom that meant "this belongs to . . ." Hardy souls cut down the bee tree which, since it was hollow, smashed when it fell, and much of the honey was lost. Everybody connected with the expedition was thoroughly stung.

OUTDOOR WORK

The pioneers seemed to hate trees. Foreign travelers were astounded at the destruction an American could wreak with an ax. But the ax was too slow for clearing land, because so many trees were giants. A man cut down those up to a foot thick and grubbed out the brush with a mattock. The big fellows he girdled, and after a year or two, he burned them where they stood. But the stumps didn't burn; he plowed around stumps for years.

Good cabin logs and those that would make good fence rails the settler snaked out and stored. The most durable woods for fence rails were chestnut, blue ash, honey locust, white oak, and alas, black walnut—which might have been put to better use. Honey locust would last twenty-five years, but splitting it was a tough job. A good man could split seventy-five ordinary rails a day, but he'd do well to split forty out of locust. Logs for rails ran twelve or fourteen feet long measured by a two-foot rule scratched on the ax handle. The rail-splitter started his split by driving an iron wedge into the wood with a maul near one end of the barked log. This separated the grain for a couple of feet, and he extended the fissure to the far end by driving in several wooden wedges,

The sap, thickening as it cooked, boiled all night in an iron pot in front of a half-faced camp. Some of the syrup was further boiled in the morning and "grained" into sugar in molds. Such sleep as the workers got, they caught in cat naps while the sap was running, but nobody minded that. The whole business was a lark, and to sit in the camp in the firelight and drink spicewood tea with maple syrup was pure bliss for a backwoods boy. The tea was made from the swelling buds of the spicebush and was probably very good.

Bees came to America with the English colonists and they preceded the frontier westward. Some people domesticated hives in "bee gums" but more often they depended on finding a wild bee tree. In either case, they were unable to extract the honey without destroying the colony, and one wonders that the species survived.

Boys hunted bee trees with acumen and guile. A bee, loaded with nectar, circles two or three times and then flies straight as a bullet to its hive. A little honey dropped on a hot stone attracts bees, and by watching them a hunter could establish a direct line toward a hive. More heated honey, a little way to right or left of the line, produced a second line; the intersection of the two located the hive. The finder claimed the tree by cutting his initials into its bark, perhaps beside

51

Wedge, glut, and maul

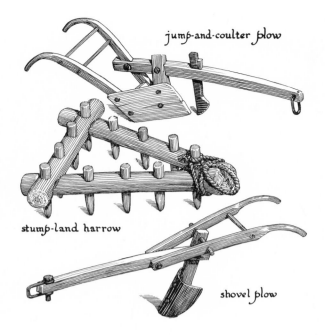

jump-and-coulter plow

stump-land harrow

shovel plow

ting. The next tier lay on the ground rails and zagged at an opposing angle; all ends extended rather irregularly beyond the crossing. Continuing, the fence was laid up as a crib. Two short poles, slanting from the ground toward the fence, braced each intersection and were held in place by the top rails which rested in the V's where the braces crossed each other. This device was later dropped as useless, but early fences seem always to have had it.

BEEF CATTLE

We associate cattle herding with the western Plains and, of course, the climax of it was there, but untouched land at the creeping edge of the frontier was used to graze cattle, even when all of that land was forest. The woodland "cowboys" of Pennsylvania, Kentucky, and Ohio lacked glamour; but they rounded up their herds on horseback, they branded and earmarked calves, and they drove their "cow-beasts" East to sell them. The animals were lean and stringy, particularly after a long drive on short rations; often they were fattened on grass in cleared lowlands for a summer before they were slaughtered.

FARMING

Not only was newly cleared ground cluttered with stumps, it was also matted with tree roots that made deep plowing impossible. But in that

called gluts. Tupelo gum and dogwood, which don't split readily themselves, made good gluts. The initial operation divided the log in half lengthwise. The railmaker split and resplit the halves to make rails three or four inches thick. Most of them were roughly triangular in section; many were crooked or even slightly twisted because the splits followed the grain of the wood.

Batches of rails were dragged to the fence site by passing a log chain around them and hitching a horse or an ox to it. Modern rail fences have posts and run straight along a boundary, but the frontiersman, with space and wood to waste, preferred worm fences. These zigzagged along a strip six or eight feet wide. The ground rails, all zigged at the same angle, rested on stones to retard rot-

Laying up a worm fence

rich soil it wasn't needed. The "jump-and-coulter" plow was made entirely of wood except for the iron colter that cut roots. The man at the plow handles had all he could do to hold the implement down; a boy drove the oxen. After a couple of workings with the colter plow, a shovel plow was substituted that merely stirred the soil.

Corn was and long remained the primary crop. In the first years, with little ground cleared, a turnip patch went in one corner of the cornfield and a watermelon patch hid in the center of the lot. All cultivating was done with hoes; but there wasn't the variety and quantity of weeds then that plague farmers today, because their seeds had not yet been spread by mixture with sown seeds. At harvest time the ears were pulled from the corn and heaped in a long pile for a corn-husking bee, which wasn't much like the later kind that involved kissing games.

All the men and boys in a neighborhood gathered for a corn husking. It began at dusk with the choosing of two team captains and a swig of whisky for all hands, taken from a tub with a gourd dipper. The captains placed a fence rail across the pile of corn at a point they agreed was its middle. The tossing of a chip, bark on one side and bright on the other, served to select the team members and assign each team an end of the pile.

Each husker used a husking pin, a small spike fastened across the palm, to help him tear off the papery covering of the ear. Once it was loosened, he turned the husk back and used it for a hand-hold as he broke the ear from its stem. Husking began in the middle of the pile with each team determined to undermine the rail and make it fall to their side, thus lengthening the pile of the other team. Cheating, though resented, was expected. Feet pushed unhusked corn across the barrier, the rail was covertly nudged, and delay was created by throwing husked ears short so as to bury the unhusked ones. These gambits were challenged and denied and were the causes of impromptu fights.

Once the rail was on the ground, the arguments stopped and the teams went to work with speed as the sole object. They helped themselves along with frequent libations and with a kind of rhythmic chant that could be heard a mile on a still night. A shout hailed the husking of the winning side's last ear, and that team paraded its captain around the still-husking losers on their shoulders. Then everybody sat down to a potpie supper.

Taking corn to the mill for grinding was a boy's job. It was often a trip of ten miles or more, and if he waited for the grinding, he was gone all day. Sometimes the miller would trade meal from his stock for the corn, holding out the tenth that was his grinding fee. When the mill was busy and

Husking pin

Scythe hammer and anvil

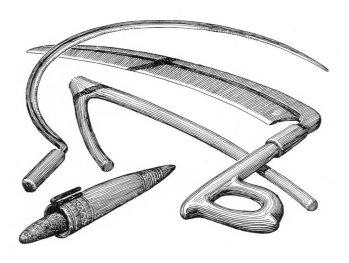

A reaping sickle; a seft and mat hook;
a whetstone and the cowhorn scabbard
in which it hung at the reaper's belt

and handsomer. In rough fields with stumps and stones scattered around, it was a better implement than a scythe or a grain cradle. A scythe man carried a hammer and an anvil along with his whetstone, but he couldn't be forever stopping to beat nicks out of his blade.

Horses or oxen or even cows were sometimes used for threshing; they were guided around a post to tread out the grain in the classical way. More often men threshed with wooden flails on the dirt floor of a log barn. Wooden floors were no good for threshing, because grain fell through the cracks. The threshed wheat or rye was poured onto canvas to let the breeze winnow the chaff out of it.

VILLAGES AND TRADES

Few settlements deserved so dignified a name as village; they were hardly hamlets. They centered on a "station" (fort), a mill, or merely the crossing of two trails. Mays Lick, which still flourishes in Kentucky, accumulated around a salt spring. It boasted a meetinghouse set in a two-acre burying ground, a store, and two taverns, which last were certainly no more than dog-run cabins; that is, two cabins built end-to-end with a roofed "breezeway" between them. Mays Lick was the center for several hundred families, so a few crafts-

there was no stock on hand, the boy might have to come back next day for his meal.

Hay was cut with scythes, and one corner of the field was left standing to provide next year's seed. Wheat and rye were harvested with sickles, and perhaps with the old Dutch *segt* (Americanized into "seft") which had a scythelike blade and a short handle and was used to cut off bunches of straw gathered together with a wooden "mat hook." The eighteenth-century harvesting sickle was larger than a modern sickle, more slender,

Tinker

Assembling a big barrel with the simpler kind of cooper's windlass

men gradually moved into it: a blacksmith who was also horseshoer, gunsmith, and when need arose, wheelwright; a carpenter, no small part of whose business was making coffins, to measure and quickly, overnight; a tanner; a cobbler who mended boots and shoes and could make them in his fashion—he also doubled as harness maker; and not least, a cooper, who could turn home-rived staves into barrels, pails, and tubs.

Some tradesmen settled nowhere; they traveled continually from cabin to cabin. There was the peddler, leading a pack horse or two laden with pots and pans, needles and cutlery, who was willing to trade for almost anything the housewife could offer. There was the tinker, mounted on a pony that was burdened also with a pair of huge saddlebags filled with his master's tools, molds, and materials. The tinker could plug the hole in a leaky basin or fashion a new handle for an iron dipper, and he could melt and recast pewter spoons, plates, and bowls in the molds from his baggage. Even better, he could retail the gossip of the countryside. One little picture comes down to us of such a man, small, middle-aged, bashful, and full of personal oddities.

The cooper made "wet" barrels for liquids and "dry" barrels that were not watertight, for flour and other granular materials. Cabin-made barrel

staves were rough planks rived out of logs. The cooper shaped them to his needs with drawknife, hand adz, and plane. It took skill to taper the sides toward the ends just enough, and to bevel the edges just enough so that when all the staves were pulled together they would lie perfectly against one another.

The finished staves were straight. To assemble them into a barrel they were stood on end in a temporary hoop that could be contracted or expanded; then the cord of a cooper's windlass was carried around their flaring upper ends and tightened to draw them inward. The older windlass, like the one illustrated, was a clumsier tool than another kind that tightened the cord by means of a crank turning a vertical shaft. With the lower ends of the staves confined and their wide midsections bearing against one another, the draw of the windlass bent the staves and brought the assembly at once into the familiar barrel shape. The first of the permanent hoops went on just below the confining cord and was driven down toward the bulging middle of the barrel to hold the strain the windlass had gained. Hoops were strips of hickory or ash notched near each end on opposite sides so that one notch could be hooked in the other, with the overlapping ends tucked under the hoop. It took nice judgment to space the notches so the hoop would be exactly the right size for its location on the barrel.

A barrel had at least one head, usually two. Probably, in that day of big trees, a barrel head

could be made from a single board; nowadays two or more boards have their edges doweled together. The cooper marked out the head with a big wooden compass, cut the circle with a narrow saw, and carefully beveled the cut edge all the way around. He scored a groove inside the barrel near the ends of its staves to receive the beveled head. The groove was made with a croze, a curved plane used only by coopers. A couple of smart mallet taps sprung the head into place, and it was held there by the addition of more hoops. When the lower end of the barrel was headed, the cooper replaced the temporary construction hoop with a couple of permanent ones. Last of all, a two-headed barrel received a bunghole in one end and a spy hole on one side, both made with a pod auger and provided with wooden plugs. A barrel, say for cider, lay in a rack on its side with its spy hole up and its bung, a spout for drawing off the liquid, protruding from the lowest point on the front head. The barrel was filled through the spy hole, and its contents could be measured there either with the eye or with a dip stick.

Pails and tubs, and piggins with one long stave

Croze and compass

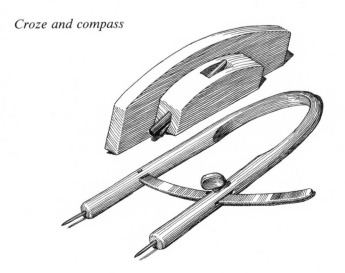

to serve as handle or hanger that were used for maple-sap buckets, all had the same construction as a barrel except that they tapered from top to bottom, instead of both ways from the middle as a barrel does.

SATURDAY

Nearly everybody came into the village on Saturday to buy, to sell, or to swap. If there was no special reason, they came anyway, for excitement and a glimpse of their fellow men. The one store where most of the trading was done necessarily carried a general stock—a pretty skimpy one in early days, when all imports arrived on pack-saddles. By 1790 wares were more plentiful, and the Mays Lick store offered a small selection of groceries, drugs, hardware, dry goods, hats, leather goods, books, stationery, and of course ammunition. Stationery included handmade writing paper in foolscap sheets about twelve by fifteen inches; wafers, which were small disks of dried gelatin used to seal folded letters, for envelopes were unknown; and slates and slate pencils for school use. A panel of smoothed slate, framed in wood, could be written upon on either side with a stylus made of a softer slate that contained talc, whose marks could be readily erased.

Books were either religious or practical. In addition to Bibles and hymn books, and perhaps *Pilgrim's Progress,* primers, spellers, arithmetic books, and almanacs were available. No one could live without an almanac to give him the phases of the moon so he would know when to plant things. Even babies were weaned by the almanac.

Most store purchases were paid for in corn, hay, eggs, or such home products as maple syrup and barrel staves. When any real money changed hands it was paper money, printed at that time in fractions as well as in multiples of a dollar. If there was no other way to make change, it was done with "cut money," created by clipping a piece off a bill of larger denomination.

Men and boys with nothing to do amused themselves in town on Saturday with horse races, not run on a closed course, but on a straightaway, "from yer t' thur." Cockfights and dogfights were arranged, and so were man fights of the uninhibited kind that have been mentioned. The taverns sold whisky by the drink, and the store sold it from a barrel for twenty-five cents a quart, so most of the men became excessively merry.

Law was informally administered by 1790, and on some Saturdays two or three justices of the peace held court in the village simultaneously. Real, stern justice was still administered directly by the citizens, however. Horse thieves were warned to leave the neighborhood at their first offense; at the second they were beaten and their cabins were burned. A murderer or other desperate criminal was shot out of hand, usually in a gun fight, and a medieval touch was sometimes added by decapitating the body and exhibiting the head on a pole at a crossroads.

SUNDAY

The excitement of Saturday vanished in the peace of Sunday morning. Families from beyond walking distance came mounted or, rarely, in wagons; there were as yet no carriages. They tied their horses early to the meetinghouse fence. Everybody was cleaned up, but there was little formality in the clothes they wore. Pap had his boots blacked with soot and grease and he carried a walking stick, but he wore no coat to church in summer. Ma went in calico, wearing a cherished black silk bonnet over a white linen cap with tabs that tied under her chin. Sis went in calico, too, and in a sunbonnet, but bare of foot as was Bud, who proudly sported a short fustian roundabout (corduroy jacket).

There was no Sunday school. Instead, the time before service was for neighborly visiting among the graves and for serious conversation on the bench in front of the church. There was more of the same at noon when the congregation ate the lunches they brought along, for all who came to the morning session stayed on for the one in the afternoon. The Baptist meetinghouse at Mays Lick was built of logs, but it had the first shingle roof in the neighborhood. Although its wooden benches inside were backless, the church was an improvement over the barn that had previously served for meetings. The ritual adult immersion of the Baptists was not performed in the church

but in a stream some distance off to which the congregation adjourned in a long equestrian procession. There were many Presbyterians and Methodists in Kentucky, too, and a small group of English-speaking Roman Catholics, who were the only members of their sect nearer than the French settlements in Indiana. Since the Revolution was but newly past, the Church of England wasn't highly regarded on the frontier and the change of its American members into Episcopalians hadn't penetrated the wilderness.

SCHOOL

A fair percentage of Kentucky settlers could make shift to read, as is attested by the publication of a newspaper, *The Kentucke Gazette,* in Lexington in 1787. The spelling of its name was modernized two years later. There were schools of a sort that early, but they had their ups and downs. Attendance was spotty because when work was at hand the children obviously had to stay home and help with it. Schoolmasters, seldom much more learned than their oldest pupils, drifted in, stayed a while, and departed, sometimes trailing scandal behind them. When the master left, the school closed.

Classes met in an ordinary log cabin, but because light inside was essential, some spaces between logs were left unchinked and were covered with oiled paper. A "turner's chair" (Windsor) and a crude desk were provided for the schoolmaster. The children sat on puncheon benches. They not only recited lessons aloud, spelling and reading in unison, but also studied vocally. Since the pupils weren't all at the same stage of learning, a Babel resulted that some—who had learned their three R's that way—thought was beneficial; they claimed that it improved speech and concentration and strengthened the vocal cords.

Mathematics went no further than the multiplication tables, which could be chorused, and the famous "rule of three," which held that, in matters of proportion, the product of the means is equal to the product of the extremes. The spelling book was Dilworth's and, a little later, Webster's. The New Testament, chorused "verse about" by teams, served as a reader; this was before the days of the great McGuffey. At each day's end the teacher

held a "spell-down" that ended when only the champion was still standing.

The schoolmaster enforced good behavior and attention to lessons with frequent floggings and slappings and made much of an incongruous elaboration of manners. On entering the schoolroom in the morning every boy was required to bow from the waist to the master, and every girl to drop a curtsy. If a traveler passed while the children were at recess, the whole student body lined up at the roadside to bow to him in unison. Pupils brought their dinners with them in baskets and spent the noon hour playing games and romping.

PARTIES

Daniel Drake says that dancing wasn't popular in Kentucky, but one must remember that he knew only a small group of the settlers. Certainly they never missed a chance for socializing. Just as they made play of corn husking and cloth fulling, they also made a "do" of the quilting party, at which the women helped a neighbor line a bedcover. She and her daughters made the top in advance by sewing scraps of cloth together to form a pattern, geometric and often beautiful. The assembled ladies spread a light pad of wool between the pieced top and a plain linen backing, and the two surfaces were stitched together all over in simple patterns to keep the pad evenly distributed.

While the women sewed and gossiped the men indulged in their usual athletics, varied by "plaguing the gaals" in the cabin. The gals ate supper first, the men devoting themselves to social drinking enlivened by jokes and horseplay. There was always a lot of singing; in fact, itinerant singing teachers were able to attract classes in taverns.

The top social occasion of the backwoods, even more popular than a funeral, was a wedding. The festivities began at the bride's home and there seems never to have been a church ceremony. Indeed, there is no mention of religion at all in any of the old accounts except one note that marriages were sometimes postponed until a parson showed up.

The Ring-tailed Roarers and their female counterparts had full scope at weddings. Those who were not invited were likely to ambush the

Shivaree

groom's party and attempt to kidnap him en route to his nuptials. The women often made a similar attack on the bride. We aren't told what happened when these forays succeeded. By established custom, the bride's father set a quart of whisky on his cabin doorstep, and from a mile away the male guests staged a wild horse race to get it. The winner carried it back in triumph to give the groom the first swig.

Both bride and groom were expected to taste at least a little of everything offered to them. About nine o'clock, the women put the bride to bed in the cabin loft, and shortly the groom's friends seized him and forcibly put him into the bed beside her. Below, the party continued through the night and occasional friendly visits were made to the happy couple. All this wasn't so horrible to the newlyweds as it may seem to you. They expected it, for they had treated others the same way. The bride was seldom a shy violet; she hadn't been raised that way.

Next day there followed the "infare," an entertainment provided by the groom's parents. The guests paired off and rode from the scene of the wedding in a procession led by the bride and groom. The infare had no ceremony connected with it; it was just another night-long party attesting the endurance of the frontier spirit. But the end was not yet.

The new couple moved to their own cabin on the third day and that night their friends organized a shivaree (charivari) to warm their new house for them. The celebrants arrived in couples, bringing along anything that would create a din. Silently they surrounded the cabin and at a signal, shouting, gunfire, pan-thumping, and the earth-shaking roar of a horse fiddle shattered the silence of the woods. A horse fiddle was a well-rosined, empty barrel energetically bowed with a rosined fence rail. That was the start of another party and for the third time the sun rose on the farewells of the guests.

"Star of Bethlehem."
One unit, about a square foot,
of a Kentucky pieced quilt.
The solid lines are seams;
the broken lines are quilting stitches.

The United States in 1790
Where the map is shaded, there were at least two people per square mile.

THE LAND ORDINANCES, 1785–1790

With the Revolution over, the old conflicting claims to western land revived. Maryland never could make any such claims; so she refused to ratify the Articles of Confederation until the land was turned over to the Federal Government as raw material for future states. She won her point, thus greatly simplifying the country's later history. By agreement, Virginia reserved a lot of western land to pay off her Revolutionary soldiers; and Connecticut held grimly to her Western Reserve, around the present city of Cleveland, until 1800 to compensate people who had suffered war losses. Georgia held out for the Mississippi as a western boundary until

1802, when she ceded to the United States as the only way out of a mare's nest of conflicting land claims.

The Government had no money and the sale of western land looked like a good way to raise some. Congress passed the Ordinance of 1785, providing for the division of the public domain into townships and for auctioning large chunks of it in the eastern states. The minimum price was a dollar an acre.

Two years later the Northwest Ordinance took care of the political development of the territory. It provided for three stages of territorial government leading to statehood. These steps and the township idea as well, served all new territories in the West except Texas and California. In the first stage nearly absolute authority was given to an appointed oligarchy of five men: a governor, a secretary, and three judges. When the population could muster five thousand free adult men, a territorial legislature was elected, and with the original officers, put the second stage into effect. The third stage arrived when the total free population (these were slave times) reached 60,000; then a constitutional convention could be held and application made for admission to the Union as a state.

Arthur St. Clair, the first governor of the Old Northwest Territory, floated down the Ohio River to Marietta in July of 1788. He hadn't much governing to do at first, but he had lots of room to do it in. His domain reached north and west almost beyond his own ken.

60

5

ROAD AND RIVER

THE WESTERN END of Braddock's Road became choked with brush after five years and was no longer useful for wagon traffic. Forbes Road, too, degenerated into a trail that ended somewhere west of Bedford (then Raytown), Pennsylvania. Pack trains to Pittsburgh used the Kittanning Path that followed the Susquehanna and the Juniata and climbed laboriously over the Appalachians to the Allegheny River. But in 1783 the old Forbes Road was cleared after a fashion and wagons began to use it; in fact, one hardy soul drove through in a chaise that year and created a sensation in Pittsburgh. Today the Pennsylvania Turnpike, smooth, wide, and fast, follows the general trace of Colonel Forbes's road.

In 1783, the Pennsylvania Road, as they called it, was rough, narrow, and very, very slow. Its "paving" was plain dirt studded with boulders and stumps; the only artificial surface was in the swampy spots. There, a bumpy corduroy road made of logs laid side by side had only the merit of

bridging the utterly impossible. Streams had to be forded, but a ferry crossed the Monongahela River at Pittsburgh. Much of the trail was so narrow that wagons couldn't pass, and whichever vehicle was the lighter was often lifted bodily off the road by the combined strength of the travelers caught in the bottleneck. The trail was anything but straight, for it detoured around all large obstacles. Arduous as it was, this road was free of danger from Indians; it frequently shook wagons to pieces, but it was the only road they could use and it was a shorter route to the West than the Wilderness Trail, which was gradually abandoned.

Even before the Revolution ended, squatters pushed west of Pittsburgh and some people, incredibly brave or incredibly foolhardy, floated down the Ohio to get to Kentucky. About three hundred boats went down the river in 1780, but that was after Clark impressed the Indians at Vincennes. River travel remained risky for years, but thousands of people took the risks.

THE TRAVELERS

Almost all of the migrants were poor; otherwise they'd have stayed home. Families on the road had sold most of their possessions and borrowed all the money relatives and friends would spare to buy a vehicle and equipment. The outfits were horse-drawn flatbed wagons or big-bodied New England carts, with two yoke of oxen and no way of braking except by chaining a wheel. There were also some six-horse freight wagons. The difficulties of getting over such a road stagger the imagination, but fortunately, mutual hardship breeds helpfulness in human beings.

Some people preferred braving the danger and discomfort of cold, and traveled by sled in the winter because deep snow smoothed the road. They risked not only freezing but also being left by a thaw with no usable vehicle. A horse or an ox might flounder through snow, but a cow made heavy going of it and pigs and chickens were helpless. It is solemnly stated that children sometimes *drove* poultry along the trail; anyone who has ever tried to urge a hen may have some trouble crediting this. There were no inns at first and few travelers could have afforded them anyway; at dusk they built their fires and camped, and in the rain they camped without fire.

Few of these people were new immigrants; they were the excess offspring of the eastern United States, where population was doubling itself every thirty years and industrial progress was not. Families were in the minority. Most of the travelers were young bachelors looking for opportunity. They hoped to mark a western claim—even one to which they had no legal right—build a cabin, and then go back home to marry a waiting sweetheart.

A good many Virginians and Marylanders went west on the Cumberland Road, which was Braddock's, renamed for Fort Cumberland where it started, and unconnected with the southern gap. The defeat of the Iroquois Indians, who remained faithful to their treaties with the English in the Revolution, opened a way through the Genesee Valley in New York and along the shore of Lake Erie; but its terminus, in Connecticut's Western Reserve, wasn't a safe place for white men until after 1794. A good many settled in upper New York; it was frontier then, too.

THE FLOATING FORTS

Not everybody going west went all the way to Pittsburgh by land; some turned south to Redstone Old Fort, on the Monongahela, above the Forks of the Ohio. A boat was needed to go beyond either place, and not just any old boat; it had to be large enough to carry all of a party's dunnage and animals, and it had to be defensible. Travelers could build boats (trees were free), or they could buy them from hatchet-and-saw builders. Some people had to sell their draft animals and wagons to help pay for a boat, even though they preferred to take those things along. Small

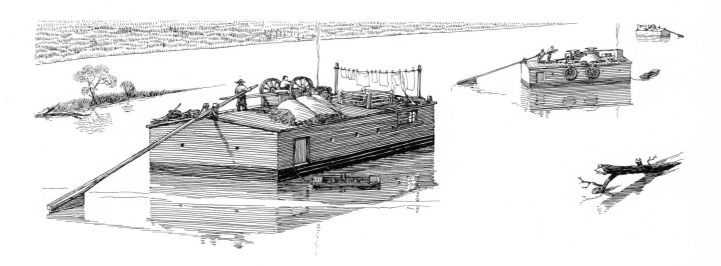

groups often joined forces to buy or build a boat, and people with no money could usually get passage in return for labor. Supplies were obtainable at high prices in Pittsburgh, and the prosperous might hope to start downriver in a ready-made craft after a delay of little more than a couple of weeks. Those who built their own ark might spend the better part of a year at the job.

The ark had ancestors on eastern rivers and was itself the ancestor of a long line of flatboats. Its form evolved on the Ohio to serve the special need. It was made in various sizes, from twenty feet long by ten wide up to sixty feet by twenty-five, which would have been nearly big enough for Noah. Such boats sold for about four dollars a foot, so the smallest came to a then staggering eighty dollars. The hull of an ark was a rectangular scow built of squared timbers eight or ten inches thick; loaded, it floated with some three feet of freeboard. The timbers had to be finished with care so they would lie close enough to permit calking. The hull certainly leaked, so there must have been a low deck to give bilge space. No old account seems to mention one, however, nor is there any word of pumping or bailing.

The house on an ark was made of four-inch planks and covered the whole hull, its walls flush with the sides and ends of the boat. The roof, too, was four inches thick and had but slight pitch so it could serve as a deck. An inside ladder reached the roof by way of a trap door. The strongly barred door in the wall at the stern was large enough to admit a horse, for this was, indeed, an ark. The walls were pierced with loopholes and sometimes with a couple of small windows that had sliding shutters.

The stern of the boat was the stable, and usually the only wooden bulkhead on board was the one that separated the animals from the people. The rest of the space was divided by canvas partitions. Just forward of the stable was a storeroom crammed with everything that had to be kept from the weather. A passageway led forward, with staterooms and a galley opening from it. In the bow was the "settin' room," which was also dining room and nursery. It was as large as space permitted. Fireplaces with stone or mud chimneys served for cooking and heating. As much comfort as possible was wanted because the voyage lasted

Settler's flatboat

weeks, and families often lived on their boats for a year or so while they were clearing land and building a house.

Audubon, the bird painter, said the roof of an ark looked like a farmyard. On it was the family wash and often a playpen for the children. Space enough for the steersman was left aft; the rest of the roof was cluttered with plows, wagon or cart bodies, various farm tools, and a haystack. Wagon wheels were lashed onto the sides. A skiff rode on the roof or, floating, was made fast almost anywhere.

NAVIGATION

It took three men to manage an ark, so far as it could be managed, for it was largely at the mercy of the current that was its only motive power. The pilot wrestled a steering oar as long as the ark, but a drifting boat is short on steerage way, since the water is moving as fast as it is or faster. Arks quite often turned themselves around and continued their stately progress side-on or stern-first.

The well-to-do hired experienced boatmen who knew the river. The poor bought booklets in Pittsburgh that gave clear navigating instructions. On the left-hand pages were good maps of the river in sections, with descriptions of the features opposite. The proper course was marked and all islands and other landmarks were shown; so were sandbars as they were when last seen, but these had their vagaries. No map could show the floating "wooden" islands or the hidden snags.

Snags were logs or whole trees, most dangerous when they slanted upstream, on which a boat could be impaled. They were classified according to their habits. "Planters," with one end embedded in the bottom, were immovable, and reached the surface or extended above it; "sleepers" were entirely submerged; "sawyers" rose and fell in a slow cycle that might keep them under water for twenty minutes; thus a boat, following another that passed safely, could still get into trouble. When other boats came down to one hung on a snag, and possibly stove in, they anchored and came to the rescue. Sometimes it took three or four days of work in skiffs with axes and saws to free a boat and patch it up; and some boats had to be abandoned. One other thing took a toll of arks going below Louisville: the Falls of the Ohio. They were actually rapids, and it took real skill and some luck to run a clumsy hulk through them.

The snag danger and the possibility of Indian attack made it wise to try to travel in groups, but the river often had other ideas. Since it was impossible to follow the charts at night and tying up to a bank was asking for trouble, the voyagers anchored in the stream. This is when the Indians attacked, but they had to do it at a disadvantage from dugout canoes. Three men with plenty of ammunition could almost always repel them. This was a good thing; otherwise there would be a lot of people in the West with no ancestors.

The hulk of an ark may yet be found, deep in the mud, somewhere between Pittsburgh and New Orleans. Until it is, not one exists of all the thousands that drifted down the river. Their owners broke most of them up at the journey's end where there was need for their timbers. The arks and their unfortified successors probably carried a million settlers in the half century before they vanished.

TRADE ON THE RIVERS

After Mad Anthony Wayne routed the Indians at Fallen Timbers in 1794, both shores of the Ohio

Flatboat for N'Awlins

River became white territory as far down as the Falls, and even below the rapids travel became less dangerous. Settlers no longer fortified their flatboats; they built flimsy houses on them and kept their livestock on an open deck forward. Some used rafts with fences around them and mere shacks amidships.

The earlier settlers on both banks raised grain and ground it into more corn meal and flour than they could use. To get the excess up the river to eastern markets was plainly impractical, so they floated it downstream and sold it in New Orleans. Neighbors joined in building a crude flatboat in the river after the harvest, and when the spring freshet came they cast off and let the current do the rest. Many of the tributary streams were too shallow normally to float a boat, but a flood would do the trick. There was a little trouble at mill-dams. The boat had to be unloaded and ridden breathtakingly over the fall by local experts who made part of their living that way. They also smashed a good many boats. Reaching N'Awlins, not only was the cargo sold but also the boat itself, for firewood. The crew walked home on the Natchez Trace that paralleled the east bank of the Mississippi, or paddled upstream in a dugout. The trip down took a month; the trip home took twice that or more. Professional flatboatmen took cargoes down for pay and worked their way back on keelboats.

Most cargo flatboats were scows with simple shelters on them. Forward and after decks were open to permit the use of steering sweeps at both ends, and footways on either side of the shanty gave space for the use of "settin' poles" to help in maneuvering the craft. Another favored flatboat was the broadhorn; again a scow, but in this case housed flush with the stern and with the sides for two thirds of the boat's length. In addition to its steering oar, a broadhorn mounted a long sweep on each side of the roof, that could increase its speed a little and help in turning or in bringing the boat to the river bank.

Because of their cheapness flatboats for cargo were used through most of the nineteenth century, though in later times the crews came home on steamboats, working their passage by loading wood for the boilers.

PIRATES

The usual criminal riffraff of frontiers here took to river piracy. Working in gangs, they took advantage of family boats caught on snags. Often they gained foreknowledge of a valuable shipment, waylaid it from some vantage point, like the famous Cave-in-the-Rock, and after murdering the crew, ran the boat on downriver and sold the cargo. Angry citizens went after them in posses when they got too bold, and shot or lynched enough of them to break up the gang.

KEELBOATS

The keelboats had eastern ancestors in the old "gundalows" and Durham boats. As with the flatboats, there were several variations under the general name; in the main it was a matter of size. The smallest, generally known as keels, were able to carry up to about twenty-five tons; barges could carry perhaps twice that; and packet boats were still larger and specialized in passengers. Keelboats traveled not only down the rivers but also up! Poling upriver was a laborious, slow business, but keelboats could still deliver a ton of goods to Pittsburgh four or five dollars cheaper than could wagons from the coast.

The small keel was some forty feet long and from seven to nine feet wide. Its carvel-built hull

Broadhorn passing Cave-in-the-Rock (now Cave in Rock)

was pointed at both ends, and like all keelboats, had a four-inch square timber running the full length of its bottom. This was for the protection of the boat rather than to keep it from making leeway, though practically every keelboat had at least one mast and a square sail. These small boats had a single house with a flat roof for loafing and sleeping. Cleats fixed to the deck on each side of it, made non-skid footways. Aft of the house the steersman stood on a pulpit, holding the tiller of a wide-bladed oar that was almost a rudder. The mast stood forward, set in the roof of the house, some twelve feet from the bow. A narrow walkway crossed the boat in front of the house. Between this deck and the bow were three or four rowing benches with tholepins beside them on the gunwales.

A barge was as much as a hundred feet long and twenty feet wide. Where a keel needed a crew of, say, ten, a barge needed fifty men, and

Walking a small keel upstream

its superstructure was correspondingly elaborate. Ahead of the main cargo shack, there was a forecastle for the crew, and on the after deck, an eight-foot cabin for the "p'troon" (*patron*), as the skipper was called. His cabin roof did duty as a pulpit for the steersman.

Packets, which reached a length of one hundred and twenty feet, had separate cabins for men and women and had "conveniences constructed on board to render landing unnecessary, as it might at times be attended with danger"; this from an advertisement in the Cincinnati *Centinal* [*sic*] for January 11, 1794. Packets were the most reliable upstream boats until 1817; they made the round trip from Cincinnati to Pittsburgh in about a month and provided "food and liquor on board at the most reasonable rates possible." This particular packet was proofed against rifle balls, loopholed, and armed with six one-pounders.

UPSTREAM NAVIGATION

Forcing a keelboat upstream against a four-mile-an-hour current required using every possible means and seizing every possible advantage. With a strong upriver wind and the sail set, life was easy for the crew; they lolled on the housetop and gained thirty miles a day. On straight stretches,

Bushwhacking

with no fair breeze, they could sometimes use the oars, but this didn't mean rowing up the middle of the stream where the current was strongest. It meant sneaking along the shore with rowers on the water side only; the land-side men pulled their share by grabbing the bushes on the bank. A boat could make fifteen miles a day "bushwhacking"

Cordelling

this way. If the bank was hard and clear of bushes, the crew shouldered a cordelle and proceeded upstream at a slow walk. A *cordelle* is a towrope, and for this maneuver, it was made fast to the base of the mast.

Where the river widened and shallow water along the banks forced the boat out into the stream, the men worked it forward along the edges of the sand bars with setting poles at a mile an hour. A setting pole was twelve or fourteen feet long and was shod with iron; it wasn't much good over a soft bottom. Each man planted his pole on the shallower side of the boat at the bow, faced the stern, and placing the pole's butt against his outboard shoulder and his feet against the deck cleats, he walked the boat under him, leaning steeply toward the stern as he did so to get the most from his effort. When the after end of the house came abreast of him, he pulled up his pole and carried it forward again on the outside footway. The men kept up a steady procession, singing as they worked to the scraping of a fiddler on the housetop.

The slowest progress was made by warping. This had to be done in rapids or where narrowing of the river increased the speed of its flow. Two men in a skiff led one end of a cordelle upstream and made it fast to a tree. The crew put the other end on a capstan and inched the boat up the line. Meanwhile, the skiff crew led a second rope ahead for the next hitch.

When strong downstream winds blew and the

Upstream flatboat

river banks provided neither bushes nor a hard path, the keelboatmen quit trying until the wind changed; they made fast to the shore or avoided mosquitoes by anchoring in the stream.

There are sharp bends in both the Ohio and the Mississippi, and when a boat rounded one of them, special tactics were used. The deep channel lies on the outside of a bend, and after rounding the curve, the water from it eddies to the inner bank, creating a short *upstream* current below the point of land around which the river bends. Water moving upstream wasn't to be missed, so the keelboats followed the inner shore to the tip of the point and rowed from there across the river, with a loss of about a quarter of a mile in leeway.

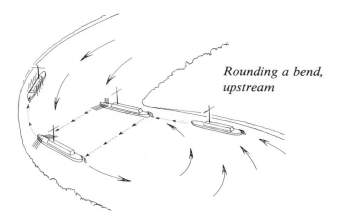

Rounding a bend, upstream

THE RIVERMEN

The earliest keelboaters were Frenchmen from the fur-trading posts along the Mississippi. Though there weren't enough of them to man all the boats after the Americans settled on the Ohio, they passed on much of their improvident, happy-go-lucky spirit to later recruits. Many of these were displaced Ring-tailed Roarers from Kentucky who hadn't left behind their swashbuckling independence or their extravagant vocabulary. A typical riverman was, rather surprisingly, honest,

generous, and roughly kind; but he was also loud, profane, belligerent, drunken, and spectacularly sinful. If the river was too low to be navigated, the keelboatmen went ashore to look for a local dance. If they failed to find one, they hunted up some deviltry. They started a free-for-all fight with some flatboatmen or broke up a camp meeting with whoops of joy. These men owned the rivers and made themselves so obnoxious that many decent settlers moved back from the water to avoid them.

OTHER BOATS

Local upstream journeys sometimes were made with small double-pointed flatboats. These were recurring trips, and paths were cleared along the banks for the oxen that pulled the boats. The animals presumably returned downstream as passengers. French planters on the lower Mississippi moved about and often took their cotton and indigo to market in big *bateaux,* which the owner steered from beneath a regal canopy and which were rowed by eight or ten Negro slaves. Some Yankee settlers, farther north, used small keelboat-sloops, perhaps thirty feet long, that depended chiefly on sailing and could be handled by a couple of men. Individual travelers moving downstream sometimes used curious catamarans, called pirogues, from the dugouts that formed their twin hulls. A shelter about eight feet square bridged the space between the hulls.

Pirogue

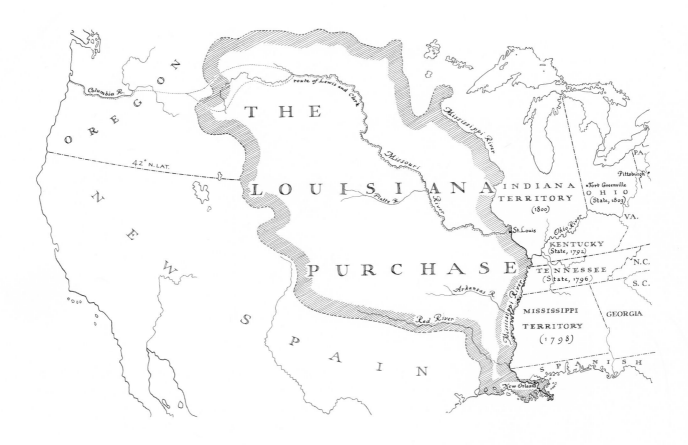

INDIAN TREATIES AND LOUISIANA, 1795–1803

The Government recognized Indian ownership of land, and Congress pretended the tribes were foreign nations and negotiated treaties with them. Western settlers saw this as foolishness: the Indians didn't understand the idea of owning land. To them, land was for everybody; allowing white men to move in didn't mean that Indians must stay out. Further, no Indian felt bound by a treaty unless he, personally, had agreed to it. The gentlemen of Congress were, as a body, sincere; still, they must have known the paltry sums they gave in return for great slices of the continent was taking immoral advantage of Indian ignorance.

Anthony Wayne met the sachems of ten tribes at Fort Greenville in 1795. With a down payment of twenty thousand dollars and a promise of about half that annually, he took over most of Ohio and part of Indiana. There were whites already settled in the area, the survey of the eastern part having begun ten years earlier. The Americans continued to spread into the Northwest Territory, making and breaking treaties as they went. The Battle of Tippecanoe further demoralized the Indians, and the shameful Black Hawk War, in 1832, finally crushed them east of the Mississippi.

THE LOUISIANA PURCHASE

By a deal made with Spain, American goods could be stored and reshipped at New Orleans without payment of duty. By 1800 three eighths of all American exports, at least a million dollars' worth, passed this way. About then, Napoleon decided for colonial expansion and induced Spain to cede Louisiana to France. When the Spanish then withdrew the "right of deposit," President Jefferson justly feared that the frontiersmen, who had to have an outlet for their goods, would attack New Orleans independently and provoke a French war. So he sent James Monroe to Paris to try to buy the town. By then Napoleon had other interests, and in 1803, he sold Monroe all of Louisiana, roughly everything between the Rocky Mountains and the Mississippi River, for less than $15,000,000. Even before it was turned over to the United States, Mr. Jefferson dispatched Meriwether Lewis and William Clark to see if there was an easy way across Louisiana to the Pacific. They found a way, but it wasn't an easy one.

68

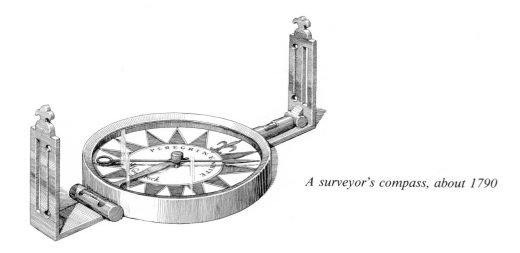

A surveyor's compass, about 1790

6

THE OLD NORTHWEST

THE OLD NORTHWEST TERRITORY, when it had all been gathered in, extended from the western edge of Pennsylvania to the Mississippi River, and from the Ohio to the shores of the Great Lakes and even beyond them, west of Lake Superior, to the Lake of the Woods. From this big domain have been taken the states of Ohio, Indiana, Illinois, Michigan, Wisconsin, and part of Minnesota.

Millions of acres in the eastern and southern parts were sold to land companies for exploitation. Most of these were honest enterprises, but not all. The Ohio Company of Associates, founded in Boston and led by stout old Rufus Putnam, bought 1,781,760 acres at an actual value of about eight cents an acre, paying one third down. The grant was later reduced when the associates couldn't keep up their payments. Putnam and a party of other Yankees built the Yankee town of Marietta—complete with Common, Town Meeting, and Congregational Church—at the mouth of the Muskingum River. This was in 1788. At the same time and for the same price, 5 million acres went to the Scioto Company, many of whom were members of the Congress that voted the grant. High-pressure salesmanship and false advertising brought over six hundred French artisans who arrived to find the Scioto Company bankrupt. They had been led to believe they were coming to a well-populated community and were appalled by the empty wilderness they found.

In 1795 Connecticut sold 3 million acres of its Western Reserve to a company named for the state that surveyed the town of Cleaveland (as it was first spelled) and then went about settlement in an orderly and successful way.

PUBLIC LAND

The survey of the public domain began where the Ohio River meets the western boundary of Pennsylvania. A line was run due west forty-two miles, and between it and the Ohio, seven numbered, north-and-south ranges of townships were laid off; each township, six miles square, was subdivided into thirty-six 640-acre (one mile square) sections. Posts marked the section corners and the nearest tree within each section became its "Witness Tree," branded on a blaze with the range, township, and section numbers. Soldiers went with the surveyors to protect them from Indians and to dispossess illegal squatters.

Squatters were hard to move. They found excuses for delay, and the army disliked being tough with them; then, too, getting them out of their cabins didn't dispose of them permanently. They merely moved farther along and squatted again; as one of them said, "All I haffen t'do t'move is putt out the fahr an' whistle fer the dawg."

The system of auctioning the surveyed land in the East only didn't satisfy anybody. The easterner bought a pig in a poke; the westerner, after traveling a thousand miles, might be outbid on

Numbered sections in a township

land he had already cleared. The whole-section lots were too large for an ordinary man to buy; he was forced either to pay high prices to a speculator for an acreage of reasonable size or to squat and take a chance of getting his land confirmed to him later, as many successfully did.

As the first Territorial Delegate from Ohio in 1800, William Henry Harrison persuaded Congress to improve things. Four land offices were set up in Ohio with authority to hold auctions, receive payments, and issue deeds. The minimum price was raised to two dollars an acre (only the leftovers, after auction, could be had at that price), but a man could buy half a section, or 320 acres, from the Government and pay it off in four yearly installments. The minimum acreage was reduced to 160 in 1804; and again, to 80, in 1817. Even so, people made deposits on more land than they could pay for with the "profits" of the first hard four years. Everybody was in debt to the Government. In 1820, the acre price was reduced to a dollar and a quarter, at the end of a period when nobody had a dollar and a quarter.

The necessary five thousand males lived in Ohio by 1798, and a territorial legislature was elected. Settlers flowed in following the passage of the Harrison Land Act; a western boundary was established, and in 1803, Ohio was admitted to the Union. After the War of 1812 the flood of settlers that is called the Great Migration began and the land offices did the kind of business that is still called by their name.

THE NATIONAL ROAD

There was an acute need for roads to get people west and to keep them in touch with the rest of their country. In 1796, Congress employed Ebenezer Zane to cut trees and open a way from the bank of the Ohio opposite Wheeling to a point across from Maysville, Kentucky. This was Zane's Trace. Ebenezer operated a ferry where it crossed the Muskingum, and Zanesville grew up around him. But to use Zane's Trace it was necessary to get to Wheeling, a difficult journey by way of Cumberland. There was much discussion of improving this road; everybody in the West and East wanted it done, but the Congressional quibbling had to be gone through and a war intervened. The National Road was finished from Baltimore to Cumberland in 1814, but it didn't reach Wheeling until 1818. A branch road went to Pittsburgh.

The like of the National Road will never be seen again. The driving surface was thirty feet wide and was "paved" with an inch of crushed stone topped with gravel. Little grading was done. Trees up to eighteen inches thick were left nine inches high (yes, right in the roadbed!) and all trees larger than eighteen inches were cut fifteen inches high. However, their stumps were "rounded and trimmed so as to present no serious obstacles to carriages." Twenty-five foot strips, cleared on both sides of the road itself, provided for pull-offs and for wayside camping.

The first four-horse coach from Baltimore reached Pittsburgh August 1, 1817, and was followed for years by a steady stream of gigs, Conestoga wagons, farm wagons, horsemen, and even horse-drawn wheelbarrows and man-pushed pushcarts; interspersed among them were pedestrians with packs on their backs and herders moving sheep, cattle, hogs, horses, and mules. Many travelers took to the river at Wheeling, but many were ferried across and hazarded the rougher but faster going on Zane's Trace.

Ferrying travelers across deep rivers was one of the better ways to frontier wealth. People and wagons had to cross or turn back, so the ferrymen charged prices that were unabashed robbery and got away with it. The ferryboat was a low-sided scow, usually long enough for a big wagon and six horses. Both ends raked as far as possible for

The National Road

easy boarding and the overhang was further extended by a six-foot hinged apron, dropped on shore as a gangplank but raised to clear the water in passage. On a river with strong current, a rope stretched across the stream kept the boat from being swept away. Two pulleys ran on the rope, with an end of the ferry secured to each of them. Lengthening the stern pulley line, to set the scow at an angle to the flow, made the current help move the boat across the river, but most of the push came from setting poles. A ferry of this kind appears on the title page.

THE FREIGHT WAGONS

Conestoga wagons were conspicuous on the National Road not only because of their size but because there were so many of them. Going west

they were always loaded, but a good many came back empty, since western exports moved south by boat. Everybody was concerned about this, and the road was pushed forward to Columbus, Ohio, by 1833, and to Vandalia, Illinois, by 1852. It was headed for St. Louis, but it never got there; the stone surface ended at the Indiana line because by that time canals and railroads had apparently made the road useless. But it had served its purpose in tying the two halves of the nation together. There was a time when some westerners advocated independence from the Union or even joining up with the Spanish.

The Conestogas were finely designed and constructed for the job they did. Their ancestors were the low-wheeled, freight-and-passenger stage wagons of Europe built to carry burdens over bad roads (but not as bad as America's). The American wagon was built with high wheels so its axle

Conestoga wagon

trees would clear stumps. Its body was deeply curved, with raking ends, so the load would settle toward the middle and stay put on steep hills. The running gear was as stout as wood and iron could make it: tough oak for the perch, springy hickory for the spokes, non-splitting gum for the hubs.

These wagons were first built about 1750 by German farmers in Pennsylvania's Conestoga Valley to haul produce to Philadelphia and Baltimore. It was the famous Pennsylvania Dutch flair for color that painted the bodies blue and the gear bright red. Industrious wives wove the tow-canvas that was stretched on hoops to cover the cargo. Careful German husbandry bred the heavy black horses that pulled the wagons in teams of six, driven by a "waggoner" who rode the near wheel horse and managed his cattle with verbal commands, a single jerkline, and a smartly cracked blacksnake whip that practically never touched a horse. The Conestoga driver's position on the left of his team led him to hold to the right-hand side of the road. This forced smaller vehicles to do the same and established the national custom, though other drivers clung illogically to the right-hand seat until Henry Ford moved them over in 1909.

The wagoners were very proud of their outfits. They decorated their horses' bridles with red string, hung big fringed leather housings over their collars, and mounted a chime of bells above each pair of hames. Grain for the animals rode in the wagon, and they ate at night from a long box that hung under the tailgate by day but was set on the wagon tongue for feeding. The wagons had big brakes that bore against the tires when the driver

or his helper held down a long iron handle. The handle could be chained to lock the brakes for a long descent. It took good brakes to hold back six or eight tons on an ungraded road.

Such wagons hauled America's freight for almost a hundred years, not only in the wilderness, but near the coast as well; in fact, they were still in local use until about World War I. In the early nineteenth century there were few points on the National Road where one or a dozen of the juggernauts wasn't in view. Two men attached to each vehicle made a considerable number of wagoners. They dressed in leather boots, linsey pants, red flannel shirts, and broad-brimmed wool hats. A roistering, hard-drinking lot, they were very fond of dancing in the taverns at night, with or without feminine partners. They smoked four-for-a-cent-cigars—long, thin, and villainous—first known as Conestogas but soon shortened to *stogies*. They talked loudly and roared with mirth at very crude practical jokes. A group of them once set fire to a whisky thief but kindly extinguished him short of incineration.

THE COACH LINES

Though the bodies of private coaches hung from S springs, all public passengers rode in springless stage wagons as late as 1798. These were literally wagons, and their nine or twelve passengers sat on uncushioned boards, with no back support whatever. A coach on the National Road was a little better. It had no actual springs, but its body rode on heavy leather thoroughbraces, slung fore and aft between rigid iron stanchions. Though this suspension eased the shocks, it permitted a sickening sidesway. Nine passengers could ride in the vehicle, sitting three abreast, with those on the front seat facing backward. Roll-down leather curtains protected them in bad weather. Their luggage was lashed on a rack behind and sometimes overflowed onto the roof. Few travelers carried more than a carpetbag and a small trunk covered with deer hide with the hair left on.

The driver's seat wasn't on the roof, as it would be later on, but was attached to the front of the body only a little farther from the ground than the passenger seats. The coachman managed four reins, two for his wheel horses and two for his leaders. Those for the lead pair reached them by way of brass terrets fixed to the crown pieces of the wheeler's bridles. The driver's long-lashed whip had a stiff stock about four feet long; beside him was the iron handle that operated the brake. His costume tended to the flashy and his hat was invariably white.

The coach fare for the whole distance from Baltimore to Wheeling was $17.25, unless you were important enough for the owner of the line to chalk a mark on your hat, in which case you rode free. The coaches moved day and night on strict schedules, changing horses every twelve miles. Fresh horses replaced tired ones at a stage house in one minute; the driver didn't have to leave his seat except to stretch his legs or wet his often dry throat. There were half a dozen coach lines with names like Pioneer, June Bug, Good Intent. One, the Express, maintained the tightest schedule except perhaps for the Oyster Line, which specialized in getting Chesapeake shellfish to Pittsburgh fast enough to avoid poisoning the consumers. An Express Line coach set a record of a rattling eleven miles an hour for the 130-mile run. Such speed earned the line the ribald nickname of "Shake Gut." Individual coaches had names, too, those of famous people. One coach was named for Henry Clay, who traveled the road himself.

Coach drivers, as was true everywhere, were important people, more so than seems reasonable now. Statesmen and generals cultivated their acquaintance and vied for the privilege of riding beside them; small boys gaped at them in awe. They were likely to be "characters," even in a day when individuality was normal. They also tended to be impressive in appearance; Redding Bunting was six feet six inches tall, and Montgomery Demming, though a mere six-footer, weighed 460 pounds on the hay scale! Demming drove for the Express, and some took his quivering abdomen to be the source of the line's nickname.

INNS

Poor travelers camped along the road, sleeping in their wagons or under them if they were lucky enough to have wagons. The more affluent stopped at inns, of which there were two kinds: the stage houses, where there were beds and

McIntire's tavern at Zanesville

whisky was five cents a glass; and the wagon stands, where "Old Monongahela" was three cents, or two for a nickel, and you slept on the floor. Late-comers often had no choice but the floor, even in good places. All inns provided feed for horses and big courtyards for parking vehicles.

Although tableware was scarce at supper, the food was plentiful. There was no ordering of one's choice; everything there was to eat went on the table at once. The guest paid a flat fee of a few cents and ate his fill. Table manners lacked delicacy. Even the gentry weren't too fastidious. Fashionable travelers made use of silver toothpicks as they left the table; simpler people, if they still had any teeth, used bone picks. The evening was loud and merry but short; rest was needed to cope with travel on the National Road.

In the morning, the boniface waked his guests with a blast on a conch shell or a tin horn and everybody piled into the courtyard to wash at the horse trough, sharing a communal towel. A good many stopped at the bar on the way to breakfast for an eye-opener of "hard likker" or a "morning draft" of beer. Some didn't wait until they had washed. As a doggerel verse had it:

Our fathers of old, they lived like goats.
   They washed their eyes and then their throats.
But we, their sons, have grown more wise,
   We wash our throats and then our eyes.

Beyond Wheeling, inns were cruder. It was a tale to be told that Mr. McIntire had *beds* in his tavern at Zanesville (then Westbourne) in 1799. No one seems to have followed his example for years. Happily, a representation of Mr. McIntire's

Broadax
and hewing dog

luxurious hostelry exists. It was two two-story, squared-log houses under one roof. The doors and the only windows opened onto the dogrun between the buildings. No doubt Mr. McIntire followed custom by hanging a jug on his signpost so the thirsty illiterate could find him.

FARMS

The early days of the Old Northwest were as crude as those of Kentucky and crudity persisted for years, along with better ways. When Finley Hutton was taken to Ohio as a boy, in 1849, he saw everywhere rough log cabins with plank roofs and stick chimneys. But even in 1800, there were some squared-log houses, and corn patches were growing into farms, primitively but effectively equipped.

To build a squared-log house a man had first to square the logs. The ideal timber was eight by eight inches and could be hewn nicely from a twelve-inch log. For hewing, the log was placed across two other logs for convenient working height, and double-pointed hewing dogs were driven into them and it to hold it immovable. The hewer marked the size of his timber on the butt of the log with keel (red ocher). Then he and a helper stretched a chalked string along the log from the upper left corner of the marked square, viewed facing the butt. Snapping the taut string struck a perfectly straight line on the bark. The hewer next stood on the log and notched it every eighteen inches along the side, beyond the chalk line. He used an ordinary ax, and his notches were not quite deep enough to reach the line. Still standing on the log, he split out the wood between the notches; then he got to the ground and took up a broadax to finish the flat.

This tool had a chisel-edged blade eight inches wide and a short handle. It had been used for hewing timber from the earliest colonial days in America and long before that in Europe. Using it, the axman stood facing the butt with the log on his left. He notched the slabbed-off face of the wood as before, but instead of splitting away the wood between notches, he cut it off with his very sharp blade, leaving a far smoother surface than a split would yield. Early broadaxes had straight

74

*One way to corner
a squared-log house
so the joints
will drain*

A log house was built on the same crib princi-ple as the old cabin, but its timbers were sawn to exact lengths, and they didn't project at all be-yond the corners. Lock mortises of one type or another were carefully cut at the corners with saws and chisels, instead of the old ax-cut saddles. The best of the mortises, the kind that were used on blockhouses, set the timbers so close on each other that a ramrod could hardly be inserted be-tween them. That took a lot of timber and a lot of work, however, and few houses were built so tight. Many houses had only the inner and outer faces of the logs flatted. The usual space between timbers was from two to four inches and was chinked either with flat wood slabs staggered at a steep angle and smeared with lime mortar or with small stones carefully fitted between the logs and similarly plastered.

Timbers were pre-cut to allow for door, fire-place, and windows. The openings for doors and windows were framed with heavy sawn planks,

handles, but those of the nineteenth century usu-ally had a crook in them to offset the blade a little from the haft and save the worker's knuckles, for he worked with the blade parallel to the face of the timber. With one flat finished, the workers rolled the log over to rest on its flatted face and present a new side to be hewn.

Backwoods flutter-wheel sawmill

and windows had glazed sliding sash. These were handmade on the job; the glass for them came by water from Pennsylvania. The door, though solid, was no longer made strong enough to keep out Indians. Floors were likely to be black walnut, sawn into wide boards.

Many log houses were two stories high and had narrow corner staircases. Ceilings were low and revealed the hewn joists and the underside of the flooring of the room above. The inner walls of some houses were the exposed surfaces of their timbers, but more often walls were covered with vertical poplar boards. Fireplaces and chimneys were commonly made of rubble stone laid in lime mortar.

The size of a log unit was limited by the length of a manageable timber, a maximum of about twenty-eight feet. Longer structures were achieved by butting two units together. Often the second section was not built until the family's growth demanded it. A two-section house commonly had three rooms on its first floor and but one upstairs. The kitchen-living room took up one section; the other was divided into a large bedroom with a fireplace, and a small unheated middle room.

Most of these houses had roofs of hand-rived shakes which were simply flat slabs split off with a froe from two-foot "bolts" of cedar or red oak and not tapered or dressed at all. This made a shaggy-looking roof and it was likely to be replaced after a few years with shingles, split out in the same way, but tapered with a drawknife on a shingle horse so they would lie close and present a neat surface.

Not a few log houses are still occupied, but they go unnoticed because they have been sheathed over. Some frame houses were built early in the Northwest, especially in the areas settled by New Englanders, but their frames were not the light "balloon" affairs of our time; they were six-inch timbers, mortised-and-tennoned and pegged.

The sawn boards referred to were cut by a water mill whose saw was set in a "sash," moved slowly up and down by a pitman connected to a long-throw crank turned by a water wheel. Already slow, the rotation was slowed further with big wooden gears. At every stroke of the saw, a ratchet beam, connected to the sash, engaged a toothed wheel and pushed the saw log against the blades. Most sashes had two or three blades that took half an hour to cut the length of a twenty-foot log. The simplest mills had a single saw. The crank moving it was directly on the shaft of a "flutter wheel," or undershot wheel, which was backed up to a natural waterfall.

THE BARN

The farmhouse was the center of a small solar system of outbuildings all geared to the busy life of the place. The barn was the largest structure, perhaps sixty-six feet by thirty-four; its walls were sixteen feet high built with full-length logs hewn flat on two faces. Standing in the wall with their flats vertical, it took only seven of them to reach the eaves. The logs rested on a stone foundation. In the middle of the structure the barn floor was

raised just high enough to bring the sill of the wide haymow door level with a wagon bed. The mow was roughly square and was cut off by log partitions from the cow stable on one end and the horse stable on the other. Animals entered both stables by doors at ground level in the ends of the barn. The horse stable took the full width of the building, but there were fewer cows than horses, so the corncrib was subtracted from one end of the cows' domain. Like that of the mow, the corncrib door stood wagon-high above the floor of the wagon shed. When sudden rain threatened, a load could be run quickly under the shed and kept dry. The wagon shed was also the carriage house if the family boasted a gig or a chaise.

CORN

Corn land was often plowed in the fall to give the frost a chance to break it up. The farmer used a wooden plow with an iron share, or if he were very prosperous and newfangled, he used a cast-iron plow. In the spring he worked his ground with an A-shaped harrow set with iron teeth driven through its wooden frame. When he had "rubbed" the land with a weighted puncheon drag and harrowed it again, it was ready for planting.

A single-shovel plow served to lay off a grid of "check rows" three feet six inches apart both ways, the plowman sighting a distant point to keep his rows straight. Four or five boys with bags of shelled corn advanced down the field abreast, following the rows and dropping half a dozen grains at every crossing of a transverse row—"One for the crow, two for the cutworm, and three to grow." A man behind each boy used a hoe to cover the kernels. Though not mounded at all, the planted spots were, and still are, called hills. This virgin soil grew fine corn, especially on bottom land. There are tales of twenty-foot stalks. Such stalks are said to have grown two or three ears weighing a pound apiece, the lowest growing as far from the ground as a man could reach.

As a rule the farmer filled his corncrib in winter. He normally cut and shocked his ripe corn and then husked it in the field in cold weather. But sometimes he pulled the corn and invited the neighbors in for a husking bee in the barn; not the violent contest of early Kentucky, but a more bucolic affair in which the girls joined. The finder of a red ear could claim a kiss and get it accompanied by a chorus of giggles and thigh-slappings.

SCYTHE AND CRADLE

By the end of summer the mow inside the barn was stacked almost to its roof with hay. The farmer cut his hay with scythes and tedded it with wooden forks to get it thoroughly dry, because if it was stored damp, it would at best mold, and at worst it would heat, take fire, and burn the barn down. He raked the dry hay into windrows, either with a wooden hand rake six feet wide or with a horse-drawn flop rake, also wooden. This implement had two opposed rows of long straight teeth set in a bar about nine feet long that could rotate in a light frame dragged by a horse. One set of teeth was used at a time. The teeth ran nearly horizontal and point first on the ground. When the working set had gathered its capacity, the farmer, walking behind, tripped a catch and allowed the rake to flop, that is, to turn over half a revolution. This dumped the gathered hay and brought the second set of teeth into operating position, and the wooden catch swung back by gravity in time to hold them there. The windrows had still to be raked into haycocks by hand and then pitched with forks onto a wagon for hauling to the barn.

One outbuilding was the granary where small grains—like wheat, rye, and oats—were stored.

A wooden flop rake
turning over to dump its hay

Such crops were "thrashed" with flails, and the straw from them was stacked near the barn. The harvesting of these grains was done with cradles, scythes with light wooden racks on them to catch the cut straw as it fell. Cradling was a community job. A number of men worked across a field side by side, swinging their cradles rhythmically and dropping their cuttings in small piles behind them. The men loved the work, for though the cradle was heavier than the scythe, it was a less laborious implement to use, and cheered by amiable competition and banter, the harvesters mowed from sunrise to sunset with time out only for a gargantuan dinner.

A binder followed each cradler, gathering armloads of straw and binding it into sheaves with strips of linden bark. Often the binders were women. They were better at it than men, staying right on the heels of the cradler and deviling him to a faster pace than he would have preferred.

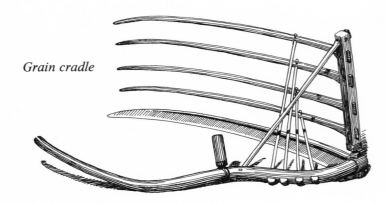

Grain cradle

Most farms had a three-sided shed which sheltered a forge and an anvil. Here minor repairs could be made on iron work, and if the farmer knew how to do it, horses and oxen could be shod. There was always a henhouse and a hog pen to which it was a boy's chore to carry water twice a day. Hogs no longer ran wild in the woods, though chickens, ducks, and geese had the run of the place, laying their eggs and nesting wherever they felt humans would be least likely to look. Foxes fed well on nesting poultry.

WATER

A worm fence enclosed the large pasture in whose midst was a spring and a stone springhouse reached by a gated path from the house. The overflow from the spring made a little brook, dammed at the foot of the pasture to make a "horse pond" where the animals drank. Between the springhouse and the pond stood another building, the still. Practically every farmer made whisky and brandy from his grain and fruit and traded them at the local store, where they were sold along with molasses and tea, like any other commodities. When the Government put a tax on whisky, many farmers on grand juries refused to indict moonshiners, some saying frankly they wouldn't punish a man for what they did themselves. The reason for the location of the still below the spring

78

was the need for water to mix with the mash in the fermenting gums. Water was also run through the worm barrel to condense the distillate in the copper worm by cooling it.

On farms where there was a spring uphill from the house, water ran by gravity to the kitchen door in wooden pipes made by boring small logs, lengthwise, with a long-shanked auger. There were also springless farms with dug wells from which water was lifted in buckets on sweeps or windlasses, or with wooden pumps bored from logs, like the pipes. But most took their water from the pasture spring, and what was needed at the house the boys carried, perhaps a hundred yards uphill, in wooden pails. In summer the housewife saved labor by doing her wash near the spring, heating water on the spot in an iron kettle.

Water from the spring ran through the springhouse in shallow channels chipped into its natural stone floor. These channels were the refrigerator for the few perishable foods. Butter and eggs were kept in lidded stoneware crocks that stood in water so cold that cream wouldn't rise on bowls of fresh milk placed in it; these were set for a while on a shelf along the wall. The tall churn stood in the springhouse to accumulate the sour cream it would turn into butter.

HOUSEKEEPING

The house had its own outbuildings. The woodshed was near the kitchen door and many chores were done under its extended roof—the

Still

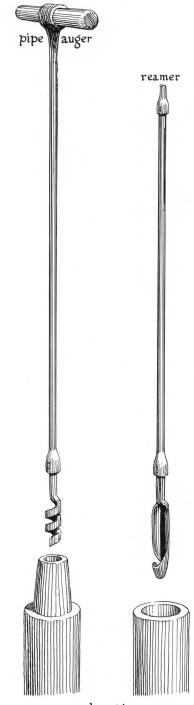

pipe auger

reamer

wooden pipe

rendering of lard, the boiling of soap, and some of the butchering. Back of the dwelling stood the smokehouse where pork cured in the smoke of a slow fire kept going for a week. Not only smoked meat but also salt meat was kept in the smokehouse, and here the farmer paid off his hired hands with the equivalent of a third of a dollar a day in sowbelly or fat back, giving them better value than the equivalent cash would buy of the same commodities at the store. South of the Ohio a farm like this would have had slaves on it, but in the Northwest Territory slaves were not profitable, and in nearly all of it, slavery was illegal from the start.

Behind the smokehouse the ash hopper accumulated wood ashes all winter from which lye was to be leached in the spring; only enough lye to make the family's soap and hominy. A little farther along the same path stood the privy, and beyond it was the orchard. Americans seem always to have tended to place these buildings near apple trees.

Spiral conveyor

The farm wife and her daughters still carded wool and spun it, but what they didn't knit into stockings, mittens, and scarves, they sent out to be woven into blankets and the coarse, ribbed cloth they called jeans that replaced the linsey-woolsey of earlier days. From jeans the frontier farm wife cut and sewed winter clothes for her whole family. Linen was still spun and woven, too, but southern cotton, boosted by Whitney's cotton gin, had cut down the use of linen for shirts and sheets.

Near the house the wife and children cultivated a sizable truck patch. It provided greens, melons, and roots for the summer table and grew some vegetables for winter storage. Turnips and cabbages kept perfectly when surrounded with straw and buried in mounded pits. Potatoes lay on the damp earth floor of a cellar under the house. Hard-shelled winter squashes and onions with their tops braided together went into the kitchen where they would keep dry and, one hoped, would not freeze.

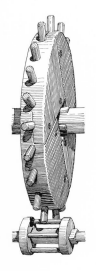

Wooden gears

The farm wife did her cooking on the hearth, as her mother had done, and she liked it that way; in fact, when cooking stoves appeared, some tried them, found them wanting, and went back to the open fire. This housekeeper could buy "luxuries" that hadn't been available to the log-cabin woman in Kentucky. Sugar and molasses came by keelboat from Natchez and New Orleans; coffee, chocolate, and spices came downriver from Pittsburgh; so did whale oil for lamps, but homemade tallow candles were cheaper.

Corn bread by no means disappeared, but the family could now eat wheat bread as well,

Fireplace, oven, and dough trough

kneaded with home-cultured yeast, put to rise in a covered dough trough, and baked in the stone oven beside the fireplace. This oven was itself a small fireplace with its own flue leading into the main one. A hot fire was maintained in the oven until the masonry around it was deeply heated; then the fire was raked out with a special hoe, and the flue was plugged. The cook slid the loaves from a flat shovel, called a peel, onto some leaves placed on the oven floor to keep the bottom of the bread from burning. She then closed the oven with a wooden door, sealing the cracks with clay, and left the loaves to bake slowly to thick-crusted excellence.

The farmer sent his wheat to be ground into flour at a mill on a creek near the farm. Here the stream was dammed, and its water was led from the millpond by a race to turn the twenty-foot overshot wheel that ran the millstones. A local millwright built the mill, taking all summer to hew out the parts for the wheel and peg them together, constructing and setting up the big wooden gear and the small "lantern" it drove to turn the millstones faster than the two-and-a-half revolutions a minute made by the shaft of the water wheel. From that shaft the millwright also took power to drive the spiral conveyors, made entirely of wood, that lifted the grain to the loft so it could run down by gravity to the stones. The same power turned the silk-covered bolting drum that separated the flour from the bran.

CLOTHES

Most farms had cobbling benches of the sort now cherished as coffee tables, and on such a one the farmer repaired the family's footgear, patching uppers with an awl and a "waxend," which was a hog bristle waxed to the end of a linen thread, and pegging patches on "taps" (soles) with a broad-faced hammer and wooden shoe pegs. When repair reached its limit, a professional in the nearest village made new boots and shoes, using leather the farmer supplied from his share of the hides he took to the tanner. In most cases the shoemaker's work was paid for with extra leather.

The shoemaker measured the feet he shod and if his stock had no last the right size, he whittled one out himself and perhaps cut new wooden patterns for the uppers. Though his products were the right size, it is said he made no distinction between right and left feet, and his customers faithfully interchanged their shoes from day to day to make them wear evenly.

We often lose sight of the old meanings of the words. What we now call an oxford was a *shoe;* anything with a top higher than the anklebones was a *boot.* Shoes had laces joining rows of eyelets, or they had latchets serving only two eyelets, or they had buckles, but buckles were disappearing. In the East men frequently wore shoes; in the West only the wealthy wore them, and they seldom, because boots were more practical. Sturdy shoes were worn by women in winter and on summer Sundays; bare feet were much more comfortable.

Some men still clung to homemade shoe packs, and no doubt many farmers made wooden-soled clogs to wear in the fields. But leather boots were replacing both wherever they could be had. A man's work boots reached above the calf of his leg and had leather loops on their tops for pulling them on. They were quite tight in the leg and a pronged bootjack was needed to get them off. Boots had very thick soles, pegged on. Some prosperous farmers wore lighter, lower calfskin boots to Sunday meeting.

A description of the clothes worn in the backwoods early in the nineteenth century has to depend on scattered phrases in old writings and a few crude sketches. The clothes were homemade

81

and hence simple, with little or no attempt to follow fashion. Fine gentlemen changed from knee breeches to tight pantaloons and then to very loose "trowsers" and back to tight ones again, but such fancies affected the frontier very little. The thinning of the game wiped out buckskin leggings except in the "fur back," and many Northwest settlers, who were eastern men, never wore them at all. The full, calf-length "long shorts" that covered a laborer's legs in the eighteenth century probably persisted a while along the Ohio, but they gave way to less floppy pants that just missed reaching the ankle. These were either tucked into boot tops or worn loose over boots.

The coats of the gentry changed from the "shadbelly" that swept in a long curve from its neck to the end of its narrow tails and couldn't be made to cover a waistcoat to a "swallowtail" coat, tight-fitting, short in front, and cut roundabout to meet its long tails just east of the kidneys. Tattered and rumpled examples of these coats show in early sketches, but surely they were leftovers from eastern life, as the hunting shirts that some men still wore were the leftovers from forest life. The coat a farmer's wife made for him was loose and cut straight around, a little shorter than a hunting shirt, hitting the wearer just below his hipbones. Such coats were for cold weather and were usually worn with scarves and mittens. On an ordinarily cool day a farmer got enough warmth from his waistcoat worn over a full-sleeved shirt. He often knotted a handkerchief around his neck with the knot in front.

Footwear,
first quarter of the 19th century

Little girls were covered by tentlike garments that had no hint of a waistline, or they wore shorter duplicates of their mothers' dresses. Boys wore pants, neither long nor short, that reached to their calves. These were topped on Sunday by a short jacket. This outfit, with slight variations, served boys everywhere through the whole nineteenth century.

PEOPLE

The melting pot boiled cheerfully in the Old Northwest, mixing up Americans of British ancestry as well as those of Continental origin. There were, at first, cells of Virginians, New Englanders, Pennsylvanians, and so on. The evidence of origin is marked on the towns they settled and the houses they built; but a sense of isolation undermined old allegiances, and having mutual problems and similar viewpoints, the people became Westerners in less than a generation. Those of foreign birth were caught up with the rest. The French and Irish quickly began to lose their national identity. There were British-born settlers fighting on the American side in the War of 1812! The Germans tried at first to stand apart, but they

A wealthy landowner;
a farmer and his son
in Sunday-go-to-meetin' clothes

In summer the farmer sensibly wore a wide straw hat, and in winter a fur or wool cap with flaps to cover his ears. For Sunday, if his financial position allowed anything "store-boughten," he had a wide-brimmed hat of felted wool with a low crown. The brim was rolled at the sides when it was new, but a little time and weather relaxed the roll to an undulant floppiness.

The farmer's wife, glimpsing or hearing of the clothes of a lady of fashion, made the waistline of her own long dress something higher than her natural one, but she didn't make her skirt tight enough to interfere with walking, as the lady did. When she was dressed up, the frontier woman sometimes wore a white muslin fichu around her shoulders. Whenever she was outdoors she wore a wide-skirted sunbonnet of the same kind that protected her sisters across the whole breadth of the continent. If one of its ancestors was the poke bonnet, the other was the riding hood that was also a cape; women still had such hoods, reaching below their knees, for wear in cold weather.

The distaff side

soon forgot all about it and became interested members of a community in which any man was literally as good as another. The West became fiercely patriotic, more concerned over the British impressment of American seamen than were the citizens of the seaports. Everybody developed an excited interest in politics because it was the means by which the West could get the cheap land and the roads it wanted.

But however self-conscious and political these people were, this was still frontier. Curious contrasts show up: A judge, just and learned, hears his cases while clad in a hunting shirt and buckskin leggings; and hard by the courtroom, his neighbors enjoy a game of billiards on a table freighted by wagon and boat from Philadelphia. There were many of these tables; billiards and pool were a prime amusement in taverns. It was still frontier all right; not seldom a man who came west alone to seek a new home for his family, found a new wife instead; and simply forgot about his first one.

Except on the rough fringes, weddings were quite decorous affairs with only a mild shivaree to recall past glory. A barbecue on the Fourth of July, which still meant something real to these people, was the principal secular celebration. Everybody from miles around came into town; families rode in wagons, or parents rode on horse-

back, carrying the babies, while the older children walked. Young blades bestrode their nags, and their wives or sweethearts rode pillion behind them, with fresh white dresses covered by a blanket. The militia held its muster and paraded to fifes and drums in such order as skimpy training could achieve. For a climax, the files fired a volley, augmented by a blast from a wooden saluting cannon that sometimes exploded in its enthusiasm. Then, as now, politicos delivered themselves of fervid oratory that called a spade anything but a simple shovel, their stentorian voices audible to the farthest edges of the crowd, who, by the way, loved it, even if they didn't always understand it. Beeves, sheep, and hogs were roasted over pits, toasts were drunk, and reels and cotillions were danced to fiddle music until the stars paled.

RELIGION

Twenty thousand people came to the first camp meeting, at Cane Ridge, Kentucky, in 1801, and the idea spread like a forest fire in a drought; camp meetings sprouted all over the Northwest. A meeting lasted a week or so and the congregation camped in tents, wagons, and lean-tos in the woods around the meeting ground. Twenty preachers, most of them Methodists, exhorted in relays by day, and in the light of flaming torches, by night. They spoke from log platforms, sometimes two or more at the same time, in different parts of the grounds. Perhaps "spoke" isn't just the word; they shouted and threatened, moaned and cajoled, whispered, whimpered, and wept. Only a few of the evangelists had any education; they were short on logic and long on emotional appeal; they moved their hearers to hysteria, to violence, and to physical collapse, but not often to brotherhood and mercy.

Possibly such lurid results could be produced only in these backwoods on people starving for emotional outlet, or in some jungle under the spell of a witch doctor's tom-tom. The repentant, the "saved," the possessed, if you like, gibbered strange "words"; they twitched, they danced (this is not exaggerated), they spun around and fell into quivering unconsciousness—and were laid out on straw in the "glory pen" to recover. Strangely, people who came merely from curiosity, even the horse thieves and worse in the shadows beyond the torchlight, were often disturbed willy-nilly. Participants sometimes had attacks of the "shakes" weeks later.

A notable preacher was Crazy Dow. Equipped with a bulging umbrella and riding a sway-backed nag, Dow offered salvation or damnation to the whole West and South. He was skinny, filthy, and unkempt, with shoulder-length red hair and a red beard that hid his chest; but he was a showman of stature and his harsh voice, portentous and coarsely comic by turns, could hypotize an audience—and sell quantities of Dow's Family Medicine. But he wasn't just a charlatan; he made no fortune, and

he drove his frail body with the zeal of a fanatic.

Though the circuit rider did his share of camp-meeting shouting and sometimes mistook hysteria for spiritual rapture, his dedication to his calling was complete and unassailable. He took no heed to the morrow and made his rounds in all weather, at all seasons, praying, visiting, exhorting, with no thought of reward this side of Jordan. His preaching circuit usually took about six weeks to complete, and a new round started at once. He traveled alone on horseback, with a Bible, hymn book, and sometimes a few tracts in his saddlebags, which often held not so much of personal possessions as one extra shirt. If he was lucky, he owned a big cape to cover him from rain and cold; lacking a cape, he put his head through a hole in a blanket.

On some Sundays he preached in log churches, on others he held meeting in somebody's cabin or barn; in between he exhorted impromptu, mounting a stump or a wagon bed wherever two or three listeners were gathered together. He was a Methodist, a Baptist, or a Presbyterian. If he was the last, he might meet hostility, simply because he was an educated man. A few congregations severed their ties with the Presbyterian Church because of its insistence on an educated clergy. Probably all of the circuit riders could read, but beyond that, the education of most didn't better that of their hearers. No matter; they were actively on the side of the angels, a needed force for decency and morality.

TOWNS

Because of the square-grid layout of all but the oldest parts of the Northwest Territory, roads followed township lines and tended to run north-and-south and east-and-west in perfectly straight lines, six miles apart. This shows clearly on road maps of the states in the area. Most of the breaks in the pattern are caused by the irresponsible behavior of streams. In time hamlets grew up at many of the crossroads, but the first of them were on the watercourses.

Some streams were "roads" in themselves, but even shallow ones could be made to turn water wheels, and below the best spot for a dam a town

might start, attracting its own roads in defiance of the surveyors. An earlier pattern repeated itself: The gristmill or the sawmill was the nucleus around which craftsmen first, and then tradesmen, grouped to serve a sizable area. Presently the needs of these artisans and merchants demanded service. An enterprising soul began to drive a big ox wagon to the nearest larger center, perhaps on the bank of the Ohio. At first he made a trip every two weeks, then weekly, and if the place still grew, the wagon became a train of wagons. So the miller's tithe of flour and the tanner's share of hides went to market to be sold, and with them went the farmer's hams in barrels, his whisky in kegs, his wife's butter in firkins. The cooper and the blacksmith had to take on apprentices, and presently a coppersmith and a potter were busy, too. Soon the wagons were bringing glassware, broadcloth, velvet, fiddles, snuff, spectacles, gloves, candlesticks, hats, books, and a hundred other things that people had done well enough without but now felt they had to have.

MONEY

Cash was still scarce in the West and now it became essential for trade. Personal promissory notes circulated as cash, but they were awkward, espe-

cially for small transactions. So groups of prosperous men joined forces to start private banks that among other functions issued their own notes in fixed denominations, down to small fractions of a dollar. This was fine at first and the bankers found they could issue four or five times the value of the actual gold they owned without, normally, being caught short. The First Bank of the United States served to keep this in check because the locally issued notes accumulated there, and the small bank knew that any post might bring a demand from the big one for redemption in hard gold coin.

The West, used to piracy and mayhem, was now introduced to new forms of knavery. Anybody who owned a press printed notes for the banks; hence any printer could make a credible counterfeit, and some did so. The promoter didn't pass his fakes in the town of their supposed origin but in near-by settlements where the name of the victim bank was known. The duped bank seldom suspected the counterfeits until it counted more redeemed notes than it had issued; by then the culprit was elsewhere, and there was no organized police system to find him, even if his identity was known.

The same vanishing act served the so-called saddlebag banker. A respectable-looking citizen rode into town with a bundle of freshly printed "money" under his coattails. He opened an office and generously made loans on personal notes without security; these notes he discounted with a local shark for honest money and left at once to place a new order with his printer.

The financial balance wheel was lost when the charter of the Bank of the United States lapsed in 1811. Then the British burned Washington in 1814, and western banks and a great many eastern ones, too, refused to redeem the notes they had issued. The paper money still circulated, but it lost value, so prices went up and up. Nobody understood what was happening; they took the rising prices for the bright face of prosperity and plunged into expansion, borrowing heavily to buy land priced at twice its real value.

Reality asserted itself eventually, as it always does, and by 1819 everybody was flat broke; to call a man a banker was to call him a scoundrel, though bankers had been no more shortsighted than anyone else. Of course nobody could pay off the mortgage on his land. Even the prudent were caught in the squeeze with the rest, and the banks were forced to try to save themselves by foreclosures. These were unpopular. Every man saw himself tomorrow in the position of his neighbor today. So he and the other local men attended the foreclosure sale armed with big, ugly weapons. Bidders vanished like snow in May. In 1816 a second Bank of the United States was chartered and some restrictions were put on private banks,

though not enough to end the trouble finally. The real prosperity of a growing area asserted itself, but the banking system was still given to nervous twitches, and it panicked every twenty years or so.

UTOPIAS

The romantic picture of the West that appealed to Europeans and to many Americans, didn't stop with Kentucky. The Northwest Territory, where cheap land lay far from the temptations of civilization, struck the leaders of visionary groups as a perfect refuge. The Mormons stopped there for a while; but before them came the Shakers, who established five communities in Ohio, and the German Rappists, who built a town on the Wabash in 1814. Both of these sects abjured marriage and kept their men and women apart; hence they were dependent for survival on new recruits, and when these failed, they withered on the vine. After ten years, the Rappists sold out and moved back east. Robert Owen bought their town to try out his theory of communal living. He recruited a thousand people, including some of notable attainments. Everybody was to share the work and the profits and be assured of the opportunity to expand his soul in the arts and sciences. But human nature came along, too, and New Harmony cost the wealthy Mr. Owen a pretty penny before it faded away.

New Harmony (after a sketch made in 1831 by Charles Lesueur)

THE "PERMANENT" INDIAN FRONTIER

Dragoon

The forts built along the permanent frontier became the sites of towns and cities. From the forts six thousand soldiers worked at the tough job of keeping the Indians inside the compartments allotted to them. On paper, white men were supposed to keep out of the area; actually traders and fur trappers paid no heed to the frontier from the start, and in a short time settlers were crossing it at will. The operation began about 1825; by 1840 the line was a farce, and by 1844 it was a myth.

Lewis and Clark, Stephen Long, and the few others who first saw the Great Plains made glum reports of their fertility. As a result, the whole far West, except for a strip just beyond the Mississippi River, became fixed in the public mind as the "Great American Desert," uninhabitable for people with white skins.

The Indians east of the river had been reduced to impotence, but they still occupied land the invaders wanted. The solution was obvious: move 'em out, put 'em in the "desert," and think about something else. Of course there were already Indians in the plains, but they could be made to move over. This was adopted as official Government policy, but it wasn't easily carried out. Treaties made with tribes on both sides of the river guaranteed the Indians "a permanent home forever." Often the bulk of the signatory tribe knew nothing about the treaty, so it was fraudulent at the outset. When treaty failed, massacre disposed of a good many; others were removed by force, some in irons. Smallpox, cholera, and even measles contracted on the move killed off hundreds, but about 100,000 unhappy Indians who had originated east of the frontier line ended up behind it. The line was beyond the Mississippi. It skirted around Arkansas and Missouri, struck north to the eastern end of the Iowa-Minnesota border; from there it followed the Mississippi and turned eastward, south of Lake Superior.

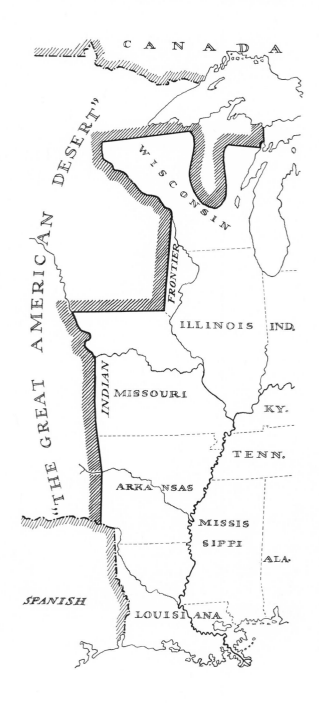

87

7

THE COTTON FRONTIER

THE NEW USE of water power for spinning yarn and weaving boomed the English textile industry; it demanded cotton and more cotton, and Southern planters, now equipped with the cotton gin, were happy to oblige. It had taken a man all day to remove the seeds from a single pound of the stuff by hand; with Whitney's gin he could clean a hundred pounds in the same time. Raw cotton, much heavier in seeds than in fiber, was placed in the gin to lie against a grid of parallel wires spaced just closely enough to prevent any seed from passing between them. When Whitney built his first model, he set hooked wire teeth in rows around a wooden roller; the teeth, passing between the wires of the grid, pulled the cotton fibers through the grid as the roller turned, tearing it from the seeds and leaving them behind. Cotton quickly clogged the teeth, so Eli mounted four long brushes on a shaft which he belted to rotate faster than the roller and in the opposite direction. The brushes thus swept with the hooks, instead of against them, and cleaned the cotton from the teeth as fast as it accumulated. An increase of size over the original model, a better power source than its hand crank, and the substitution of a bank of circular saws (which have hooked teeth) for the wooden roller and its bent wires were all that was needed to make the cotton gin a practical machine.

The growers' problem was space in which to raise the plants. Bad agriculture had already worn out many plantations east of the Appalachians, so the planters moved their slaves over the mountains. From Georgia and the Carolinas they went into what is now Tennessee, Alabama, and Mississippi. They bought cleared land from pioneers who moved farther west, and the slaves cleared more thousands of acres.

It wasn't a healthy kind of settlement. The landowners were short on civic virtue, interested only in turning land and labor into cotton and quick money. Such towns as struggled into life were poor things, offering no bait to crafts or trade. The planters shipped cotton from their own wharves down the rivers to Mobile and New Orleans. They bought in those towns and lived like lords within their own gates. Outside those gates gathered a group of scoundrels as thorough as could be found unhung, attracted by the chance to grab Indian land. This was the country of the Five Civilized Tribes, the only Indians who showed real signs of taking to the white man's ways. They were ruthlessly uprooted from their farms and exiled westward.

Florida at this time extended all along the Gulf Coast to New Orleans and, north of the town, it reached the Mississippi River. Wilted Spain was in no position to defend it, and there's no doubt that the United States wanted it but found no excuse to take it. Andrew Jackson, old Ring-tailed Roarer that he was, needed no excuse. On his own initiative, he marched his army through and took the place in 1818. The Government backed him without blushing—much.

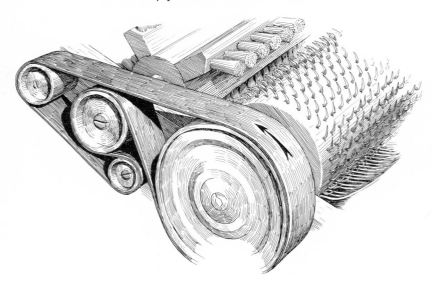

*The mechanism of
Eli Whitney's first cotton gin*

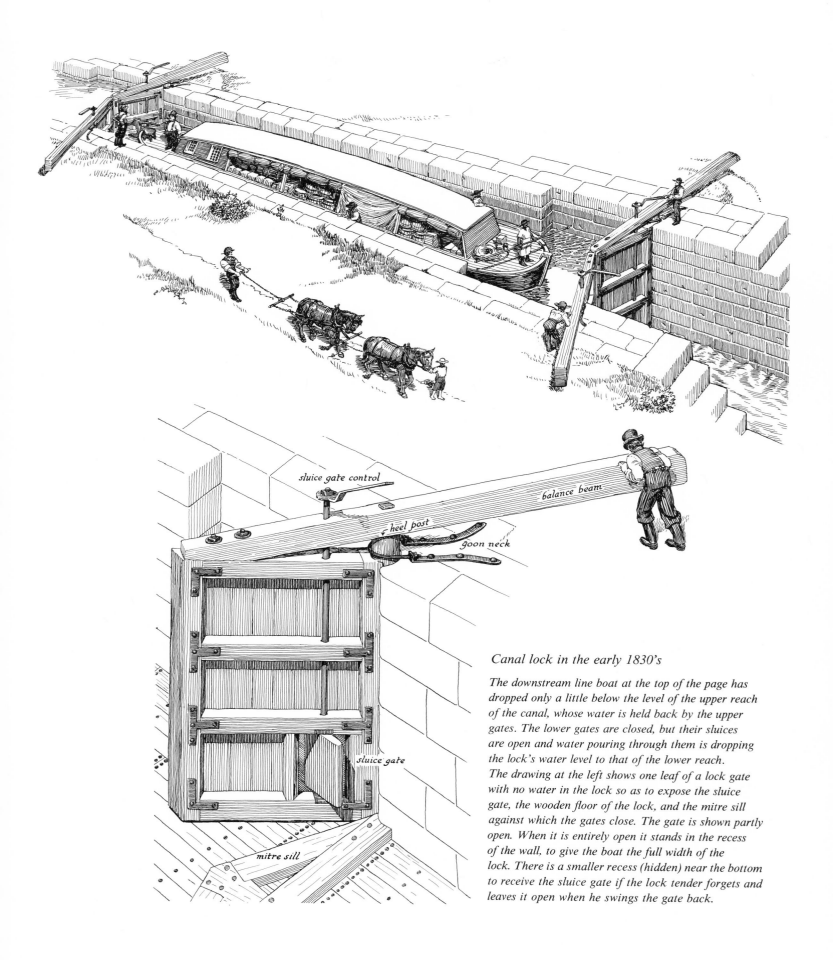

sluice gate control

balance beam

heel post

goon neck

sluice gate

mitre sill

Canal lock in the early 1830's

The downstream line boat at the top of the page has
dropped only a little below the level of the upper reach
of the canal, whose water is held back by the upper
gates. The lower gates are closed, but their sluices
are open and water pouring through them is dropping
the lock's water level to that of the lower reach.
The drawing at the left shows one leaf of a lock gate
with no water in the lock so as to expose the sluice
gate, the wooden floor of the lock, and the mitre sill
against which the gates close. The gate is shown partly
open. When it is entirely open it stands in the recess
of the wall, to give the boat the full width of the
lock. There is a smaller recess (hidden) near the bottom
to receive the sluice gate if the lock tender forgets and
leaves it open when he swings the gate back.

8

SHRINKING DISTANCES

STEAM NAVIGATION

As an army must move its supply base forward to keep up with its front line, so new jumping-off places, always farther west, were needed to support the frontier. Behind the forward bases the country was filling up and the settlers had ever increasing needs. The wagons and the flatboats were too slow and too limited in capacity to deliver all that the West wanted to buy and certainly all that the East wanted to sell. Everybody demanded better transportation.

Robert Fulton's steamboat, the *Clermont,* paddled her way up the Hudson in 1807. Four years later, one of Fulton's partners, Nicholas Roosevelt, built the steamboat *Orleans* at Pittsburgh and took her on a leisurely demonstration voyage down the Ohio and the Mississippi. She unnerved the town of Louisville by blowing off steam in the middle of the night; the townsmen thought a comet had fallen into the river. The excitement she created in the clearings as she passed downstream was nothing to the stunned amazement of the keelboatmen when they saw her move upstream against the current of the Mississippi, at *three miles an hour,* which everybody had agreed was impossible.

The *Orleans* was about 116 feet long and 20 feet wide, as long as a packet and as wide as a flatboat. She settled down to a run between New Orleans and Natchez but passengers, fearful of boiler explosions, mostly stayed off her and merchants, wary of the newfangled, clung to the keelboats. After three years she struck the inevitable snag and sank; but her engine was salvaged and put into another boat, the *New Orleans.*

Enterprise, a sternwheeler, made the first trip upstream from the Mississippi delta to Pittsburgh.

But she didn't convince the skeptics, because she didn't breast the main stream but took advantage of slack water over flooded country. In 1816, however, the *Washington* made a convincing round trip under normal conditions between Louisville and New Orleans in thirty-seven days, twenty-five of them needed for the upstream trip. Her builder, Henry Shreve, pioneered the flat-bottomed river steamer that would "float on a heavy dew." He was thought a little "tetched" when he predicted a ten-day upstream trip, but by 1840 it was being done in a shade over five and a half days.

These boats all burned wood, as river steamers did for a long time. Squatters on the banks cut the wood. The steamboat blew her whistle and pulled over to the shore. Her crew and those passengers who were working their way toted the fuel aboard and stacked it near the boilers, which stood on the open deck. The squatter tallied his cords of wood by moving his hand along a notched stick and sometimes, maybe, his hand slipped over two notches at once. At night he maintained a bright fire on the bank so the skippers could find him. Steamers commonly went overland in flood time, both to avoid debris in the current and to reach a source of wood. Very low water was worse for them than flood. They not only had all the snag troubles that plagued flatboats, but theirs were worse, because the steamer hit a log at higher speed and did herself more damage. Sometimes in summer the Ohio was so low that steamboats couldn't enter its mouth and upriver passengers were landed, to proceed on foot as best they could.

In 1818 a sidewheeler was launched on Lake Erie; she was called by the name the Indians gave her, *Walk-in-the-Water*. Her sixteen-foot paddle-wheels could move her at eight miles an hour in a

The Walk-in-the-Water.
Where her helmsman stood is a mystery of the sea.

flat calm, and a few yoke of oxen often had to haul her out of the port of Buffalo at the head of the swift Niagara River. Nevertheless, she could carry a couple of hundred passengers and their possessions to Cleveland and Detroit. It took her ten days to make the farther point, but that was a lot faster and more comfortable than the same trip by land.

THE ERIE CANAL

Passengers going west by the *Walk-in-the-water* reached Buffalo by the Genesee Road that ran up the Mohawk Valley and struck west through Oneida to Lake Erie. This was the only route to the West that crossed no mountains. It was possible to use a boat on the Mohawk River as far up as Fort Stanwix (Rome); a lock had been built around the rapids at Little Falls in 1796.

Wooding up, about 1835

Governor DeWitt Clinton is rightly given credit for promoting the Erie Canal and seeing it through to completion; but the daring dream of a ditch 362 miles long was Elkanah Watson's back in 1810. Thomas Jefferson and most other people thought it "little short of madness." Perhaps it was. The powerful equipment that would do such a job today was unknown and special tools had to be developed to cope with the problems of the canal: oversize root-cutting plows pulled by many horses; horse-drawn scoops for moving earth; remarkable horse-powered machinery for pulling stumps and trees. Irish immigrants provided the human labor and did the job in eight years, locks and all. Sections were opened as they were finished and the "ditch" was making a profit long before it was complete.

Seventy-two locks achieved a total lift of five hundred feet between the Hudson River and Lake Erie. The locks were twelve feet wide and ninety feet long with an average lift of about seven feet.

Packet boat on the Miami Canal

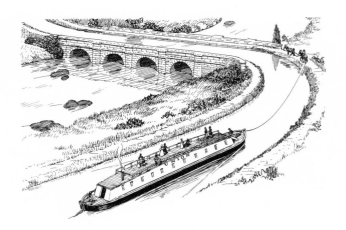

Canal boats had to be small enough to enter them. The side walls of each lock were stone and its two double gates were wood, opened and closed by hand. An upstream boat entered a lock through its lower gates, with the upper ones closed to hold back the water above. Once in, the lower gates were closed and small ports—called wickets, or paddle gates, or sluice gates—in the upper ones were opened to allow water to run in and fill the lock to the level of the upstream reach of the canal. Then the upper gates were opened wide and the boat passed on toward the lake. A downstream boat was usually waiting its turn and entered the lock at once. The upper gates swung shut behind it, and the lock was drained through the wickets of the lower gates to bring the boat to the level of the downstream reach.

The waterway was wide enough for boats to pass but not wide enough for them to turn around; to do that they had to go to the nearest turning basin, a kind of artificial harbor. The canal was four feet deep with sloping earth banks so that, though it was forty feet wide at the surface, it was only twenty-eight feet wide on the bottom. The current was barely perceptible and the water was always muddy, which was the least unattractive thing about it.

Canal boats were quite like keelboats in appearance and were pulled by horses or mules walking the towpaths on the banks. Since there was a path on each side, passing was no problem; but overtaking with both teams on the same path required some fussing with towropes, rudder, and setting poles. "Line" boats for freight and ordinary passenger boats moved at a mile and a half an hour and tied up at night; de luxe packets moved night and day and went a little faster because they were pulled by more and better horses. Much time was lost at locks, where fifty or sixty boats might be waiting their turns. Packet boats offered a women's cabin forward; the men slept in the main cabin and were routed out early so the crew could set up breakfast, which was cooked in the galley at the stern. In good weather the passengers spent the day on the roof of the cabin enjoying the scenery at leisure.

The canal was a howling success. Thousands of tons of freight moved both ways on it. It reduced the time between New York and the West by a third, cutting freight rates in half; it sharply thinned the traffic on the Mississippi and on the National Road. Since canal boats were towed by steamers on the Hudson to and from the Erie's terminus at Albany, almost the whole western trade went suddenly to New York City and played no small part in making it the American metropolis. An improved version of the Erie still operates as the New York State Barge Canal.

If a canal was good at one end of Lake Erie, why not at the other? By hiring the Irish "broadbacks" to dig between rivers, Ohio built two canals simultaneously to connect her river with the lake: the Ohio Canal from Portsmouth to Cleveland; the Miami Canal from Cincinnati to Toledo. These served, as did the Erie, not only for

through transportation but also to open up the country along their routes. Indiana also built a canal—the Wabash and Erie—which, after some obstruction by Ohio, was joined to the Miami.

THE PENNSYLVANIA SYSTEM

New York's sudden monopoly of western trade flabbergasted the other Atlantic ports and they thrashed around desperately for any means to recapture a share of it. Philadelphia was the first to get into action, beginning the astonishing Pennsylvania System in 1826 and completing it in 1834, though it was in partial use earlier. It is sometimes called the Pennsylvania Canal—the major part of the distance to Pittsburgh was covered by canals—but in order to operate locks it is necessary for water to flow by gravity; running it over a mountain range stumped even the most boundless enthusiasm but didn't extinguish it. The Pennsylvania System was part canal, part rail road, and part something that was entirely its own.

A steam railroad had begun operation in England in 1825. There were rail roads in the United States that early, but they were merely smoother substitutes for ordinary roads. The coaches that rode their iron-shod wooden rails had flanged

Moving half of a canal boat over a mountain

The Pioneer Fast Line

wheels but were pulled by horses in the orthodox way. Such a rail road was the Pioneer Fast Line, the first leg of the Pennsylvania System, which conveyed passengers from Philadelphia to Columbia on the Susquehanna River. The state built the road and rented the use of the rails to the Fast Line and to others who hauled freight on them.

The second section was a canal 172 miles long between the Susquehanna and Hollidaysburg; it had in that distance 108 locks, but it stopped at the mountains. The Portage Railway covered the thirty-six and a half miles to Johnstown, but one stretch of that line climbed 1,400 feet in a mile and

no team—or no locomotive, for that matter—could haul a car up such a grade. An idea of Robert Fulton's solved the problem. Horses and stationary steam engines did the work by turning winches at the top of a series of inclined planes. Endless belts made of hemp hawsers three inches thick moved slowly up and down the inclines, and the cars were hitched onto them. There were ten inclines, five on each side of the ridge. The canal between Johnstown and Pittsburgh had sixty-six locks. Despite all this pulley-hauling and shifting, the Pennsylvania System did well because it was shorter and more direct than the Erie Canal. Its total length was 394 miles, and goods transferred from an Ohio River steamer at Pittsburgh were in Philadelphia in four days. In time the canal boats were built in sections and hauled piecemeal over the inclines on cars, without being unloaded.

EARLY RAILROADS

Some Virginia and Maryland gentlemen long cherished a plan to navigate the Potomac River and somehow get through to the Ohio. The startling success of New York and the activities in

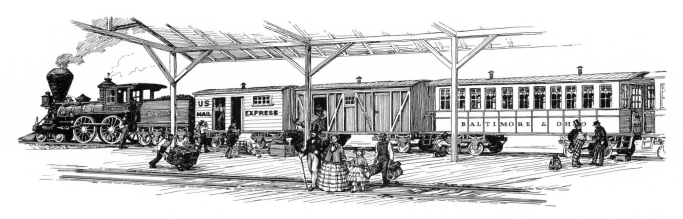

Pennsylvania persuaded them to build instead a canal paralleling the river. When the Baltimoreans in this group realized their town would be left on the sidelines they pulled out, discarded canals entirely, and plumped for a rail road. The two projects started the same day, July 4, 1828, with President John Quincy Adams shoveling for the canal, and ninety-one-year-old Charles Carroll, the only surviving signer of the Declaration of Independence, wielding the spade for the rail road. The rails went on eventually to Ohio and points west; the canal quit at Cumberland because it was useless to go farther. Canals had had their day.

The founders of the Baltimore and Ohio Rail Road intended to pull their cars with horses, but they reckoned without one of their number, Peter Cooper, who mounted an old pumping engine on a flat car in 1830 and produced Tom Thumb, the first locomotive built in America. Tom was able to pull a couple of cars at a breathless twelve miles an hour. This experimental engine never went into regular service, nor was it the first locomotive in this country; the Stourbridge Lion, built in England and run at Honesdale, Pennsylvania, preceded it by more than a year. The first American-built locomotive on a regular run operated in South Carolina between Charleston and Hamburg. Unfortunately, a fireman who was annoyed by the sound of escaping steam tied down the safety valve one day and blew himself and the engine to kingdom come.

Early English locomotives burned coal and ran on perfectly straight, level tracks. America had quantities of wood but had as yet mined little coal;

also, there were very few places in the East where tracks could be laid either straight or level for any distance. So the Americans built wood-burning engines with gigantic balloon stacks to catch sparks, and with coupled drive wheels to get them up steep grades. They also had swiveled front trucks that allowed them to take curves without jumping the tracks. The British deplored such "opportunist" innovations, "as loose-jointed as a basket."

Steam railroads started up by dozens, radiating like spokes from the larger centers of the East, but with the exception of the Baltimore and Ohio none of them covered much more than forty miles. Their purpose was to tap the countryside; if they joined two towns, it was by accident. A traveler could make some use of them by changing from one to another or bridging a gap by stagecoach. By 1842 he could get from Boston to Buffalo by rail (except for a ferry across the Hudson), but he had to use ten different railroads, none paying any heed to the schedule of any other.

In Ohio, the town of Sandusky was annoyed at not being chosen as the terminus of a canal, so it decided to correct the situation by building itself a railroad. As a starter, it had a locomotive shipped in, the first west of the Appalachians. All locomotives had names then, and this one was called Sandusky. The gauge of its wheels was measured and the tracks of the Lake Erie and Mad River Railroad were laid accordingly, four feet ten inches wide. Every railroad had its own gauge.

The tracks of the Baltimore and Ohio reached Cumberland, Maryland, in 1842, and Parkersburg, West Virginia, in 1856, the same year that a road from Cincinnati got to the Mississippi. In 1857 the Through Line to St. Louis was announced. It was a combine of six roads and the only thing that went through was the passenger; no car could do so because of gauge differences and some unbridged rivers.

If the constant changing was a nuisance, it was at least a relief from the misery of "riding the cars." There were no de luxe accommodations on trains as there were on the steamers and canal boats; the seats were thoroughly uncomfortable. In spite of the balloon stack, sparks flew in the open, unscreened windows in summer and burned holes in the passengers' clothes. In winter each car

was heated by a single stove, kept literally red hot regardless of outside temperature. The introduction of dim, oil-burning headlamps persuaded the railroads to run at night in an optimistic, devil-may-care way. In the fifties, sleeping cars were introduced. These were admirable to some and disgusting to others, especially to women, who detested sleeping "in the same room" with twenty or thirty men. With all their drawbacks, the railroads still moved more people and more goods faster than they had ever been moved before. Without them it would have been almost impossible to supply the jump-offs for the mass migrations to the far West.

SOUTHWESTERN BOUNDARIES

The Treaty of 1819 which made Florida American also set the boundaries between this country and the Spanish possessions in the West. The northernmost line ran east from the Pacific along the forty-second parallel almost to Nebraska; then it ran south and east in big steps to the mouth of the

Sabine River on the Gulf of Mexico. All of what is now California, Nevada, Utah, Arizona, New Mexico, and Texas, most of Colorado, and parts of several other states, was Spanish. In 1821, Spain lost her grip entirely, and the whole area became Mexican.

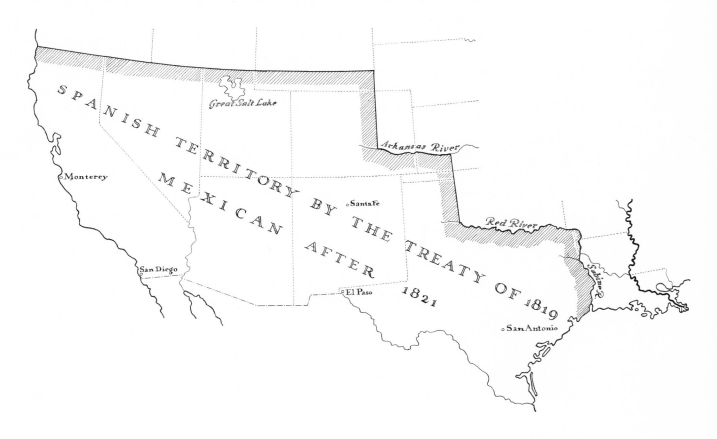

*Pierre Laclède's house
at St. Louis*

9

BEYOND THE MISSISSIPPI

MISSOURI

THERE IS LEAD in Missouri. The French learned about it from the Indians and crossed over from their settlements on the east bank of the Mississippi as early as 1720 to mine it. Salt springs, as well as lead, sparked the first west-bank village of Ste. Genevieve, settled in 1733 some sixty miles below the mouth of the Missouri, opposite Kaskaskia in Illinois. The habitants did their mining twenty miles inland and sent the pigs of lead to the river in the form of U-shaped collars on the necks of pack horses. Later, solid-wheeled, wattle-bodied carts, called charettes, carried the metal. The Yankees called them "barefooted carts" because they had no tires.

Pierre Laclède Liguest, who was known by his middle name, founded St. Louis in 1764 as a trading post for the fur company of which he was a partner. Actually, Laclède made himself comfortable in Cahokia, on the east bank, while his thirteen-year-old stepson took a gang of men across the river and built a house for him. The boy was called Chouteau, or Choteau, a name prominent in the fur trade for a century or more. He put the post on top of a bluff, an excellent idea in that locality.

Laclède had scarcely moved in when the Seven Years' War ended and St. Louis and all the land around it became Spanish; but few Spaniards ever lived there. Missouri became even more French when slave-owning Frenchmen moved in from Indiana after the Northwest Ordinance of 1787 forbade slavery north of the Ohio. Then the Spanish Government offered eight hundred acres of land to anyone who would pay a forty-one dollar survey fee—it could be done on the installment plan—and found plenty of takers who spoke English. They became Spanish subjects, which didn't change them much, and they were supposed to become Roman Catholics, but nobody insisted. These Americans were interested in farm land and they headed for the country, where they built standard dog-run cabins, leaving the towns to the French fur traders and rivermen, the logs of whose cabins stood vertical in their walls. By 1800 there were more American Spaniards than French Spaniards, but Mr. Jefferson made them all Americans in 1803.

Having lost his land in Kentucky and finding the place "crowded," Dan'l Boone pushed west just before 1800 and joined his son on the Missouri River. The Spanish, astonishingly—for they didn't like Yanquis—gave him 8,500 acres of land and made him a syndic. He and his sons boiled the water of the Licks of Missouri, freighted its salt down the river in pirogues, and sold it at St. Louis.

St. Louis in 1800 was little bigger than the trading post it had been thirty-six years earlier, but things were about to happen. Its location made it the main base for western travelers and the center of river traffic, especially steamboat traffic. It was the jumping-off place for Lewis and Clark and most of the early western explorers. When the jump-offs for settlers and trade moved farther west, St. Louis remained their marshaling yard.

In 1812 an area about equal to the present State of Louisiana was set up as a separate territory, and all the rest of the great purchase became Missouri. Shortly there was a rush across the river by cotton planters looking for more cheap plantations, and in three years land that had brought ten cents an acre jumped to eight dollars an acre. The population jumped too—to sixty thousand by 1820—and demanded statehood with the right to own slaves, since most of them already did. This was a touchy matter. Eleven of the United States allowed slaves and eleven did not, which gave each side equal Senate representation; neither side was willing to have the balance tipped against it. The result was the Missouri Compromise by which Maine, with no slaves, came into the Union along with slave-holding Missouri, and slavery was outlawed in any future state north of the southern boundary of Missouri. Such pairing continued; thus Arkansas and Michigan became states together in 1836.

Homemade Texas chair with a rawhide seat

Cimarrón *(not all of them were black)*

TEXAS

Spain did little for her colonies beyond feebly policing their borders. In Texas her settlers raised ferocious cattle for their hides and what little beef they themselves could eat. The total Spanish population of all Texas was never more than four thousand, including half-breeds. Early maps show a "Great Space of Land Unknown" east of San Antonio. Herds of horses and *cimarrón* cattle ran wild in it. It tempted Americans. When Mexico took over its own destiny in 1821, Stephen Austin was able to get himself confirmed *empresario* (in this case, "autocrat,") of a grant his father, Moses, had wangled from the Spanish. It was as big as a small state, and was near where Houston is now. Stephen agreed to bring in three hundred families, but he bettered that; in ten years five thousand people lived on his land.

Americans didn't get Texas land free, but the payments were small and were spread over a reasonable six years during which they paid no taxes. Each man got either 177 acres of farm land or 4,428 acres of grazing land. A few settlers came from as far as New England, but most of them were southerners interested in cotton growing but not averse to shipping a little live beef to Atlantic coast ports in special shallow-draft sailing vessels. Many came to Texas reasonably prosperous and brought slaves with them. Some were indigent squatters.

The first Texas houses were dog-run cabins and even as late as 1850 they remained the commonest dwellings. Householders made much of their own furniture; crude stuff, but not so crude as that in the woodland cabins. Chairs had frames

98

and rawhide seats; chests were reasonable copies of those other people brought with them or of those remembered from back east. When better houses appeared with prosperity, a man built a house like the one he'd grown up in; thus, porticoed plantation houses, square Yankee houses, and porch-surrounded Creole houses stood contentedly in the same settlement. The Germans who followed the first settlers built whole towns of typically German houses, some of them maintained as "Sunday houses" by farmers whose land lay some distance away and who occupied them only on weekends.

All the settlers in Texas had to be technically Mexicans and Roman Catholics, and for most of them this required a distasteful hyprocrisy. Friction between them and the real Mexicans came into the open as soon as the Americans became a majority, and there were a couple of short-lived revolutions. Sam Houston, six feet six and clad in gaudy raiment, ran away from his wife and a distinguished northern career in 1832 and came to Texas with the fixed purpose of freeing it from Mexico. After four years he accomplished his aim at San Jacinto, by whipping a shocked superior force whose rule book didn't allow for attacks by the weak on the strong. In the fight Houston captured the Mexican dictator Antonio López de Santa Anna and forced him to recognize Texas as an independent nation. That wasn't what the Texans really wanted; they were Americans. Almost at once they voted overwhelmingly for annexation; but the fact of slavery in Texas and a hesitation about provoking a Mexican war made the United States cautious. So with no particular relish Texas had to perform as an independent republic for nine years before she was made a state in 1845.

THE BLACK HAWK WAR

This was the result of another Indian treaty to which a few members of the Sauk tribe "touched the goose quill," but which the majority repudiated. The treaty was twenty years old when the white men took advantage of it to move into the Sauk land in western Illinois. Part of the tribe under Black Hawk fought back and were eventually forced across the Mississippi by troops under General Winfield Scott. The incidents of the "war," including the rout of 350 soldiers by forty Indians and the white massacre of an undefended party of women and children, leave the United States with little cause for pride.

General Scott banished the Sauk, the Winnebagos (who earned their bad reputation), and the Fox, who "permitted" the Sauk to fight. He sent them all to the Iowa River, taking their Illinois land and also a strip about fifty miles wide west of the Mississippi. The strip was known as the Black Hawk Purchase because the General agreed to pay the Indians twenty thousand dollars a year for thirty years. Black Hawk lived out his years in Iowa among white neighbors who accepted him as the great gentleman he was.

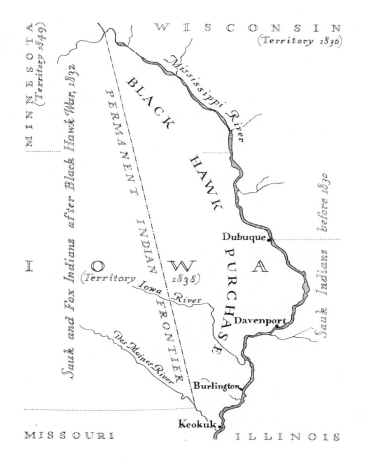

99

THE IOWA SQUATTERS

Julien Dubuque was the first recorded white settler in what became Iowa. It wasn't the Iowa Indians but the Fox who in 1788 granted him almost two hundred square miles of land fronting on the Mississippi. Here he set himself up as a feudal baron, operating his Mines of Spain with Indian labor and shipping lead to St. Louis in his own fleet of boats. The clustered shacks of his miners marked a site for the city that bears his name.

The Black Hawk strip became public domain on June 1, 1833. A law forbade settlers to enter such land until it was surveyed, but the law was in the East and many on the frontier had never heard of it. Before dawn of that June day, improvised ferries began conveying wagons across the Mississippi at three different points; between the ferries, squatters crossed everywhere in skiffs, towing their swimming horses. They blazed their claims near streams where there was wood for cabins, fences, and fuel. The grass-covered prairie was magnificently fertile, but it was hard to plow. That first year most of the squatters spaded up a patch for a vegetable garden and planted "sod-corn" on a larger area, merely punching holes in the turf for the seed. They shot deer and buffalo on their land and caught fish in the streams. Most of the women went back across the river to spend the winter with friends and relatives in Illinois. The men who stayed in Iowa nearly starved, and cholera broke out among five hundred of them who holed up in Dubuque.

The real work of breaking the tough prairie sod began in the spring of 1834. Not less than four and preferably six oxen dragged a coltered wooden plow that clogged with roots every few feet and had to be cleared by hand. In 1847 John Deere beat a circular-saw blade into a steel plowshare that wouldn't clog. He started a factory, but by then the hard work was finished in Iowa.

BUCK AND BRIGHT

In both the East and the West more oxen than horses served as draft animals through the first half of the nineteenth century. They were snail-slow but less nervous than horses and, pound for pound, an ox could outpull a horse; he also did well on a lower grade of food. The big Devon ox, solid red and wide-horned, was introduced into Massachusetts in 1800, but few of his kind reached the frontier. The common ox of forest and prairie was smaller, of miscellaneous colors, and looked something like a lean and scrubby shorthorn steer.

Oxen are stubborn and sometimes balky. Because they can't sweat, they become overheated and have to be rested until they cool off; but they were handier in stump ground than horses and they wouldn't lunge, as horses would, when the plowshare hit an obstruction. Oxen had another advantage: no reins were needed to control them, so a man's hands were free to grip his plow handles. Oxen pull by pushing against the wooden yoke of ancient shape that rests on their necks just ahead of the shoulder hump. There were single yokes as well as double ones, though few oxen will work alone. The pair of a span were devoted companions; in fact, the death of one meant endless trouble persuading the survivor to work with a new mate.

All oxen recognized one or the other of two names: *Buck* for the near, or left-hand animal; *Bright* for the off, or right-hand, one. Very likely Adam's famous off ox was named Bright. Control of a team was verbal, so the naming system avoided confusion; any driver could address any team familiarly. The animals stopped on "Whoa" and backed on command, though backing was hard with a yoke. They turned right on "Gee" and left on "Haw," as Adam's team probably did. Unfortunately, oxen sometimes ran away, and all the driver could do to stop them was jump up and

100

down and swear; he had no string on them whatever.

An ox wore a two-piece iron shoe on each cloven hoof. His tough foot will hold a shoe longer than a horse's hoof will, but while shoeing a horse is fairly simple, shoeing an ox is a major undertaking. Because of his great weight and his small feet, an ox can't easily stand on three legs as a horse can. The shoeing job was done in special stocks equipped with a windlass and a wide sling to take most of the animal's weight off his feet. The hoof to be shod was strapped to a block while the operation, in itself painless, was performed. Settlers who couldn't get iron, protected the hoofs of their oxen with rawhide boots.

The bovine species has a natural liking for children. Hence, youngsters have immemorially trained oxen to the yoke. A pair of altered bull calves, gentled and handled from birth, began their training as soon as they were weaned. Wearing a little yoke of light wood, the steers (as they were called until they were full grown) played with the children at learning commands and presently at pulling small burdens. At a year and a half the span was put to light work; at four they graduated as oxen.

THE CLAIMS CLUBS

There were fewer lawless characters among the early Iowa settlers than was usual on the frontier. These were serious farmers; but they were all lawless in the sense of being beyond the jurisdiction of courts and having no formal laws to govern them, so they did what they could without laws. They allowed a murderer to choose twelve men from a panel of twenty-four to try him. There was no judge, and if the jury found the accused guilty, they helped to hang him.

Since there was no legal way of registering the ownership of land, these communities created an extralegal way. They formed "claims clubs" with elected officers who recorded all owners and boundaries and registered transfers of land, for land was bought and sold with no ghost of a title beyond the club records. The clubs did their work so well that some years later a high court validated their archives as land titles.

The Government surveyors finished their work in 1838; two land offices opened and offered the sections at public auction. The prospect of losing the land they had improved dismayed the squatters, and the clubs went into action. Groups of quiet men, with rifles hung in the crooks of their arms, stood silent while the secretary of their club entered prompt bids of the minimum price of a dollar and a quarter an acre for each man's land as soon as it was described. The sympathetic auctioneer was a local politician, dealing with voters who might elect him. He asked for no further bids but immediately said "Sold," and entered the transaction in his book. Club members suppressed any nonsense from an outsider with an urgent invitation to leave the territory; any backtalk earned the interloper a coat of tar and feathers, or worse if he talked too loud. No jury that could be drawn in Iowa would convict a club member. Congress recognized the situation in 1841 and passed the Preemption Act, legalizing the squatter's right to buy his land in advance of auction for $1.25 an acre, provided he had lived on the property and improved it.

The Indians knew the fertility of the prairie land, and the white settler, seeing no forest and no resulting stumps, knew it for God's gift to the pioneer. True, the sod was tough, springs were scarce, there was too little timber, and no acorns to fatten hogs; but once the sod was broken, the soil grew fabulous corn that would fatten hogs far faster than acorns if not better.

Independence, Missouri, in its heyday

10

CARAVANS TO SANTA FE

Zebulon pike looked for the headwaters of the Red River in 1806 but fell upon those of the Rio Grande instead. The Spanish fell upon Zebulon and jailed him for a while in Santa Fe. He took notes on what he saw and when he got home he published the first account the United States had seen of the settlements in the Rio Grande valley. He mentioned the possibilities of trade. Santa Fe was the largest town in the valley, and it was 1,500 miles from Vera Cruz on the Gulf, its nearest port. Squealing ox carts took three years for the round trip; they brought back fantastic luxuries for the wealthy rancheros, but no common things for the everyday use of ordinary people.

A man named McKnight followed Pike's hint and took a pack train loaded with goods to New Mexico in 1811; but he was too soon. He also landed in the *calabozo,* and the soldiers took his

stock away from him. In 1821, as soon as Mexico became independent, William Becknell tried it. These two trips, made alone through unknown country, part of it desert and all of it occupied by hostile Indians, demanded fortitude of a high order. Becknell got home with enough profit to encourage others to try, and went again, with wagons, the following year. For a couple of years the ventures were sporadic; then a regular caravan organized itself and made yearly trips until the railroad put it out of business more than half a century later.

THE JUMP-OFF

Conestoga wagons, or Pittsburgh wagons (as they called them in the West), drawn by four or six yoke of oxen or as many mules, carried the trade goods. The early outfits started from whatever jump-off was most convenient—Boone's Lick or Franklin—but after 1827 most of them used Independence, Missouri. Its twentieth-century fame rests chiefly on one genial citizen, but once it was the point of departure for the great majority of travelers to the hinterland. Steamboats reached it on the Missouri. The importers who sold the wagon men "notions" to take to Santa Fe and the sutlers who sold them groceries brought their supplies in by the river. Independence was a busy place: wheelwrights built and repaired wagons; farriers shod oxen and mules; saddlers and harness makers found plenty of work; blacksmiths mended

yokes and chains; gunsmiths tinkered with firearms, often modernizing flintlocks.

GUNS

Joshua Shaw of Philadelphia perfected his percussion cap for firing guns in 1816. It was a little copper cup with a bit of fulminate of mercury in its bottom. The cap fitted on a steel nipple, drilled with a hole that reached the chamber of the gun barrel. The gun's trigger released a hammer which hit the cap and exploded the fulminate to flash through the hole and set off the gun's powder charge. The gun still had to be muzzle-loaded;

A SMALL ARSENAL OF EARLY WESTERN ARMS

"Arkansas toothpick"

THROWING KNIVES

standard throwing knife

Bowie knife for close work

*A thrown knife traveled
end-over-end to its target*

*The mild and quiet Colonel Bowie probably didn't design this toadsticker;
he gave it his name by way of the mayhem he did with it.
Fighting, he and others held it like a sword
rather than like a dagger.*

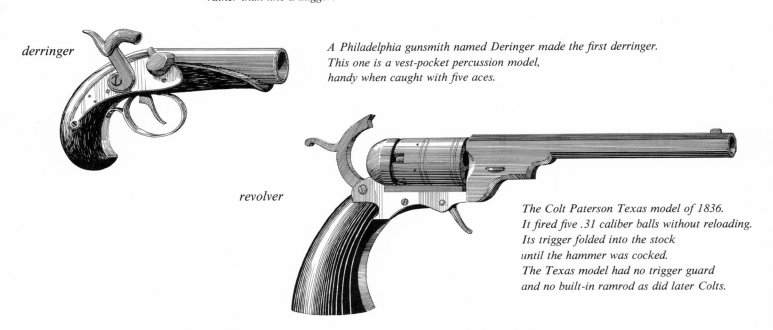

derringer

*A Philadelphia gunsmith named Deringer made the first derringer.
This one is a vest-pocket percussion model,
handy when caught with five aces.*

revolver

*The Colt Paterson Texas model of 1836.
It fired five .31 caliber balls without reloading.
Its trigger folded into the stock
until the hammer was cocked.
The Texas model had no trigger guard
and no built-in ramrod as did later Colts.*

but percussion was a simpler and much surer way of igniting a powder charge than was flint and steel. It was easy to convert a flintlock to percussion, and so many thousands were changed that flintlock guns are quite rare now.

Naturally this better way of shooting was in great demand in the West. Percussion rifles, muskets, and carbines gave a shade of extra advantage over the Indians. Percussion pistols flourished in all sizes, from snub-nosed derringers that would fit a gambler's vest pocket and little "pepperboxes" with five rotating barrels to single- and double-barreled horse pistols a foot and a half long. Colt's Patent Repeating Pistol, 1836, which had a single barrel and five muzzle-loading chambers bored into a revolving drum, used percussion caps, one for each chamber. Every man on the frontier carried some kind of gun and the percussion cap usually fired it until breechloaders came in after the Civil War.

THE TRAIL

Wherever the Santa Fe wagons started, they all headed for Council Grove (Kansas) about 150 miles west of Independence. The road that far was safe, and there was good grass and water there. The venturers made last-minute repairs at the rendezvous and organized the caravan for travel and for defense against the Comanches. They took to the trail as quickly as possible with the object of completing the round trip between the last snow

of spring and the first one of autumn; there was barely time to do it. One of the caravans had 230 wagons and a hundred or so was usual; they averaged fifteen miles a day at best. The round trip was more than 1,700 miles, and time was needed at Santa Fe to rest up, repair damages, and dispose of the cargo. The trail wasn't a straight one, since it had constantly to turn aside for water. The wagons parked in a circle at night, head to tail, with their tongues swung inward toward the center. They thus formed a respectable rampart against Indian attacks which were usually nocturnal and which forced an unceasing vigilance to forestall surprise.

SANTA FE AND THE RANCHOS

It is startling to realize that Coronado was in Kansas less than fifty years after Columbus made his landfall. The first white town north of the Rio Grande was San Juan de los Caballeros, an Indian pueblo that Don Juan de Oñate renamed when he moved into it in 1598. Santa Fe was built about thirty miles farther south in 1610. The whole town was constructed of sun-dried mud "bricks" a foot and a half long. The place was laid out, as were all Spanish towns in the New World, according to standard plans issued to colonial governors. The governor's "palace" was finished by 1610 and still stands unchallenged as the oldest structure of the white men in the United States. Its crude façade, colonnaded with wooden posts, formed a whole side of the town's plaza, or central square. Shops, dwellings, and at least two chapels faced the other three sides. Behind them were more mud houses, and the whole town was surrounded by a defensive wall of adobe.

The wealthy rancheros lived on their vast lands, farming a little and herding some cattle, but specializing in the raising of sheep. The house of such a *patrón* was also a fort. It sheltered and protected his family to the last cousin thrice removed. The rooms of the *casa* were built, one story high, around a patio upon which all their doors and windows opened. The back walls of the rooms formed the outer fortress wall of the place, with no opening in them except one strong wooden gate wide enough to admit an ox cart. The gate

"Sala"

had a small door cut into one leaf for convenience.

The *casa* roof was adobe spread over brush and supported by cedar beams brought down from the mountains. The roof extended beyond the walls on the patio side and rested on posts to make a shaded walkway around the court. Families were frequently so large that additional connected patios were needed to house them. Still more courts were added as servant quarters and stable yards, for these people, as the saying goes, "lived on horseback."

The rooms were sparsely furnished with crude, homemade articles except for an occasional chest or a cherished mirror that had miraculously survived the bumpy cart trip from Vera Cruz. Chairs were heavy and straight-backed, with rawhide seats. Beds had rawhide "springs" and wool-stuffed mattresses. The principal room, the *sala*, quite dark and rather high-ceilinged for coolness, had in one corner a small fireplace for chilly weather. The main feature of this room was a wide adobe bench, covered with skins and blankets, that ran the length of one wall. Though a poor man's house had but one room for all purposes, it had a similar bench and fireplace.

A mounted *patrón* was a sight of splendor; from

Santa Fe

the flat *poblano* on his head to his nine-inch rowel spurs he wore velvet and silver. His medieval saddle and its leather-housed stirrups were silver-mounted and his bridle was ornamented with more of the same metal, mined by Indian slaves in the mountains. The peon, though he sported no silver and couldn't approach his *patrón* in sartorial glory, wore the same short jacket and the same knee-length pants, buttoned up the sides and held at the waist with a wide sash. Below them white drawers showed above high moccasins that did duty for the caballero's flaring leggings, called "winged boots." Both men carried serapes behind their saddles. These are bright woolen blankets with head-slits cut in them.

Though the *patrona* often wore imported silks and velvets and always carried the household keys at her belt, the form of her clothes was much the same as the bunchy cotton skirt and blouse that a peon woman made for herself from cotton she grew, spun, and wove. Both of them wore black shawls over their heads in public. The amount of chest exposed by the peon women bulged the eyes of the American traders, whose own women were buttoned up to the neck. The Americans were also startled by the coat of red clay that the New Mexican women put on their faces to protect them from the sun just as the Indian women did.

TRADING

One man who made the trip to Santa Fe with a caravan doubted if the crusaders beheld Jerusalem with more joy than the wagon men first glimpsed the mud walls of the little outpost. The whole town turned out to greet the traders, and in the evening put on an impromptu fiesta, complete with fandangos. The wagoners made proper gifts to officials, who reciprocated by charging them only 40 per cent import duty, instead of the legal 60 per cent. After that the Americans sold the stuff they had brought, right from the wagons, at retail, in the streets: needles and pins, knives, spoons, tools, hand mirrors, cotton cloth, thread, thimbles, shawls—anything of value that wasn't too large or too heavy.

On the home trip the wagon carried raw wool, tallow, beaver and other skins, all of low quality, and gold and silver ingots. The gross business seems small now—$130,000 to $450,000—and one boom year, following a hiatus caused by politics, it hit a million and three quarters. The profit ran from 10 to 40 per cent, enough to keep the caravans returning. The men who went kept their eyes open; their reports revealed the military weakness of Mexico and shot holes in the myth of the Great American Desert.

Patrón and peon

The map locates the more important trading posts approximately; many subordinate and temporary posts are omitted. The two sketches show the outside and inside of a post, based on paintings of Fort Laramie by Alfred Miller. The fort was built in 1834 and was first called Fort William for William Sublette of the Rocky Mountain Fur Company. Miller painted the first wooden structure, not the adobe fort the American Fur Company put up in 1845 on a slightly different location.

Fort Laramie, exterior

Fort Laramie, interior

11

THE FUR TRADE AND THE MOUNTAIN MEN

LEWIS AND CLARK started up the Missouri River in 1804, but they were not the first white men there. Theirs was the first public report, but on their return trip they met fur traders coming in. The traders had long used the river as a highway, though not very far up. Many were French *voyageurs* following the trade their forefathers started almost two centuries earlier. Loading two dugouts with knives, glass beads, and rum, they paddled and poled their way upstream and traded with the Indians for pelts until their stake was gone. However much the Indians hated the white men, they could not resist the temptations the traders offered them. Furs were bulky but a few poles lashed across the dugouts made a floating platform that would bring them home.

Many later traders traveled both up and down the Missouri in big cargo-carrying dugouts hollowed out of soft cottonwood logs. These were the

commonest boats on the river. Some were as long as thirty-five feet by four feet wide and had short masts and small sails. Other men abandoned the small dugouts they paddled upstream and brought their cargos back in bullboats like those of the Indians but much larger. They made a light frame of saplings and stretched over it a cover of bull-buffalo hides sewn together and caulked with fat. Indian bullboats were circular and very cranky; the traders made theirs oval, but they still weren't what you could call handy. They were leaky, they became waterlogged, and they were easily punctured, but they could carry three tons of skins and still draw only ten inches of water.

Larger expeditions came downstream in mackinaws that looked like flatboats but were actually rafts. A mackinaw was sixty feet long and fifteen feet wide; it had vertical sides and carried a high

Cottonwood dugout

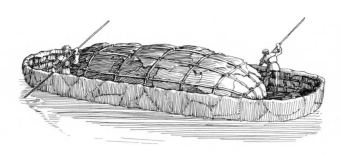

Bullboat

mound of covered furs amidships. The skipper handled a big steering oar from the top of a tower and shouted orders over the fur heap to four rowers on benches in the bow. They rowed from dawn to dark, singing to pass the time, and lay to overnight. The mackinaw's ends were rounded or pointed instead of being square. Water came through the raft's logs, so the cargo rode on a platform built a foot above the deck between two bulkheads.

THE BEAVER AND THE "COMPANY"

In the early nineteenth century every gentleman in Europe or America wore a beaver hat, even though it cost fifty dollars. The hatters stripped the soft underfur from the hides by hand and matted it into a beautiful felt with very hot water; then they shaped it over wooden molds. The demand was great enough to bring the trappers six dollars for a beaver "plew," and at that they were cheated on the price by the fur companies. Buffalo hides made fine lap robes to use in sleighs and buggies; no winter turnout in the East was considered elegant without one. These

two items made the backbone of the fur trade, but there were of course many other valuable furs: marten, mink, fox, otter, bear.

John Jacob Astor founded the American Fur Company in 1808. He saw possibilities in the far West as soon as he read the reports of Lewis and Clark, and he tried to get there first. With no faint thought of conservation, his trappers cleaned out the Old Northwest Territory ahead of the pioneers. They finished off Wisconsin and made a good start on Minnesota before either place had any white population. Astor sent a ship around the Horn in 1811 and set up a trading post, called Astoria, near the mouth of the Columbia River in Oregon. Part of a land expedition to the place reached it after great hardships; but it all came to very little because the British were already trading in Oregon, and when the War of 1812 came along, the Astorians felt suddenly lonely and sold out to them. Nevertheless, the land expedition had scouted the Missouri valley, so Astor moved his western headquarters to St. Louis.

The American Fur Company distinguished itself for chicanery at a time when nobody's morals were over-nice, in business at least. It used any means to squelch competitors and made a 50 per

Mackinaw

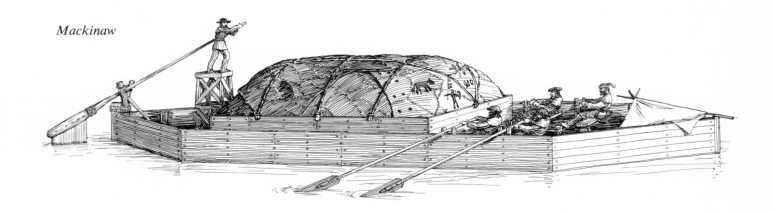

cent profit by methodically cheating on everything it bought and sold. It took over the Missouri River and practically "owned" it from 1822 until it was no longer useful in 1846. The company forced the white trappers who worked for its chief competitor, a changeable organization best known as the Rocky Mountain Fur Company, to operate in the rugged country beyond the river valley; they were the "mountain men," most of whom were free lances.

THE COMPANY POSTS

Astor's company had trading posts all along the upper Missouri and on some of its tributaries, such as the Platte. It built Fort Union at the mouth of the Yellowstone in 1829; Fort Benton, built several years later, was halfway across Montana. All the posts were forts, and like the earlier Kentucky stations, almost impervious to Indian attack. Fort Uinta was the only one ever taken. A high palisade surrounded an enclosure a couple of hundred feet square and a fighting platform hung on the inside of the fence about five feet from its top. Two blockhouses, set at opposite corners, mounted light cannon on their ground floors and sometimes, as at Fort Laramie, there was a kind of fighting tower over the gate and a loop-holed passage inside with a second gate at its inner end. Dangerous customers had to do business in the passage. Houses for the officers, barracks for the rank and file, warehouses, and the trading store, under the sights of concealed guns, stood in the quadrangle. Men stationed at the post planted a garden outside the walls when it was possible and also picketed their horses outside in times of peace.

In its first years on the Missouri, the company supplied its posts and freighted its furs with keelboats under tougher conditions than either the Ohio or the Mississippi offered. In addition to the

usual snags and to far more than the usual bends and loops, this river refused to lie still in its bed. In a week's time it might make a new loop miles long where nobody remembered one before, or cut across the neck of an old loop and shorten itself by a day's journey. Its sand bars shifted overnight and a navigator, making yearly trips, had to relearn the river on each one. It sometimes took nine months to get a keelboat up to Fort Union.

A steamboat, the *Yellowstone,* first made the 2,500-mile trip to that point in 1833, and other steamers followed it from then on. These boats started from St. Louis with a hundred or so wildly mixed passengers: Indians and trappers, scientists and adventuring noblemen. Time hung heavy on their hands. They took pot shots at game on the banks and sometimes disembarked and walked across the neck of a long loop to join the vessel on the other side. Once in a while everybody had to lend a hand to pull the boat off a sand bar.

Fuel was a constant problem; there were no wood-cutting squatters here, and green cottonwood was poor stuff. A pilot stopped at any time to pick up a likely drift log. Few tried to navigate the Missouri at night, and while the steamer was tied up a professional hunter went ahead to get meat for the galley. He hung the carcasses of his kill in sight along the bank and a skiff put off to get them, finally picking up the hunter himself in mid-morning. Except for this meat, the passengers ate salt pork and flapjacks.

A post official often rode downstream on horseback to meet the steamer a couple of days below his station. This gave him time to transact business with the company agent on board, as the boat stayed at a landing only long enough to transfer cargo and submit to Government inspection. One of the jobs of a company pilot was to smuggle in the liquor (raw alcohol) that was "indispensable

to the fur trade." The inspectors usually did what they could to avoid seeing it and they were aided by such dodges as setting the stuff ashore, concealed in barrels of flour, until the inspection was over, or moving the kegs from one side of the boat to the other, ahead of the inspector.

The traditions of the fur trade were French, so the two chief trading post officers had Gallic titles: the *bourgeois*, who was in charge, and his principal deputy, the *partisan,* who handled operations in the field. The man who really did the trading was known simply as the clerk, though he was an important personage. The company employed trappers, called *engagés,* paying them four hundred dollars a year and outfitting them; all the pelts they took were company property. In addition, the organization bought furs from free trappers and sold them supplies, cheating them blind on both transactions. Trappers paid as much as 2,000 per cent above the cost of goods in St. Louis; sugar was $1.50 to $4.00 a pound, a steel trap brought $15.00. The Indians, though cheated even worse, supplied more furs than the white trappers.

THE RENDEZVOUS

William Ashley was the principal figure in the outfit that became the Rocky Mountain Fur Company. His mountain men, free trappers, worked mostly in the Tetons and the Wind River Mountains and beyond them in territory claimed by the Hudson's Bay Company. Ashley arranged to have his men come in July, 1825, to the Green River valley in western Wyoming where there was

water and pasture. To them there he brought a pack train of mules and horses along the banks of the Platte River, up its North Fork, and then up the Sweetwater River and over South Pass on the Continental Divide, a trail along which many thousands would follow him. Ashley's animals carried heavier burdens than those of the old Pennsylvania pack trains over far more rugged country on a longer trip. The packs contained traps, guns, ammunition, tools, blankets, clothes, coffee, and sugar for the trappers; and for the Indians: beads, vermilion paint, knives, prefabricated tomahawks and war clubs, fish hooks, and the steel awls they used for sewing and valued so highly. There was tobacco for everybody and keg after metal keg of alcohol, to be diluted and sold as "whiskey."

This first rendezvous set the pattern for the future. The trading and carousing lasted until the supplies and the furs were exhausted along with the participants. The mountain men worked alone in the wilds for at least a year without liquor, often without tobacco, and sometimes with very little food; when they came down from the hills they staged an almighty binge that ended only when all the liquor was gone. As the last hangover faded, the trappers returned, broke, to their mountains, and the caravan took a king's ransom back to St. Louis.

The American Fur Company realized what it was missing and sent a pack caravan of its own to the rendezvous of 1832. A couple of years of vicious competition froze out the opposition as usual. Not until 1835 were the first wagons sent over the divide. The company held a rendezvous, usually at Jackson's Hole, every year until 1839.

By then the area was pretty well emptied of everything but buffalo; and the silk hat, cheap and shiny, put an end to the demand for beaver plews just in time to save the animals from joining the dodos.

A mountain man left a rendezvous in a complete outfit of new clothes, even though he might not pay for it until the following year. By the end of the fall trapping season, in November, it was worn to rags and rotted from being constantly wet. When he holed up in some valley for the winter it was time for his Indian "wife" or a squaw hired as a tailor to make him new garments of buckskin. The leather wasn't the tawny stuff of the Indians' regalia; it was smoked black to make it as nearly waterproof as possible. His moccasins, fur-lined for winter, had rawhide soles and were identical with those of the Plains Indians. Indian, too, were his leggings and breechclout. His hunting shirt followed the pattern of Kentucky, but the squaw decorated it with porcupine quills or with the fur traders' glass beads she was learning to use. If possible, the trapper wore a blue cotton company shirt under his hunting shirt and he sported either a wide-brimmed hat or a kind of turban made with a big bandanna (a French touch; the early fur traders at St. Louis tied up their heads in blue handkerchiefs). He loved bizarre ornament and often wore feathers in his hair, but even if he had worn a war bonnet, nobody would have taken him for an Indian because of his ragged beard.

The mountain man set his beaver traps under shallow water because the animals are aquatic, because the water didn't retain his own man-scent, which was strong, and because a trapped beaver drowned quickly and so couldn't chew off his caught foot and escape. The trapper thrust a pole through the ring on the trap and into the pond bed to hold the trap and mark it. Beavers lived on bark, and since there was plenty of that along the banks, no food bait would attract them. Instead, the trapper arched a willow twig over the trap, with its ends in the pond bottom and its crown just above the water surface. He smeared the exposed part of the switch with castoreum, a strong beaver scent that he extracted from the glands of earlier catches and commonly called "medicine." This stuff he carried in a plug-stop-pered horn bottle, and the musky smell of it followed him on the wind. He or his squaw cleaned the plews and stretched them on willow frames to dry. Each one was marked with the trapper's personal symbol and would be marked again by the company that bought it from him.

No men on earth were more completely free than these mountain men, which was the way they wanted it. They were the original rugged individualists, acknowledging no restraint but their own and no law but that of survival. A hard lot, few of them could read; but they were fine horsemen and marksmen, as good as the Indians at the Indians' game—and better. They retained a strong trace of the Ring-tailed Roarer; but these were men. It is customary to compress them all into the same mold and say that the mountain men took from the West but contributed nothing to it, that when they left, it was as if they had not been there. True, they drew no maps, but each of them had an excellent map in his head and he missed no opportunity to fill in its blank spaces in talk around campfires. They found South Pass, the easiest way over the Continental Divide into Oregon, for everything northwest of the pass was Oregon, including all of Idaho. The wagons of their later caravans marked some kind of road up the Platte and the Sweetwater. Mountain men were the scouts, Kit Carson among them, who guided explorers and military expeditions; and one of them, Jim Bridger, set up a private fort in the back country to provide the last anvil east of the Columbia River.

Beaver trap

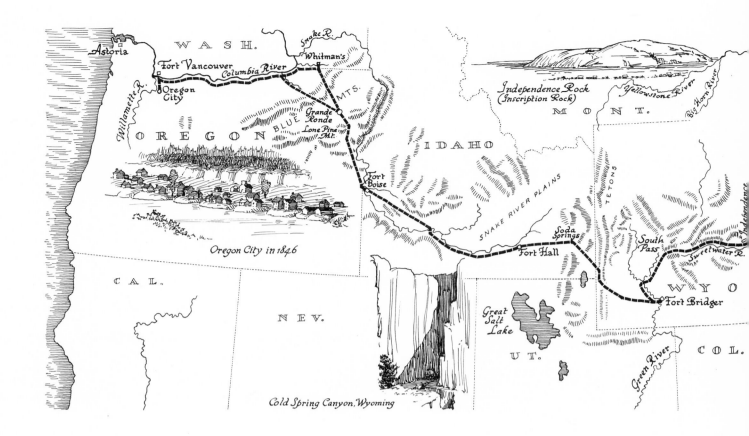

Oregon City in 1846

Cold Spring Canyon, Wyoming

12

THE BITTER ROAD TO OREGON

THE MISSIONARIES

THE FLATHEAD and Nez Percé Indians sent a joint delegation to St. Louis to ask for teachers to instruct them in the white man's religion. This was unique. Perhaps the delegates didn't use just the flowery language attributed to them by the Methodist *Christian Advocate* for March, 1833, but no matter; the request sparked a flame of missionary zeal and turned a new page in American history. Jason Lee, a Methodist, went out with the fur caravan the next year, but for some obscure reason he decided to pass up the Indians to whom he had been sent and went on west to build his mission in the green valley of the Willamette River, in Oregon, where some retired Hudson's Bay trappers seemed to him to need spiritual guidance.

Marcus Whitman, M.D., and the Reverend Samuel Parker, backed by the Presbyterians and Congregationalists, came out with the caravan of 1835. Parker went on to Oregon and came home on a ship by way of Hawaii. He wrote a book at sea, *Journal of an Exploring Tour Beyond the Rocky Mountains*. Dr. Whitman, seeing that the Indians were sincere and estimating the size of the job, went back east for reinforcements. He returned a year later with a wagon; a new wife, Narcissa, who could charm, equally, a Scottish baronet or a turkey-necked trapper; and another couple, Henry and Eliza Spalding. These two wives were the first white women to cross the Rocky Mountains; the wagon was the first wheeled vehicle to cross them. It broke an axle beyond Fort Hall, and Whitman took it the rest of the way through Idaho as a cart, but the gorges of the Snake River did it in. The doctor was trying to prove that a wagon could go to Oregon, and in spite of his fail-

114

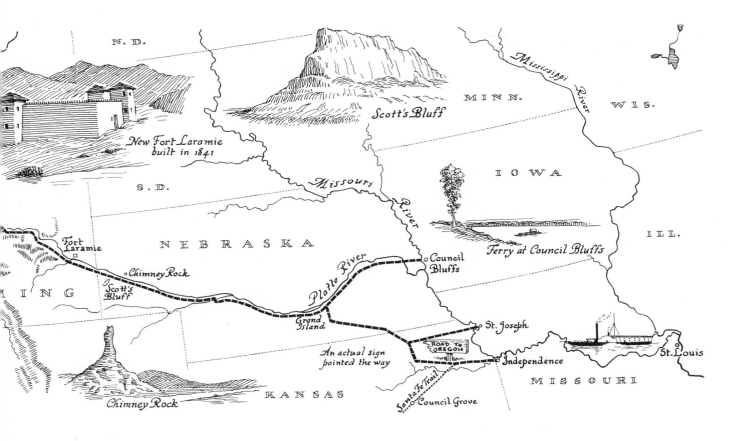

ure, he was right. He built his mission, Waiilatpu, on the Walla Walla River twenty-five miles upstream from the Columbia. Nez Percés were scarce in his area; he sent Spalding to them, farther east. Whitman converted a few Cayuses. In 1847 some he hadn't converted murdered him and Narcissa, but not before he did noble work as a good Samaritan.

The volatile mind of Hall J. Kelley, a Boston schoolmaster, took fire from the first reports of Oregon; all through the twenties he extolled the place in print and on platforms as a paradise without flaw, though he hadn't been there. (He went to Oregon later and was mistaken for a cattle thief.) The missionaries wrote letters home when they could and reported to their boards, and some of what they wrote was published; so was Samuel Parker's book, in 1838. The East heard a lot about Oregon during the thirties, and it sounded like a Promised Land, another Caintuck.

A trickle of immigrants came each summer. Jason Lee brought out a few teachers, artisans,

and farmers in 1834. More farmers came in 1839, and that year some people came around the Horn, by sea. In 1842, a Government Indian agent headed a party of 130 with eighteen wagons. The following spring the dam burst and a thousand people with 120 wagons and five thousand assorted animals collected at Independence for the start. Nearly all of them were from west of the Appalachians, and a good many were Missourians.

ORGANIZATION OF THE WAGON TRAIN

Such people had some notion of what they faced and made careful preparations for the journey. Few families came to Independence singly; most were units of groups that had been fitting themselves all winter. At the jump-off they organized on a military basis, electing officers and a council of elders whose decisions were law. They grouped the wagons in two divisions, each with a captain, and both subdivided into platoons of four

wagons each. The council also hired a mountain man as "pilot" to find the way, select camp sites, and act as advisor. Dr. Marcus Whitman, returning from a trip east, also traveled with that first trek. He and the pilot knew the trail and the minimum supplies needed. And who understood better than Whitman the maximum practical load for a wagon?

The council, acting on their suggestions, required that each man have at least one rifle of an effectively large bore, flintlocks preferred to cap rifles because it was easier to repair them. Each gun was supplied with four pounds of powder, twelve pounds of lead, and a mold to cast its bullets. Further, every man had to carry a canteen, a "butcher" knife (hunting knife), and a tomahawk. Most of the men had horses and they were advised to get a Spanish (Western) saddle and a long picket rope to stake the horses for grazing at night.

Hunting would supplement food on the way; but each wagon carried a barrel of flour, half a bushel of beans, ten pounds of rice, twenty pounds each of sugar and coffee, and 150 pounds of bacon. On board also were a ten-gallon water keg and some spare ox shoes, a year's supply of woolen jeans, extra shoes for everybody; and two woolen blankets apiece. Plows (for these were farmers)

and other implements and tools the settler took at his discretion, so long as he didn't overload his wagon and risk hurting his oxen. Mules pulled a few of the wagons, but two or three yoke of oxen each, served the majority.

Most of the early wagons were Conestogas, but though the old freight wagon could stand the punishment of the trip, it was very heavy; its curved body was difficult to build, hence expensive; and the same curves made it uncomfortable for passengers. The standard prairie schooner was an ordinary farm wagon with extraordinarily sturdy wheels. Its flat body was bolted solidly to its under-carriage. The shocks of bumping over rocks passed directly to the passengers with nothing to soften them; walking was often less tiring and a lot less painful than riding. The canvas cover was lashed on over its frame, but it wasn't often tied down tight; even with the sides of it raised, the interior of the wagon was an oven under the summer sun.

THE OREGON TRAIL

The divisions started, as the fur caravans had, early in the spring, but not so early that pasture at high altitudes would still be covered with snow.

This starting question became what the cowboys called "a hair in the butter." Later, when five thousand or more were using the trail every year, if your division was too late, the pasture had been eaten. The Indians, by the way, believed there could be no white people left in the East. The first half of the trail was the old one used by the fur companies. It began at Independence and struck northwest through Kansas and Nebraska, picking up a tributary trail from St. Joseph before it reached the Platte River near Grand Island. A good many later travelers came from Council Bluffs, Iowa, to Grand Island. The way west along the Platte was reasonably level on either bank as far as the forks, just east of where Nebraska meets Colorado; there the Oregon Trail took the North Fork, past Chimney Rock and Scott's Bluff to Fort Laramie, 667 miles from Independence. The American Fur Company had recently rebuilt the fort of adobe, and supplies could be bought there at the usual cutthroat rates. It was a place to rest a day or so, repair wagons, and put gear to rights, for beyond Fort Laramie the hills became mountains.

The trail still followed the Platte, described as "a thousand miles long, a mile wide, and an inch deep," but it wasn't dependably shallow. The wagon trains forded it from time to time. The operation was complicated by the difficulty of driving reluctant cows across and by the stubbornness of braying mules which sensed the quicksands and feared them. Sometimes an ox floundering in these traps would give up and let himself sink to his death; beyond that, the sands were no worse than a monumental nuisance. In the mountains the river narrowed in canyons in which wagons could sometimes use the stream bed for a road, but occasionally the trail had to detour around one. The mouth of the Sweetwater was something like 140 miles from Fort Laramie, and the wagons turned westward up its valley, past Independence Rock where many travelers scratched their names, to South Pass. Beyond the pass the streams flowed west and their alkaline waters were unpleasant to the taste and disturbing to the intestinal tract. The word *pass* suggests a high-walled gorge, and South Pass—called the Gateway to Oregon, though it is in Wyoming—should certainly look dramatic, but it doesn't. It is merely a hump, open and wide, an easy road for the wagons. That wasn't true of all passes on the trail. Sometimes days were lost wrenching wagons through steep and stony places by doubling up teams and heaving on ropes and levers. From South Pass the way ran along Green River about 125 miles southwest to the fort Jim Bridger had built when the fur trade faded. He put it there to serve the immigrants he foresaw were coming, and it benefited everybody, including "Old Gabe" Bridger himself. His fort was another oasis where men and animals rested before undertaking the next leg of two hundred odd miles to Fort Hall. Hills, rocky ground, and the scarcity of grass and good water as well as game made the passage across Idaho the hardest part of the trip. Many animals died of heat and thirst, and some wagons were broken beyond repair. Here some families faced the harsh necessity of abandoning all their possessions and going forward empty-handed, on the charity of others, to a goal that had lost its shine. It is for the help they gave such people that Marcus Whitman and John McLoughlin, the Hudson's Bay factor at Fort Vancouver, will be honored as long as men can remember.

Fort Boise, a Hudson's Bay outpost, was on the

Fording the Platte

Snake River in Idaho near where the Oregon border is now. The Snake flows into the Columbia, but the deep canyons of its lower reaches are impassable. The wagons turned off and followed the Burnt River valley as far as they could, then struck northward, past Lone Pine Tree Mountain, to rest a while in the beautiful valley that Canadian trappers named the Grande Ronde. Most of the people who were still in good shape as to health, animals, and wagons, crossed the Blue Mountains to the headwaters of the Umatilla River and followed it to the Columbia. Those in need of help took the longer route by way of Marcus Whitman's mission on the Walla Walla. They, too, had to cross the Blue Mountains which killed many a wagon that had made it through Idaho. Some families settled at likely points along the Columbia, sometimes because they could not possibly go farther, but most of the early immigrants went to the trail's end in the valley of the Willamette River.

wagon to pull in alongside the first. The men unyoked the oxen at once and turned them out to graze; the animals were tired and hungry, and as long as there was grass they wouldn't wander too far. Horses and mules were picketed or hobbled with a short rope that limited the stride of their forelegs. The travelers chained their wagons together for the night as a rampart and the captains posted guards, every man taking his turn. Once in a while the Indians silently murdered a guard in the night; they stole stray animals when they could. (The whooping Hollywood "attack on the wagon train" isn't all romance, but it came later. Only in desperation did the Indian notion of warfare include rushing a hundred well-armed men in a strong position.)

While their husbands attended to the animals and set up the tents that nearly every wagon carried, the women brought out their tinderboxes, and the children gathered whatever fuel was available—often buffalo chips (dry dung)—until

THE ORDER OF THE DAY

The 1843 caravan took five months to get to Oregon and only seven people died; two years later, when three thousand people started up the Platte, seventy-five were buried at the trail side. No count was kept of broken wagons and only the vultures counted the reeking carcasses of oxen; but the tale would have been worse without the ordered discipline and the planned routine.

Toward evening the pilot and a group of young men rode an hour ahead of the wagons and selected a camp site. While his helpers dug water holes beside a stream the pilot marked out a circle about a hundred yards in diameter for the camp. He became expert at judging the size of his circle, and we are told that when he led the wagons around it, there was exactly room for the last

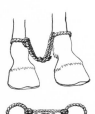

Rope hobble

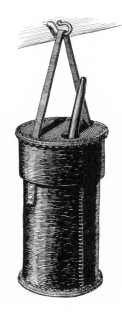

The leather tar bucket that hung from a wagon's rear axletree held a mixture of pine tar and tallow for greasing the wheels. Mineral grease was unknown.

Fort Boise was passed. Striking a light with flint and steel was an exasperating business, and whoever got her supper fire started first, passed embers to her neighbors.

Nobody loitered long before turning in after supper because reveille was at four in the morning. Men detailed for the job scattered at once to round up the oxen and bring them into the circle while others unchained the wagons. Tents were struck and stowed, breakfast was eaten, oxen were yoked; the women and children were in the wagons by ten minutes of seven, waiting for the bugle on the hour. The platoon that led the division yesterday brought up its rear today, unless another platoon started late and hence was automatically assigned to the tail end—and the dust. Men and boys rode horses or mules unless they had ox teams to drive or livestock to herd; then they walked. The pace was slow.

THE BUFFALO

As soon as the caravan started, outriders posted themselves as daytime guards and ten or more young men on horses set off to hunt for meat. They often had a long trip because the Indians drove buffalo and other game away from the trail. The overland caravans probably couldn't have made the trip had there been no buffalo in the West, but there were 60 million of them, more than of any other large animal on earth. Since adults weighed from 1,200 to 2,000 pounds, they made an abundant source of excellent meat. These animals have good ears and keen noses, and they are hard to kill; but they are stupid, they have poor eyesight, and they can't run as fast as a fairly good horse.

Until midsummer the buffalo scattered in small bands of twenty or thirty; the big herds gathered later in the year. Most of the time cows yielded the best meat, but they were lean and stringy in early summer; a young bull was the best choice then; old bulls were always tough. The hunter

approached a band from its down-wind side to keep his scent from the animals until he could get within three hundred yards, if possible, before they ran; once they did that, the hunt was a race. An educated buffalo horse knew how to do his part with very little direction. He dodged the lunges of bulls and overtook the selected quarry from its right side to give the hunter's rifle a chance at the one spot, behind the right shoulder, that was vulnerable enough to bring the animal down immediately. No rifle ball of that time could penetrate the mass of hair and the thick bone of a buffalo's head, and rarely could one do fatal damage to the spine.

The scholarly calm of missionary Samuel Parker was once disturbed by a primitive urge to shoot a buffalo. He *dismounted* in range and wounded a bull! The animal would certainly have charged and killed a more sinful man, but this time he ran away.

The mountain men took only the tongue, hump, and hump rib, leaving the rest for the wolves and coyotes. But they were epicures of buffalo, each man consuming eight pounds of it a day. Men hunting to feed a thousand people took all the ribs and probably the haunches, too, though they were tough.

ON THE TRAIL

With luck the hunters rejoined the wagons at the "nooning" in time to provide the women with meat to broil or fry for dinner. Hump meat, which was boiled, and thick ribs, which were roasted, they probably cooked at night when there was more time. Nooning was only an hour's pause, and the oxen stayed in their yokes. It was the time for the council to meet if there was need. In a succession of noonings, the immigrants of 1843 devised a form of future government for their settlement. The train moved even slower in the afternoon. Tired animals lagged; tired men napped in the wagons if possible, and the women and boys took over the driving until they sighted the pilot with his circle marked out for the night.

Such a day of steady progress was rare beyond the Sweetwater. When trouble hit one wagon, its whole division was delayed until it was righted; a single wagon couldn't be left behind as an invitation to attack. All wasn't invariably peaceful within the platoons either; the people brought their human cussedness with them. Quarrels broke out between families and even within families; one couple split so determinedly that they cut their wagon in half and proceeded to Oregon in two carts! On the other hand, friendships, welded by mutual hardships, caused families to settle near each other, helping one another. Inevitably their children married. Many an Oregonian can trace nearly all of his ancestors to the same platoon.

Once on their land, the Oregon settlers did well; it was good land, blessed with adequate rain. Further, it was wooded land of the kind they knew in the East. No one had to learn new ways of doing things, as the grassland settlers did; a man could clear his place, build his cabin, and start farming between the stumps just as his fathers had done.

THE PATHFINDER OF THE WEST

Dashing Lieutenant John C. Frémont, U.S.A., had the good fortune to marry Jessie Benton, daughter of the senator from Missouri. In 1842 the lieutenant, guided by Kit Carson, led an exploring party through South Pass. Jessie "ghost wrote" a book from his notes on the trip that intensified popular interest in the West. The next year Frémont and Carson tried to find a more direct pass through the Rockies. Failing, they used South Pass and went to *Great Salt Lake, which Jim Bridger had assumed was the Pacific Ocean when he floated into it in a bullboat. Frémont struck north from the lake to Oregon and south again to California, then almost unknown in the East. The book about that trip earned him his Pathfinder title, though he had found no new paths. He was an able man, however, and Jessie's descriptions and his maps were accurate. The books were useful guides for Western travel.*

Nauvoo

13

THE HARRIED SAINTS

THE PROPHET

ACCORDING TO THE Book of Mormon, two of the lost tribes of Israel came to North America: a good tribe, the Nephites, and a bad one, the Indians. Evil triumphed and of the Nephites only the prophet Mormon and his son Moroni were left alive. They wrote the Book on gold plates and buried them about 400 A.D. In 1827 an angel showed Joseph Smith where the plates were hidden and provided him with a remarkable pair of spectacles that enabled him to read the Hebrew immediately in English. Smith also received divine revelations, one of which directed him to lead a movement to reconquer the Promised Land from the Indians.

The gold plates of the Book vanished, but Smith published his translation and sold it from door to door. It converted many readers in upper New York State, and in 1830 they founded the Church of Jesus Christ of Latter-day Saints with Joseph Smith as its Prophet. The Saints wished to build a new Zion in the West, and as a way station, they

picked Kirtland, Ohio; but some went on to Independence, Missouri, to make a start on Zion there. At Kirtland they built a Temple and houses, laid out farms, and started stores and a bank. They remained apart from their gentile neighbors but did business with them. The Mormon Bank, like all other private banks, issued paper money and couldn't redeem it in the panic of 1837. The colony was unpopular and rumors of polygamy, then unfounded, were already circulating. The Saints were forced to sell out and move west to join the builders of Zion, who meanwhile had also had trouble and moved north of the Missouri River to a place called Far West. The Governor of Missouri shortly evicted all Mormons from the state.

In 1839 Joseph Smith bought a deserted village on the Mississippi in Illinois and named it Nauvoo. The Saints built a new Temple on a hilltop, and a community of industrious, dedicated people was soon thriving. Missionaries, some working in Europe after 1840, brought in converts, and in six years the town became the largest in the

Part of Salt Lake City, about 1850

state, with a population of twenty thousand. Polygamy was practiced at Nauvoo as a result of an earlier revelation of Smith's; this was widely suspected but was not publicly admitted until 1852. The Mormons then believed that single women could not attain salvation, and since the sect had more women than men, it became a man's duty to grant grace to several women by marrying them. Some of the extra partners were wives in a spiritual sense only, but many were fully married; there was a need of children to carry on the work of the Church.

Polygamy was intolerable in a monogamous society, so it was always the readiest rock to throw at the Saints; but the Illinois farmers found other grievances against them. The Mormons voted as a solid block and easily controlled state politics for their own advantage. Within their community, their law was for the benefit of Mormons, and criminals frequently became "converted" to escape a less prejudiced authority. The gentiles persecuted the settlement with increasing violence, burning barns and houses and raiding outlying farms, even injuring people. Hostility reached such a pitch that Joseph Smith and his brother were charged with treason on no evidence and jailed in Carthage under guard of the state militia, who somehow failed to prevent a mob from murdering both men.

EXODUS

Brigham Young was strong enough to hold most of the flock together after Smith's death. Young was already an Apostle, and on the strength of his one revelation, he became President. It was revealed to him that the Mormons should move

west beyond the civilization that repudiated them. He said nothing about a destination, but he owned a copy of the Frémonts' second book. With their usual energy, the Saints turned Nauvoo into a wagon shop; they built wagons even in the Temple. They sold everything they could to buy more wagons, oxen, and supplies for the trip.

The greatest single migration in American history began when the first outfits crossed the Mississippi ice in February, 1846. By mid-May sixteen thousand of Young's following were on the Iowa shore and only a thousand of them, too old or too poor to travel, stayed in Nauvoo. Four hundred wagons pushed ahead in the spring mud and made Council Bluffs on the Missouri by July. The next divisions moved more slowly, making long stops to dig wells, build camps, and plant crops for the use of those who followed them. Most of the families reached the Missouri by autumn; those who didn't, wintered in the prepared camps on the Iowa prairie. The younger men and women worked for local farmers, others sold things they could make, and Mormon bands gave concerts to raise money. A brass band, or any music, was a rarity in that part of the country. The poor souls who stayed behind in Nauvoo were driven out in the early fall; they camped on the west bank of the Mississippi in utter destitution until wagons came back and rescued them.

The main body of the Saints spent a miserable winter on the Missouri collecting their resources to go farther. They lived in huts and caves on an almost unrelieved corn-meal diet, and scurvy broke out among them. They had some help from the Potawatomi and Omaha Indians who, like them, had been ejected from their homes. Brigham Young took seventy-three wagons westward in April of 1847 to mark a road and find the new Zion. He followed the north bank of the Platte instead of the south bank, which was the Oregon Trail, to avoid the gentiles as far as possible and in search of undisturbed pasture for the thirty thousand Mormon animals. Every ten miles the vanguard set up a guidepost, often with a written message on it. These pioneers went up the Sweetwater, through South Pass, and crossed the Green River on rafts the thirtieth of June. At Fort Bridger they left the Oregon Trail and struck southwest, though Jim warned them against the kind of country they would find. Soon, Young detached forty-four wagons and pushed ahead. They had to camp once, long enough to build a passable road through a canyon. On the nineteenth of July two advance scouts topped a hill and looked down on the Salt Lake Valley. Young, who had the Frémonts' book in his luggage, joined them and spoke his famous line, "This is the place."

THE PROMISED LAND

The place didn't look much like Zion, in spite of the silver sheet of bitter water in the distance. Sagebrush and cactus covered the land; there were no trees except in the mountains and along the few streams. But this was the place. The men unyoked their teams, went to work at once on an irrigation ditch, and planted a crop of late potatoes. Within a month they "broke, watered, planted, and sowed upwards of 100 acres with various kinds of seeds." Then they went to work on adobe huts, built in a close group and fortified. Most of the first year's crops failed because they were planted too late. Grasshoppers threatened to destroy the next year's plantings, and the Saints saw a miracle in the great flocks of sea gulls that arrived and devoured the bugs.

By September, 1847, fifteen hundred Mormons reached the valley, but the bulk of the brethren were still on the Missouri. It took five years from the day the first wagon left Nauvoo to get them all to Utah. Hundreds were buried by the way, but Mormon surveyors methodically noted the exact latitude and longitude of every grave. Even when all of the Nauvoo Saints were at Salt Lake City the troubles of the trail didn't end. Many English converts came in by way of New Orleans and started west on foot, pulling hand carts.

Numbers of them died of exhaustion, and the rest were at the point of starvation when help reached them.

When the Mormons left Nauvoo, the Great Salt Lake was in Mexico, but though they didn't know it, they planted their first potatoes in United States soil. Congress wouldn't admit Utah as a state because of polygamy; so in 1849 Brigham Young set up the extralegal State of Deseret. In addition to Utah, it included Nevada, Arizona, and southern California. Utah, cut down to size, was admitted to the Union in 1896, six years after the Mormon Church repudiated polygamy.

In the meantime the colony went as far as enterprise could go to become self-sufficient. It built miles of irrigation ditches. The Church established dozens of outlying communities, sending selected people to develop them as a religious duty. They opened iron mines; they started various kinds of mills; and they began cooperative stores that are still in operation. Missionary work continued, requiring a means of communication, and some supplies could be obtained only in the East. So the Mormons ran a freight line of wagons to the Missouri and also operated their own postal service. Not all of the story is so good: Travelers passing west through Utah were, after all, hated gentiles, so perhaps there was some excuse for selling them food at prices that took their wagons and left them to convert their teams to pack animals, or took both wagon and team and made the buyers pedestrians. But nothing can excuse the deliberate murder of a whole wagon train of Arkansans at Mountain Meadows in 1857. If the Church did not instigate it, it nevertheless made no effort to punish the known criminals until many years after the event.

14

ALTA CALIFORNIA

MISSIONS, PRESIDIOS, AND PUEBLOS

Russian fur hunting in Alaska disturbed the Spanish in the mid-eighteenth century. Sitka was far from New Spain, but sea otter could be caught as far down the coast as the latitude of Mexico City. The Russians? Who could tell what they might do? The Spanish king's *visitador general* decided to create a buffer state by colonizing Alta California. A combined religious and military expedition under Gaspar de Portolá reached San Diego Bay in 1769. The soldiers built themselves a presidio, and Father Junípero Serra founded the Mission of San Diego de Alcalá. Portolá explored northward, found Monterey harbor, which he was looking for, and discovered San Francisco Bay, which merely annoyed him because he couldn't get around it. Fifteen years later a chain of twenty-one missions extended from the base of Point Loma north to Solano beyond the Golden Gate. Father Serra founded nine of them himself; he and his fellow Franciscans converted six thousand Indians and taught them skills they had never needed before.

Portolá built a second presidio at Monterey, and two more were built at San Francisco and

The Mission of San Luis Rey de Francia

Santa Barbara. In an effort at civilian settlement, three towns, or pueblos, were established: San Jose, Nuestra Señora la Reina de los Angeles de Porciuncula, and Branciforte, which became Santa Cruz. Settlers willing to come to California were a poor lot, enticed only by the *situado,* a government handout of $125 a year to each man, which encouraged an already well-developed laziness. Living was easy; the settler cared little about the crop he planted as a formality on his outlying acreage. He lived in utter squalor in a mud hut in the pueblo, sleeping on its floor, cooking out of doors, and squatting on the ground to eat.

The mission fathers had idealistic intentions of carrying on Junípero Serra's work of Christianizing and educating the Indians. Unfortunately they went about the job by dominating the simple people and doing all their thinking for them. These Indians were not the best specimens of their race. They lost their natural way of life and gained no initiative that would help them to adopt a new one. They did as they were told; when they didn't, they were whipped for the good of their souls. On a diet of porridge, they herded cattle and sheep, worked in the fields and vineyards, wove cloth, built churches, and decorated them with some remarkable painting. The missions owned thousands of acres and waxed rich on free labor; it probably never occurred to the padres that they had enslaved their converts.

GAY PROSPERITY

Under Spain a few individuals got large grants of land despite the protests of the Franciscans, who insisted that all California belonged to the Indians, to be held for them by the missions. But California became Mexican in 1821, though she didn't find it out until a year later; and in 1834, Mexico began taking the missions away from the fathers and granting their vast land holdings to private enterprise. What happened to the Indians, who had learned nothing but the white man's sins, is a sad story that will not be told here. At the end of ten years the last mission was secularized, and the gay and carefree life of the *Californios* was in full swing. It was a swing with gusto and charm.

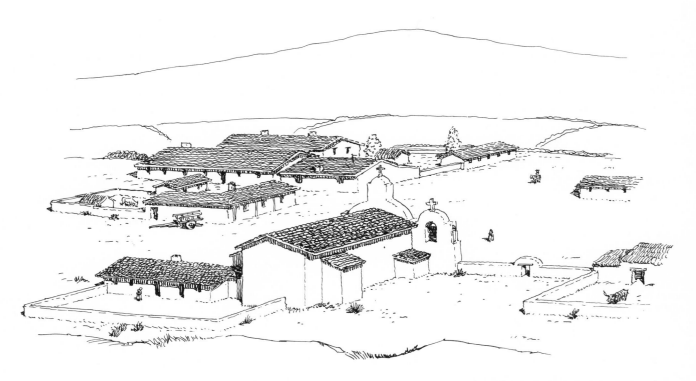

The pueblo of Nuestra Señora la Reina de los Angeles de Porciuncula as it looked in 1847

The *patrón* of every estate dispensed an open-handed, my-house-is-your-house hospitality. He welcomed and entertained any traveler according to the wayfarer's station in life. Did he not bring news and a new ear to listen? Did the guest need a new horse? Well, if he *must* leave, take one and welcome; and here, too, was a little gift of money for his journey. *¡ Vaya con Dios!*

Though small, Monterey, Santa Barbara, and San Diego became active social centers. Rich men had houses in them, *casas de pueblo,* not greatly different from the houses of rich men in the country. Like the New Mexican houses, they were built around at least three sides of a square court, but in California the outside walls had windows in them; this was a later time and the need of fortification had passed. A country house was a *casa de campo;* it stood on a rancho if its patron herded cattle, on a hacienda if he was a farmer. There were wooden *casas,* but most of them had three-foot-thick adobe

"Casa de campo"

walls. In early days thatch covered the roofs in the south and hand-split shingles those in the north; but after a mission priest succeeded in firing roof tiles, molded from red clay over an Indian's thigh, most people used them to keep out the rain.

A happy, reasonably innocent, if largely illiterate, social life went on among the *casas*. People thought nothing of riding forty miles to a party; fun was worth any time or distance and the host was happy if his guests stayed a week. Sometimes, where the ground wasn't too rough, ladies traveled in cushioned *carretas* hooded with thatch to keep off the sun and drawn by oxen, but at no creeping ox pace. Springless though the *carretas* were, they bumped along at an axle-screaming full gallop, a pace easy for the lean, long-legged Spanish cattle, though impossible to heavy Yankee oxen.

The ladies in the carts wore Chinese silks and home-woven cottons. A few of them left their bell-shaped dresses plain, but most of them orna-

outside seam. Embroidery ornamented both garments, and they sported silver buttons far in excess of practical need. The horseman plaited his well-oiled black hair into a queue that hung below the bright head cloth he wore under his *poblano*. A small gold ring hung in the lobe of one ear. His wide, red satin sash showed all the way around below the edge of his jacket. The gaps at the sides of his pants exposed his loose white drawers and his boots, armed with sharp rowels so large he had to remove his spurs to walk.

THE RANCHOS AND TRADE

When the rancheros took over, the Mexican and Indian vaqueros went right on herding the same animals they had tended for the missions. These men were the centaurs who showed the American cowhands how the thing was done. They were the

mented their party dresses with rows of ruffles from hem to sash. Over her simple shirtwaist, a *señorita* draped a fringed shawl; if she was lucky, it was an embroidered Chinese one that had come to Acapulco by the Manila galleon. Her mantilla was black lace, and she draped it over a high fan-shaped comb. She carried a painted fan, and the heels of her shoes were red. Of course her dark eyes were either languorous or flashing; and frequently she was fat.

The dashing caballero cantering beside the *carreta* preferred velvet for his short jacket and his flaring trousers that were split to the knee on the

127

first masters of the mustang and of the *reata*, with which they roped even grizzly bears. Since no one worried about the condition of the cattle, the vaqueros lived an easy life except at branding and slaughtering times. Trick riding was a workaday part of their roundups, the name of which, *rodeo*, they handed on to the modern contest.

Lacking a market, cattle had no value as meat. Any hungry white man (woe betide the Indian who tried it) was welcome to kill an animal and take what meat he needed, so long as he hung the hide where its owner's men could find it. Rancho cattle were tough and stringy, but they had

enough tender morsels to make a meal. The vaqueros slaughtered them from the saddle with long knives and then waded into the hardest work they did: skinning the animals and rendering their fat. They left the carcasses for the vultures and coyotes, taking only the hides and tallow. At first Mexico allowed no foreign trade with California; everything went south in *carretas* or by boat. But Yankee ships that landed for wood and water did a small, illegal trade even as early as 1800 in Spanish times. The *Californios* acquired a vague idea that the United States was a suburb of Boston.

New England shoe factories could use many hides, and a real trade in them began after restrictions relaxed. American ships came around the Horn stocked like department stores with luxuries for an eager market. San Diego was the main port for shipping hides, but comparatively few left any port; loading them through the surf avoided needless bother with export duties. The vaqueros simply dumped the skins on the beach or on a cliff above the beach, and it was up to the ship's droghers (in the old sense of driers) to get them on board. The

crew worked at this, but many Kanakas were brought from Hawaii as extra hands. The droghers waded into the sea with bundles of hides balanced on their heads and put them into longboats lying just beyond the breakers. On board the ship or sometimes on an offshore island, they scraped the hides clean, salted them, and dried them for stowing in the hold. Often it took two or three years for a ship to complete a cargo, and when she did other ships were happier if they passed on her windward side.

GRINGO SETTLERS

In 1814 John Gilroy, a young Scot, became ill on shipboard and was set ashore at Monterey. He embraced Roman Catholicism the same year and shortly afterward married a California girl. In time he acquired a rancho, but he was too fond of the bottle and he lost his land. Others improved on his pattern. American seamen jumped ship and converted themselves into *Californios*, Spanish or Mexican, depending on the date. Most of them took, or had given them, Spanish versions of their names; and all who were Protestants had to change their religion. Some took up ranching, some trade, and many of them held Mexican offices. American agents for ships lived ashore and sometimes elected to stay there: Abel Stearns became a rich merchant; Thomas Larkin—who broke the mold by marrying an American widow he met coming around the Horn—stayed as a trader, as the first United States consul at Monterey, and as the secret agent of President James K. Polk.

The most interesting of all these first American Californians, not only in the light of future events but in his own right, is John Sutter. Of Swiss origin but an American citizen, he settled in the Sacramento valley in 1840 and bought out the Russian fur-trading post just north of San Francisco which the Americans called Fort Ross. Around his own fort he developed New Helvetia, covering many square miles. He irrigated land, built a gristmill and a distillery, set up a tannery and weaving operations, and ran a launch down the Sacramento River to San Francisco. He was called a "hospitable, visionary, improvident land baron," and hundreds also called him blessed.

His fort was a way station for immigrants, but John Sutter didn't just wait for guests to arrive; when he heard of trouble he sent out relief parties to bring people in, sometimes from far to the east in Nevada. His help was needed. There were three hundred Americans in California in 1840, mostly farmers, and more of the same arrived every year; but in small parties who had no well-marked trail to follow and no long line of traveling companions to aid them. The worst tragedy was that of the Donner party of 1846. They took a new trail, against advice, and they took it too late. Cold weather caught them in the high pass that is named for them. They suffered in hovels under snow so deep that when spring came the "bushes" they had cut for firewood were found to be the tops of tall trees. The survivors had Sutter to thank for rescue. Of eighty-seven, thirty-nine died; and fewer would have made it, but that the living ate the dead.

BOUNDARIES AND "MANIFEST DESTINY"

In 1818 England agreed to the forty-ninth parallel of latitude as at least a part of a western boundary between the United States and Canada. The line began at the Lake of the Woods on what is now the Minnesota boundary and ran west to the Rockies. Everything beyond the mountains was vaguely called Oregon; neither country knew much about it, so they decided to "occupy" it jointly. The Oregon of 1846 was a more definite place, and despite an absurd political slogan, "Fifty-four-forty, or fight," that would have given this country half of British Columbia, the forty-nine-degree line was carried on west to the Strait of Georgia.

By 1846 the myth of the Great American Desert had faded; the whole United States became aware of the possibilities of the West and convinced of a "Manifest Destiny" to dominate North America. President Polk agreed with them. When Mexico ejected an envoy of his who was trying to buy the territory north of the Rio Grande, the President sent troops under General Zachary Taylor to the bank of the river. This was invasion, but when the Mexicans attacked Taylor war was declared.

General Taylor moved south toward Buena Vista; General Kearny invaded New Mexico; and Admiral Sloat, who was waiting for a signal off the California coast, took Monterey. Shortly afterward Winfield Scott came ashore at Vera Cruz, marched inland, and reduced the defenses of Mexico City. That was the end of the Mexican War. Mexico was forced to recognize the Rio Grande as the Texas border, which she had insisted it was not, and to cede to the United States all of the territory south of Oregon and west of Kansas. She was paid 15 million dollars for it. In 1853 the Gadsden Purchase of land south of the Gila River completed the United States' boundaries as they stood for more than a century.

Placer mining with a "long tom"

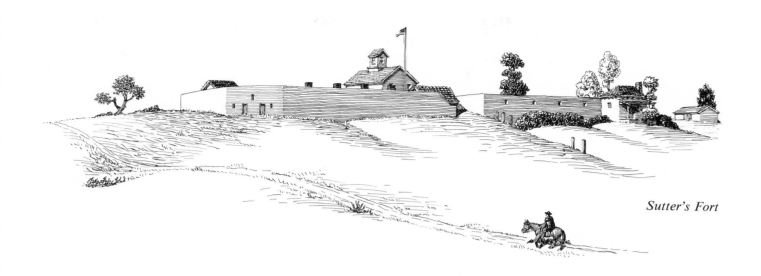

Sutter's Fort

15

EL DORADO

IN 1848 JAMES WILSON MARSHALL, building a sawmill for John Sutter at Coloma on the south branch of the American River, cut the mill's tailrace across a bend in the stream. One day in January he saw golden flecks on its sandy bottom. He took three ounces of the stuff to Sutter, and the two of them convinced themselves, correctly, that it was gold. Sutter was troubled. He vaguely foresaw this as disturbing his Eden, so he swore Marshall to secrecy; but workmen at the mill had seen the glitter and Sutter himself was a poor secret-keeper. With no particular fanfare, the story shortly appeared in the San Francisco newspaper. The rush began in May and by late June San Francisco and Monterey were almost deserted and poor Sutter's land was overrun with more squatters than he could possibly evict.

The first discoveries were all placer deposits in stream beds and banks eroded from bedrock higher up. The metal was usually distributed through the soil as "dust," though sometimes a stream deposited a rich pocket or rolled a nugget among its other pebbles. The first five men on the Yuba River took $75,000 in three months; Chino Tirador could hardly lift the gold he took from a pocket in a single day.

THE RUSH OF THE ARGONAUTS

The story hit the East in late summer of 1848 and soon crossed both oceans. There was skepticism at first, but by frost, all of the United States, much of Europe, and some of Asia suffered an outbreak of "yellow fever." Young romantics, ne'er-do-wells, middle-aged failures, and old fools all started for California. A surprising number of families went, but most of the Argonauts were very young men, many of them newly discharged from Mexican War service. The first enthusiasts went west in December and had to wait at the edge of the Plains for the grass to grow. A ship for California left in February of 1849 to go around the Horn; it was followed by fine clippers, as well as by anything else that would float—hulks some of them, to be scrapped at the end of the voyage. Many good ships, too, were abandoned in San Francisco harbor when their crews took off in a body for the diggings. The slower tubs took eight months to get around South America; the clipper record was under ninety days. The sea trip was costly, but it required little stamina beyond a high tolerance for boredom and poor food. It was the preferred way for big operators, gamblers, and

131

The head of the Chagres River in Panama

feminine entertainers, who sniffed gold they wouldn't have to dig with a shovel.

The Government subsidized two steamship lines: one to run from New York and New Orleans to Chagres in Panama, the other from Panama City to San Francisco and Oregon. The contracts were let long before Marshall started his mill, but service got under way just in time for the gold rush. Other lines jumped into the business, some operating to Nicaraguan and Mexican ports. Fares were steep, sometimes precipitous, and it was up to the passenger to get his body overland between the seas as best he could. In Panama this meant mules and native boats, steaming heat, bad food, bad water, malaria, yellow fever—the real thing this time—and often the frustration of waiting for the next over-crowded boat. Still, this was the fastest way to California, some thiry-four days from New York.

All overland trails had to go above or below the long canyon of the Colorado River, of which the Grand Canyon is but a part. Those Argonauts who started from the South naturally took southern routes. Some twelve thousand went by way of either El Paso or Santa Fe, but in 1849 alone, nearly thirty thousand took the northern route through South Pass and across Nevada along the Humboldt River, where Horace Greeley said Famine sat enthroned. There was a little grass along the river, always on the other side, and men crossed over at night to gather it for their animals.

A hundred miles or so from the Sierra Nevada Mountains the Humboldt gives up and sinks into the ground. The forty miles from there to the Carson River was bone-dry desert; eight miles east of its end opportunists did well selling water to the thirsty at a dollar a gallon. Plentiful grass on the eastern slopes of the Sierras gave the travelers a place to rest and refresh their beasts before attempting the mountain passes. One of the easiest was the Donner Pass, but people were superstitious and wouldn't use it. Many wagons broke up trying to get over the mountains, and their drivers converted the mules to pack animals, often loading them so ineptly that valuable equipment slipped off and went crashing down cliffs to ruin.

The sheer mass of the forty-niners protected them from Indian attack, but their tenderfootedness suffered enough from disease, heat, thirst, floods, and buffalo gnats. They filled the trail from horizon to horizon in wagons, on horses, behind push carts, and simply walking. They didn't organize themselves as the Oregon pioneers did, but in spite of inevitable exceptions, a good spirit prevailed; somebody always helped with a mishap, and somebody always shared food with the hungry. When a man came down with cholera, as many did east of the Divide, some stranger always stopped to nurse him back to health, or to bury him.

Packing in the Sierras

THE DIGGINGS

A new arrival's first problem was to find a likely spot for mining and mark it as his. If he claimed too much space, his neighbors quickly reduced it; but the same rough justice dealt harshly with any man who jumped the claim. To find his spot, the novice prospected along a stream by panning. He filled a shallow pan with silt and rotated it gently just beneath the surface of running water. The swirl he gave the water in the pan washed the lighter particles over its low sides, leaving only pebbles, which the miner picked out, and heavy gold dust, which settled to the bottom. This California silt nearly always yielded a little gold; unless the first sample showed an obvious strike, a man staked a claim only after he had found good "color" in a number of random pannings.

The next problem was to recover as much gold as possible by washing all the likely dirt on the claim. This took endless shoveling and something bigger to wash in than a pan. The best placer miner was an experienced ditchdigger; few Argonauts qualified. The work wore them down and discouraged them. Many felt cheated when they failed to find gold lying around in chunks to be picked up. Some quit and went home; others stayed to turn farmer in the rich valleys or went into the profitable business of supplying the miners. There were some, however, to whom the possibility of a bonanza was an irresistible lure;

133

most of these roamed the mountains behind a pack burro for the rest of their lives. Only a small few of them struck it rich.

When two men worked a claim, one shoveled and carried water, and the other washed gold in a cradle, sometimes called a rocker. It was a two-level box, about three feet long, set on rockers and provided with a handle by which the operator gave it the motion of an old-fashioned cradle. Though built as a unit, the device may be considered as two troughs, the lower full-length, the upper covering a little more than half of the lower. The shorter one was the riddle box; it served as a hopper and its bottom was perforated with small holes to allow water and silt, mixed by the rocking, to drain through into the lower riffle box. The hopper tilted just enough to sit level when the cradle was placed on a slope, as it always was, so

Cradle

that the sludge could run toward the uncovered end of the riffle box over cleats, or riffles, wedged into its bottom, and out through a slot. Heavy particles of gold collected behind the riffles.

Three men together could use a "long tom." It involved two separate boxes arranged the same way, but it had no rockers. The upper box of a tom was eight feet long and eighteen inches wide. It was placed with its closed end a couple of inches higher than its open end, which was covered with an iron strainer. A constant supply of water flowed into the higher end from a trough, a hose, or a pipe. Two men shoveled in dirt while the third stirred the thin mud constantly. The sludge ran through the strainer into the lower box and over riffles.

The sluice was a slightly later development that required no stirring. It was usually set up across a sharp bend in a stream and was a flume made of a series of connected open-ended boxes through which part of the stream flow was diverted. All of the sections had riffles in their bottoms, with a little mercury behind each to catch gold by amalgamating with it. Gold-bearing gravel was shoveled into the upper end of the sluice, and dirty water ran out the lower end. The pitch of the sluice was quite steep, at least eight inches to each twelve-foot section, so the water ran through it quite fast and carried away fairly large pebbles. The whole sluice was from two hundred to a thousand feet long; very little gold got all the way through and the run could go on for six days before the operators had to stop the water and remove their take. Distillation recovered the mercury, which could be reused. Miners eventually improved the sluice method by damming a stream and putting the water pressure they generated into canvas hoses to wash down gravel banks.

Everybody guessed from the first that there must be a mother lode from which the streams washed all this gold, and even in 1849 some quartz mining started in the Mariposa district. This was not for the romantic; it was even harder work than placer mining. The hard rock of the vein had to be quarried and then crushed to fine grit and mixed with mercury. Fortunately, mercury as well as gold was mined in California. At first the miners crushed the quartz lumps by dragging big granite blocks back and forth across them with mule power, or by rolling them with a stone wheel trundled round and round a pivot. Later, stamping mills reduced the ore to powder; these were big hammers powered by water wheels or steam engines. Quartz mining didn't end when the gold rush was over; it produced about 50 million dollars a year for fifteen years and flourished to the end of the century.

THE ROARING CAMPS

The forty-niners were reasonably decent boys, though loud, boisterous, and full of practical jokes. Most of them loved to gamble and they drank too much; they sang raucous songs and held dances at which, there being no women, men with patched pants acted as "ladies." When the boys heard of a real woman in camp, they rushed to take a respectful look at her, sometimes offering to pay her husband for the privilege. They lived in tents and slapped-up cabins and, all in good fun, gave the camps weird names like Murderer's Bar and Delirium Tremens. Their numbers swamped local peace officers, but their own group action enforced law enough to keep them in some bounds. Anybody could do as he pleased so long as he didn't hurt anybody else. The rules the forty-niners made to regulate their mining claims ultimately became part of the national code.

The magnet of many men with loose gold soon attracted the dregs of the world—crooked

gamblers, prostitutes, thieves, murderers—and the miners dealt rough justice to them. They selected judge and jury and tried suspects on the spot. At Dry Diggings, not far from Sutter's sawmill, five men were caught in the act of a gang robbery. There was no jail to put them into, so the pick-up court ordered thirty-nine lashes which were applied with enthusiasm. Then somebody charged three of the men with an earlier crime. Evidence was offered. Perhaps it wouldn't have satisfied a real jurist, but it was convincing enough to string the three up to a near-by oak and to get Dry Diggings a new name, Hangtown. A more solemn generation changed it again to Placerville.

Once, a man washing his face in a stream found himself looking at a gold nugget as big as his head. The feverish hope of something of this sort kept the Argonauts digging with aching arms, however much they hated it. Gold was everything. They cooked for themselves, hastily, living mostly on a diet of bacon, flapjacks, and coffee, though some baked bread on Sunday when everybody took a day off to wash clothes and relax. Sometimes a professional hunter brought a carcass into camp and sold hunks of venison or bear meat for a little less than their weight in gold dust. The sutlers sold at auction in small quantities, because that way they could run up the prices of flour and other staples, and once in a while some such delicacy as pickles or the herring whose boxes shod the miner's daughter in the old song:

> "Light she wandered, like a fairy,
> And her shoes were number nine,
> Herring boxes without topses,
> Sandals were for Clementine."

Miners gave appearance no thought. A broad-brimmed "wide-awake" hat, a flannel shirt— usually red—pants held up by galluses and tucked into oiled leather boots, made almost a uniform for them. Buttons were kept at minimum to save sewing, and holes were patched with any material that could be sewed on. Only wealthy men and gamblers wore plug hats and frock coats.

Next to the strike that would enrich him for life, the man with the shovel worked to accumulate enough dust for a spree in Frisco. Hang the pawky day-to-day take; it was small change compared to the bonanza that would turn up presently. To get to Frisco you clung with a dozen others to the wagon that Jim Birch drove from the diggings to Sacramento and then you took a boat downriver. Both legs of the journey put a strain on your bag of gold dust. San Francisco recovered quickly from its early evacuation and then burst its seams trying to accommodate a glut of population. Streets were literally knee-deep in mud. Bars served whisky from pitchers in tin cups at fifty cents a drink (a nickel bought one in St. Louis). Gambling joints and dance halls paid $40,000-a-year rents—for tents. Abandoned ships, hauled ashore, became rooming houses charging luxury-hotel tariffs. A man could get rid of a lot of dust in a hurry and convince himself he was having the time of his life.

WASHOE AND PIKE'S PEAK

To the forty-niners who trudged heedlessly over its rich deposits Nevada was merely a place to be crossed. Disappointed California miners panned color in Gold Creek, a tributary of the Carson River, and were annoyed by the blue mud they had to wash away. Every ton of the mud they cursed contained $3,500 worth of silver. It had eroded from quartz ledges such as those of the great Comstock Lode in the Washoe district. The rush to Washoe came over the snow of the Sierras in the winter of fifty-nine to sixty; the gold mad became the silver mad.

Placer mining was useless; the ledges ran deep and prospectors ranged over the desert pitting it with experimental holes. Few worked their own strikes; they sold them to mining companies who in turn sold stock in the prospects. Everybody, at the diggings and elsewhere, speculated in the stock. Its value fluctuated wildly with every new rumor and the people who really made money out of it were the directors of the mining companies, who knew what was going to happen next. The ledges were erratic; a thin one became a bonanza, or a rich one suddenly turned worthless.

The silver mines were deep and hot and were shored up with timber to retard cave-ins. Now and then part of a town fell into an excavation. In the lower levels, where it was hottest, men worked nearly nude, stopping every few minutes to sponge off with ice water. They made four dollars a day, high wages for the time. A few men made enormous fortunes from Nevada silver mines and took their money elsewhere to spend it.

In 1858 a little gold appeared along the south fork of the Platte River and was immediately exaggerated in the eastern press. A fantastic rush started before a thousand dollars' worth of dust had been washed. There was plenty of gold in Colorado and silver, too, but very little of it was lying around loose. Most of the hundred thousand people who followed the cry of "Pike's Peak or Bust" dragged themselves home thoroughly busted. But they founded Denver and some stayed in Colorado to start new lives. Not all mining towns were so permanent. In Colorado and Nevada, and later in Montana and Arizona, when the lodes gave out, the population left and empty ghost towns still stand in desolate valleys.

Shoring of a silver mine on the Comstock lode

Mud wagon

16

TWO THOUSAND MILES

STAGES IN CALIFORNIA

JIM BIRCH, a young man who had driven stage-coaches in New England, seized a better thing than gold mining when he hitched four mustangs to an open wagon and started passenger service in 1849 between Sacramento and the diggings on the American River. By the mid-fifties he was the principal partner in the Pioneer Stage Line, which used good horses and imported Concord coaches to run through much of California and, eventually, over the Sierras to Genoa in Nevada, a trip likely to scare a year or so off a passenger's life. The stage company graded the roads enough to make them passable but left the surfaces in a state of nature over which six miles an hour was fast.

The Pioneer coaches were the first the Indians attacked and the first to be held up by bandits. The Achomawi Indians wanted good horses, so they rushed an empty coach near the Pitt River in northern California. The wounded driver

whipped his team to a dead run that demolished the coach, but not before he gained enough distance to unhitch and ride the horses to the next change station. In spite of sixteen arrow punctures, he survived.

No one thought of bandits at first. Messengers casually tossed wooden boxes of gold worth thousands into the boot of a coach with the passengers' luggage. Experience later suggested iron boxes bolted fast under the driver's seat. Tom Bell (his real name was Hodges) tried the first robbery in 1856. A doctor who saw a quicker way to wealth than his profession provided, he organized a gang to help him. Bell planted a "miner" on a coach to "case" it, and with six men took a short cut from the station where his spy dismounted. When they stopped the stage, the messenger, in charge of passengers and mail, fired at once and knocked Bell off his horse. The passengers out-shot the bandits and saved the $100,000 booty, but the outlaws killed a Negro woman in the coach and wounded two other passengers and the driver. Angry posses quickly caught the six gunmen and then traced Bell to a hideout where they lynched and scalped him. Bell's failure by no means kept others from trying—and succeeding.

FREIGHT AND MAIL

Only pack trains crossed the Sierras before 1844 and they continued to cross them for some years after the first wagons negotiated the passes. Some trains used fifty mules to carry food, dry goods, mining supplies, and mail. It took sixteen days by muleback for mail to reach Carson City from Sacramento, and another week from there to Salt Lake City, whence it went east in light wagons by way of South Pass and the Platte, the drivers traveling by day and camping at night.

There was no mail whatever to Washoe in winter until Snowshoe Thompson crossed the passes on skis in January, 1856. Few of his customers had ever seen such things, but Snowshoe was a Norwegian; he could not only use skis, he could make them. They were ten feet long and weighed twenty-five pounds. There was no trail in winter. Thompson covered the ninety miles by following landmarks in the daytime and stars at night. He had no Government contract but operated a one-man enterprise; he carried anything—even a printing press, in parts—over many trips.

Isolated communities sprang up in the fifties along the trails that led to California, Oregon, Utah; scattered centers appeared in Kansas and Nebraska and in the Colorado valleys. The West Coast towns received some goods by sea. From San Francisco, freightmen distributed stuff inland as far as the Nevada mines in the big Washoe wagons that John Studebaker built in his factory at Placerville. Twenty mules pulled them, guided by a mule skinner with a magnificent vocabulary of profanity, a loud voice, and neat skill with a long whip that could flick the leaders' ears from the saddle on the near wheeler. He needed skill; a road in the mountains was often a mere shelf cut in a cliff above an abyss. Bells on the mules warned other wagons of their approach around a bend, sometimes in time to prevent a tie-up at a spot too narrow for passing. Turn-outs helped, but a driver hated to enter one because, once in, it might be hours before traffic let him out again.

Steamboats brought supplies for inland settlements to landings on the Missouri, hundreds of miles to the east. Huge canvas-covered freight wagons, carrying four or five tons apiece and often hitched in pairs, inched over the trails from the landings behind span after span of oxen hitched

by a long chain. A bullwhacker with a whip kept each team in order and a "swamper" manned the brakes on downgrades. Freighting was a profitable business that a man could start with a single wagon. Many did so and some grew to be considerable outfits, by far the largest of which was Russell, Majors & Waddell—with 6,000 wagons, 75,000 oxen, and a brigade of bullwhackers.

Twenty-five wagons made a "bull train" and the gaps between trains were short. They bellowed and shouted along at a pace that took ten weeks to get from Fort Leavenworth to Salt Lake City. Fast freight traveled in lighter wagons pulled by mules, at more than twice the speed and more than twice the cost. This was still unsatisfactory and everybody clamored for better roads and faster deliveries, especially of mail. Even after the

mail was speeded up by the Overland coaches and the Pony Express, and even after a railroad crossed the continent, bull trains continued to serve outlying settlements.

All sorts of transport ideas were tried. Perhaps the most bizarre was the introduction of camels for use in the desert. The army tried them for supplying survey parties; in 1856, fourteen of

them padded from Texas to Los Angeles. Private enterprise tried them, too, for supplying mines in Nevada and there was thought of using them as farm animals. Experiment proved that a camel could out-plow a mule; the difficulty was to find a farmer who would be seen *gee-hawing* such an outlandish beast. The American desert wasn't the sandy Sahara, and it cut the camel's feet; Mexican drivers didn't know how to handle them or to load them, so the animals' backs became sore, too. Finally, the camels were shot or turned loose.

THE OVERLAND MAIL

Congress authorized a mail-carrying contract to a cross-country stage line in 1857, leaving the selection of the contractor to the Postmaster General and the selection of the route to the contractor. Neither provision was carried out. Jim Birch got a temporary contract and was ordered to go by way of San Antonio and San Diego. That way took thirty to thirty-eight days and was too long, as Birch knew, but he operated the "Jackass Line" because he was assured of getting the main contract. He didn't. James Buchanan, then President of the United States, stepped in and forced the $600,000-a-year award to his intimate friend John Butterfield, a big man in the eastern freight business who had never operated stagecoaches; but he quickly found out how to do it. In the year allowed him to get organized he built 165 change stations with wells and corrals, set up blacksmith shops and built bridges, bought 1,200 good horses, 600 mules, about a hundred vehicles—some coaches, some stage wagons—and hired 750 men.

Coaches left both ends of the run on September 15, 1858, and were followed by others twice a week thereafter. The Apaches sacked one sta-

tion before the first coach reached it. The route's official starting point was Memphis because that was the Postmaster General's home town; but it really started at St. Louis and went by way of Little Rock, El Paso, and Yuma, to San Francisco, covering just under 2,800 miles. Almost everybody knew the Platte-Salt Lake City route was better, as Ben Holliday later proved, but the partners Butterfield, Fargo, and Dinsmore were afraid of snow. The stages made the trip in about twenty-one days, changing horses every eight miles in rough country, every twenty-five miles where the going was better. Most early pictures show the coaches traveling at a full gallop; their average speed of five and a half miles an hour proves they held a more sedate pace, but they held it day and night and the passengers caught what miserable naps they could. The only stops were for abominable meals at the larger "home stations" where the coaches changed drivers.

THE CONCORD COACH

Abbott and Downing of Concord, New Hampshire, built special large and heavy Concord coaches for western use. They painted the running gears yellow and the enclosed bodies barn-red, with fancy scrolls on the bottom panels and romantic landscapes on the doors. Nine passengers rode inside, three of them facing backward and three on a folding jump seat between the doors. In addition to the driver, the messenger, and an armed guard who rode on the box, three passengers had seats on the roof; sometimes more clung on wherever they could. Some luggage went on the roof, but most of it traveled in the leather-covered boot behind the body. Mail rode inside the coach, but occasionally it lay unguarded at the trail side a few days until a coach came along with space enough for it. Mail transportation was covered by the Government subsidy; passengers paid cash.

Thoroughbraces made of eight layers of heavy sole leather—the same kind that had eased stages on the National Road—ran fore-and-aft between stout iron stanchions attached to the undercarriage of the Concord and carried the entire weight of the coach body. They did a better job of cushioning shocks than would springs, and they made life easier for the horses. Stage wagons, more familiarly known as mud wagons, used thoroughbraces too. Lighter in weight and simpler in construction, these vehicles protected their passengers from the weather only with light-framed tops and roll-down canvas curtains. Mud was a consideration, but the real use of the stage wagon was on steep mountain roads; mules took them to back-country settlements that never saw a coach.

Six horses pulled an Overland stage. The driver controlled them with six reins, three held in his left hand and three in his right. At very sharp

Concord coach

corners which only one pair at a time could round, he reached over with his outside hand and shortened the leaders' rein, that of the swing horses, and that of the wheelers, successively. He flourished a long whip but seldom touched a horse with it. The usual harness of western stage horses gave them no way to hold the vehicle back on a downgrade, as ordinary harness does with its breeching. The right foot of the driver slowed the coach by pressing on a long lever that pinched brakes against the rear tires.

Though Indians always made more than a nuisance of themselves by raiding isolated change stations, they seldom bothered the well-armed stages until Civil War times. Then most of the western troops went East to fight, and trouble broke out for both coaches and bull trains; it sometimes stopped traffic for weeks. Ben Holliday had by then bought out Butterfield and shortened the route by running his Overland stages from Atchison, Kansas, to Salt Lake City; passengers changed there to Wells, Fargo coaches for Carson City. Ben was the king of all the stage men. A rough character but astute, he foresaw that the railroad would put the stages out of business. So he sold out to Wells, Fargo & Company and retired, rich, in 1864.

THE PONY EXPRESS

Few ever used its real name: The Central Overland, California and Pikes Peak Express Company. Russell, Majors & Waddell set it up in April, 1860, and ran it at a staggering loss in hope of a fat Government contract. The strain was too great; after eleven months they sold it to Ben Holliday.

Pony Express riders were supposed to weigh no more than 125 pounds; hence most of them were boys. Mr. Waddell was a pious man. He gave each rider a small Bible to carry and required an oath from each not to quarrel, drink, or swear; he also gave each man a horn to blow, and at first, a carbine and two revolvers. This armament proved too heavy and was reduced to a single "Navy" revolver, plus an extra loaded cylinder. The boys rode excellent horses, changing them at nine-to-

fifteen-mile intervals, and each rider covered a fixed section of the route, both ways.

When the rider arrived, the station keeper had a fresh horse ready, girthed with a special light saddle. The change of horses was made in two minutes, with the rider dismounting, transferring his mochila, mounting the new horse, and taking off again at an easy canter; a horse can't run full-out for nine miles. The mochila was a square of leather that covered the saddle. It was pierced with a round hole for the saddle horn and a curved slit for the cantle; attached to its four corners were locked boxes of hard leather which held the mail. These *cantinas,* as the boxes were called, remained padlocked except when they were transferred to a new rider at the end of a section; at that time the home station keeper opened them and checked their contents. If he had lost his horse to the Indians or to accident, it was a rider's duty to carry his mochila to the next station in any way he could get it there.

The Pony Express route began at St. Joseph, Missouri, and ran to Fort Laramie, to Fort Bridger, to Salt Lake City, to Genoa, Nevada, and on, through Placerville, to Sacramento. From there, mail reached San Francisco by river boat. A separately maintained detour between Julesburg, Colorado, and Granger, Wyoming, handled letters for Denver. Except in winter, the total time of passage was under ten days, with a record of seven days and seventeen hours. A half-ounce letter cost five dollars at first; this was reduced to a dollar in July, 1861, in accordance with the terms of a Government contract. The first poles for a transcontinental telegraph line already stood when the first Pony Express rider threw a leg over his mochila in April of 1860; the outbreak of the Civil War hurried its completion. Part of the express service was relaying telegrams between the two ends of the unfinished line. Those ends met on the twenty-sixth of October, 1861; two days after that, the last rider started west, just over nineteen months after the first one.

THE CIVIL WAR AND THE WEST

New Mexico never made an official decision, but her sympathies were southern; Texas, Arkansas, and Arizona formally seceded. Missouri voted not to do so, but her proslavery governor forced a secession vote through the legislature. Internal fighting broke out and Federal troops put the state under martial law. Union militia from California and Colorado inflicted heavy losses on Texas troops in Arizona and New Mexico and drove the survivors out. Kansas had the worst troubles. Bands of ruffians, changing sides at their own convenience, used the war as an excuse for robbing and murder. Since real soldiers also took what they needed to live, and since uniforms were scarce, citizens couldn't distinguish the genuine from the spurious.

When the South closed the Mississippi River, it forgot about the new railroads. Westerners, who had habitually shipped by boat to New Orleans, sent their products to the Atlantic coast by rail instead; once the habit was formed it was never broken.

THIRTY MILES AN HOUR

A railroad to reach the Pacific and open a rich trade with the Orient was already a dream early in the 1830's, when California and China seemed about equally remote from the Atlantic coast. More serious minds discussed the idea in the next decade, calling forth the famous bad guess of the New York *Herald,* ". . . ridiculous and absurd. Centuries hence will be time enough to talk of such a railroad." In the fifties the need to tie the new State of California and other distant settlements closer to the Union by fast transportation, became clear to the whole country. A wave of enthusiasm overruled the quibbles of the cautious. Surveys for five different routes were finished by 1856. The outbreak of the Civil War in 1861 eliminated all Southern routes from consideration while increasing the need for closer ties with the West. It hastened the granting of a railroad charter in 1862, and at the same time made construction almost impossible by creating a labor shortage, raising prices, and making difficult the raising of money.

The chosen route was roughly that of Ben Holliday's Overland stages. It was divided between two railroad companies: the Central Pacific, to build eastward from Sacramento; the Union Pacific, to build westward from Omaha. They were to meet somewhere; no point was fixed. Neither company expected to make money from operating its railroad; both looked for profits from construction contracts to companies they owned and from the sale of the fabulous grants of public land they received as encouragement. As further help, they had the right to cut ties and quarry stone on the public domain, and after each built its first forty miles of track with private money, the Government sold bonds to lend the railroads from $16,000 to $48,000 per mile, depending on the terrain they encountered. The grand-scale swindles of both companies are classics; their directors made an estimated $23,000,000 among them, but they built the railroad.

LAYING THE RAILS

Central Pacific, far from the war zone, started early and moved steadily ahead, though slowly, because of mountains and because nearly all tools and materials had to be sent out by sea, even cars and locomotives. The contractors licked the mountains by such devices as lowering men over cliffs in baskets to drill holes for blasting; and they licked the labor problem by importing hundreds of Chinese coolies. By 1867 the Central Pacific was out of the passes and laying track much faster.

The Union Pacific had easy going on the flat at first, encountering its rough country later. Its trouble was getting started at all; it wasn't until 1866 that the Government approved the first forty-mile stretch of track. There was no railroad connection from the East to Omaha, Nebraska, where the Union Pacific tracks started. Supplies, including food except fresh meat, came up the Missouri and moved west over the newly laid rails. Meat was shot by professional hunters who had their own troubles with Indians. So did the workers. There were ten thousand of them, mostly Civil War veterans, who drilled like troops and worked with their rifles stacked handy.

The road went forward in hundred-mile sections; that is, the surveyors kept a hundred miles ahead of the grading crews, who filled, cut, bridged, and tunneled as necessary a hundred miles ahead of the track layers. Materials for the graders came by rail to bases and then went forward on wagons. Ties, too, moved ahead of the rail layers on wagons. Most of the ties were cottonwood, processed to harden them. Rails came to the work area on horse-drawn cars. Crews unloaded four rails to the minute, carrying them ahead and placing them on the ties to be gauged, spiked, and bolted by other specialized gangs. The 4-8½″ gauge, by the way, set the final standard for all American railroads. An empty rail car was simply tipped off the track until a loaded car had passed it. It was then tipped back on and returned for a new load. The track moved forward at six or eight miles a day, and every day's work shortened

the route of the Overland stages, running between the railheads.

With the track, also in hundred-mile jumps, moved the construction base—known as Hell on Wheels—a canvas-and-framework town as gaudy as any mining camp. It was knocked down and thrown on flatcars when a section was completed; next morning it was open for business a hundred miles farther west. Sometimes it left nothing behind but trash, sometimes a nucleus for a new and permanent town, and sometimes an older settlement it had overwhelmed and corrupted shook itself and took up life again, though not quite as it had been before.

THE GOLDEN SPIKE

Each of the two railroads wished to control as much track as possible. So not having been told where to stop, they continued past each other, until Congress hastily fixed a junction at Promontory, Utah, just north of the Great Salt Lake. Here, May 10, 1869, was staged the ceremonial driving of the final Golden Spike and the meeting of the locomotives from east and west. Leland Stanford, President of the Central Pacific, swung at the spike and missed, but there was no television camera to embarrass him. Telegraph keys clicked, triggering a country-wide celebration complete with torchlight parades, patriotic speeches, and toasts drunk in champagne.

The expected rush of Oriental trade didn't develop, but the trip from Omaha to San Francisco

Snow shed in the mountains

could be made in four days at thirty miles an hour and in reasonable comfort. It was wonderful to everyone; to mountain men, Oregon pioneers, forty-niners, it was a clear miracle. Winter slowed "the cars" but didn't stop them. Trains crept through wooden sheds under the snows that had buried the Donners and supported Snowshoe Thompson. When the Eads Bridge over the Mississippi was finished in 1874, steel rails actually spanned the continent from sea to sea.

THE CLEARING OF THE PLAINS

In the 1850's the Plains Indians accepted fixed tribal hunting areas and agreed to the passage of traffic through their lands; but agreeing didn't make them like wagon trains, stagecoaches, or railroad construction crews. Above all they hated miners, who paid no heed whatever to Indian boundaries or Indian rights. Travelers and the railroad workers shot buffalo for food; often they shot them wastefully, but not so wastefully as the hide hunters after the Civil War. These men skinned the animal they killed and left the carcass to rot. They shot a million in 1870, and by 1884 they had wiped out the herds and so flooded the market that finished buffalo robes for carriages sold at three or four dollars apiece. With no buffalo, the Plains Indians starved, but for Government handouts.

The Bureau of Indian Affairs had benevolent, if often misguided, intentions; but unfortunately it wasn't in sole charge of Indian affairs. The army took a hand, too, and tended to be rough and to resent the rifles the bureau gave the Indians, sometimes better guns than the soldiers carried.

A small band of Sioux murdered six white peo-ple in Minnesota in 1862. Panic at once seized both settlers and Indians. Some Sioux fled west at once, but 1,300 of them stayed to fight and killed 737 white people of all ages. The white avengers hanged thirty Indians and made trouble for many more. The Sioux resentment spread to other tribes, and the Plains started a desperate last-stand fight, but not with any concerted plan. The turmoil and slaughter lasted well into the seventies, climaxed by Custer's tragic bid for glory at the Little Bighorn in 1876 and the bitter retreat of Chief Joseph and his Nez Percés the following year. As each tribe yielded, its survivors were cooped up on a reservation, either in their own country or in the Indian Territory, as Oklahoma was then called. Even as late as 1890, the Sioux—excited by ghost dances and prophecies of a messiah who would erase the whites and bring back the dead buffalo—started trouble under Sitting Bull. The old shaman was murdered in his tent; and the massacre of 128 men, women, and children by frightened white troops at Wounded Knee Creek, South Dakota, finally ended Indian resistance.

17

THE COW HUNT AND THE COWHAND

THOUGH HE SPAWNED no Daniel Boone, no Davy Crockett, no Kit Carson, collectively the western cowhand has been made the supreme American folk hero. He still accumulates legend, and only heaven knows what prodigies may be assigned to him in another century. The man himself was an amiable soul and highly competent at his job, but his heyday lasted only twenty years and his importance to the frontier doesn't justify his glory, nor do his mental and spiritual attainments. But no American has ever worn such dashing clothes, especially as he is now re-created. The swaggering gun fighter of screen and picture tube sometimes twangs his guitar in front of some cattle for atmosphere; to his working great-grandfather cows were the center of existence. He studied all their ways, lived with them, and cursed them for months at a stretch. "Cow," by the way, meant any bovine animal, regardless of sex or age.

THE LONGHORNS

Long before the Spanish brought cattle to California they drove them into New Mexico and Texas. The animals themselves were Spanish; narrow of face and stringy of body, vicious, self-reliant, and able to survive heat and cold. These were the *cimarróns*, or "wild ones." They raised themselves, and what profit they yielded came from their hides. The famous Texas longhorns were the descendants of these cattle. Undoubtedly they had been somewhat crossbred with stock brought in by the American *empresarios*, for the longhorns, though mean, were not as mean as the *cimarróns*. Neither the Spanish nor the original American stock had horns of such length as to account for the spread of four, five, or even seven feet of the longhorns.

American Texans shipped a few live animals by sea to East Coast ports; they even drove a trickle of them overland to New Orleans and St. Louis. The Civil War sent the cattlemen into the Confederate Army, and their herds ran wild. When the fracas ended, returning soldiers slapped brands on the nearest animals and went into business. So was born the great idea, held by a large minority, that unbranded cattle were yours if you could get to them first, and further, that cow stealing wasn't quite as criminal as horse stealing.

The Texas brush country was free to all and so vast that early herds could be kept separate. Each owner rounded up his own cows, penned them, and branded their calves. If he caught his neighbor's cow with his own, he branded her calf with his neighbor's mark; not everybody was dishonest. Such branding was done with a "running iron" or a cinch ring or a ring from the end of a wagon tongue, heated and held in improvised wooden tongs; the brand was drawn on with the iron. The made-up iron that was applied like a rubber stamp was in use, however, and had been since Spanish times.

Branding iron

THE COW HUNT

Even Texas "filled up" to the point where there was no longer room to keep herds separate, and everybody's cows grazed together, unattended, both summer and winter. The stockmen met and divided the public range of South Texas into districts a hundred miles square more or less, each with a superintendent of the roundup, or the cow hunt, as they called it. In that thick and prickly horse-high brush, it *was* a cow hunt, too. Spring and fall, every large outfit sent to its district roundup a mule-drawn chuck wagon and cowhands in proportion to its herd, with a string of horses for each man. Small ranches sent only two or three men with horses and a pack mule to carry grub, or a group shared a chuck wagon. Owners on the edges of adjoining districts also sent a man or two to pick up strays. By the time the roundup started, fifteen or twenty wagons and three or four hundred men had gathered at a central spot where there was water and good grass.

The ranchers culled beef cattle in the fall and branded calves that were born late or had been missed in the spring. This took only two or three weeks, but the spring roundup, which began late in May as soon as the grass was good, took at least a month and sometimes three. Cattle grazed in bunches over the whole district and the hands' first job was to gather them all into one enormous herd. Fortunately the men knew where to look for them, never far from water or from the chunks of rock salt that were put out for them. When a hand found a bunch, he took care not to "chouse" it; he quietly consolidated it and moved it slowly toward the roundup. He might take several days to get his charges into the big herd, guarded on all sides, milling slowly round and round and bawling loud enough to blanket speech for a hundred yards. So thorough was the cow hunt that it often caught some settler's family cow and left him with the hard choice of finding Bessie in ten thousand cattle or letting the baby go without milk for a while.

Only a couple of experts from each outfit, mounted on equally expert ponies, rode into the herd to cut out their bosses' animals. In spring they sought cows with calves old enough to eat grass but still young enough to follow their mothers. The cutter-out moved slowly among the cattle looking for his outfit's notch in a cow's ear rather than its brand on her flank, which was hard to see in the close-packed herd and might still be covered by long winter hair. The man found the cow, but once he had shown her to his mount, the pony took over the job of working her out of the herd, pressing her quietly along and cleverly putting himself in her way every time she tried to turn back. Her calf he disregarded; it would go where its mother went. Once the cow was out of the mass, another man took over and persuaded her to join the boss's cow herd a half mile away.

Cowpunchers caught calves with lariats, throwing them for branding as they had learned to do from the Mexicans. The word "lariat" itself is an Americanization of the Spanish *la reata,* though a cattleman seldom called it anything but a "rope." As used in Texas, it was about thirty feet long. The later "grass ropes" of hemp were cheaper and actually stronger than the four-strand plaited rawhide of early days. The working noose ran through a honda, which was sometimes a small eye spliced in the end of the rope itself but more often was a metal grommet. The cowhand held the coils of his rope in his left hand, swung the noose with his right, and cast it to open and fall on the animal, on a moving target, that is. One can best understand the accomplishment by trying to rope, say, a stationary garden chair with the clothesline. If it were a calf, you would make your throw from behind it, drop the noose over it, and flip the rope

146

to one side while your pony made a quick dash to the other side. The rope, made fast to the saddle horn, would snap tight and "bust the calf's legs from under him."

Once thrown, the youngster was dragged to the fire and kept down on its side by tying its feet together or by a man who put his knee on its back, pulled the calf's tail between its legs, and held on. The operation was over quickly. The flick of a sharp knife on one or both ears, a whiff of burning hair from the seared flank, a loud bawl from the victim, and it was on its feet to "high-tail" it back to the mother (creating the slang word with its action). The brands were simple combinations of letters, numbers, and geometrical shapes that could be given descriptive names. They and the various ear slits were recorded on the books of the stock associations and in the county courthouses.

Mavericks, or unbranded yearlings, belonged to the man on whose range they were found, when that fact could be determined. More often, mavericks and stray calves separated from their mothers were divided, pro rata, at the roundup. Many a man built up a herd for himself by rustling mavericks and applying his own brand to them. Stray calves he could create by the simple process of eliminating their mothers. The next easy step was the addition of the bar or curlicue that would convert his neighbor's brand to his own. Unless a man were caught with the hot iron in his hand, such artistry was difficult to prove; but a well-founded suspicion was often enough to get him a long necktie made of his own rope.

Cutting out

HORSES

Descendants of horses that had escaped from the Spanish in New Mexico ran wild on the western Plains, where the horse probably originated but from whence he vanished thousands of years earlier. Though the herds had water, and in summer, all the grass they could use, they suffered in winter; the survivors became hardy and tough but small. They acquired the name "mustang" from the old Spanish word *mesteño,* "strayed"; or they were called, more neatly, by the Spanish word *bronco,* "rough," "rude," "crabbed."

A later infusion of Spanish equine blood came from California where wild horses increased so mightily that thousands were slaughtered to save the grass for cattle. California horses worked north, and the Plateau Indians caught and mastered them. One tribe, the Cayuse, gave their name to all Indian ponies north of Texas; another, the Palouse, practiced selective breeding, the only Indians to do so. They produced the Appaloosa, dark on the forequarters and spotted over the rump, the best horse on the Plains before the Americans came.

The scrubby mustang had qualities of agility, endurance, and natural sense that were good in a cow pony, but he was too small and too slow for the job. He was also too cussed; you had to "break him all over again every morning." The white man's casual breeding that added a little Thoroughbred, Standard, or even Morgan blood to the mustang often resulted in an ideal horse for the work. He was taller, faster, and wasn't usually pretty, but he could run wild and take care of himself; normally, he wasn't impossible to break, and once broken, he could perform the tricks of the cow trade.

No horse can do continual hard work unless he eats some grain, and since the western horses lived entirely on grass, a couple of weeks under saddle brought them to the need of a long rest cure. Hence each cowhand used a string of six or eight horses, only one of which, usually, was his; the rest belonged to the outfit. They were all geldings; a stallion was too wild for the job and no American would ride a mare, though the Mexicans did. Mares, stallions, and foals ran free on the range, subject to occasional roundup for branding, gelding colts, and selecting young horses to be broken and trained.

Western horse breaking wasted no time in gentling. The animal was roped and thrown and held down by a knee on his neck and a good grip on an ear. A rope halter, called a hackamore and usually equipped with a leather blindfold, was slipped on his head. Even a wild horse is a little cautious if he can't see; and it was a good idea to cover his eyes the first time you saddled him. Before that was tried, the bronco twister stood in the middle of the corral holding a twenty-foot rope with the lunging youngster on its other end wearing himself down. When he was good and tired, they slipped the blinder of the hackamore over his eyes and tried throwing a saddle on him, and after enough tries they got it on and cinched it up tight. The twister mounted, sometimes in a jump from the corral fence, and the horse went into a mad convulsion that was really a frenzy of fright. He "swallowed his head" (threw it between his forelegs), bucked straight up, and came down with all four legs stiff; he stood on his hind legs and

Sunfishing

shook himself; he "sunfished" with all four legs to one side in mid-air, anything to rid himself of this appalling burden he didn't understand. Often he threw the rider repeatedly, and often the rider was safer being thrown than staying on, for a bucking horse can turn clear over in the air and fall on a man.

Some horses needed little breaking, and a few could never be ridden; but the average pony put up his fight, lost, and then submitted to instruction in the niceties of the cow profession. He learned that he was "tied to the ground" and must stand where he was when his reins hung from his bit in front of him; he learned to do his part of the roping rite without command. If he were especially apt, he was given post-graduate study as a cutting horse. He learned some things on his own, too: how to get over the ground by "crow hopping" when his forelegs were tied together with a hobble; how to hide behind the other horses in the corral when he knew he was wanted for work.

COWHANDS

Except in songs, they seldom called themselves "cowboys," but then, a lot of people are called things they don't call themselves. "Cowpuncher" and "cowpoke," too, they first called each other in comic derision, but only after the railroad came west. A cowpuncher, armed with a long pole, urged cows up the runways to cattle cars; a cowpoke thrust a similar pole between the slats of the cars to persuade reclining animals to stand up and avoid being killed by their fellows. "Cowhand," and more often, just "hand" was the range word. "Buckaroo," for cowhand, was the best Wyoming and Montana could do with *vaquero*.

The typical hand was young, bowlegged, easygoing, and cheerful. He was fearless, even reckless, but he was rarely lawless. He was healthy and strong; the work quickly weeded out weaklings. His reputation for taciturnity, like the Indian's, was given him by strangers; with his friends the cowhand was lively, chatty, and heartily coarse. He made twenty or twenty-five dollars a month (and keep), paid in gold and silver coins which he kept in a drawstring "poke" made of leather; he

had seen what happened to Confederate paper money and he wanted no part of it. Some few range men saved their money and in time became ranchers, but most, like the old Ring-tailed Roarers and the forty-niners, "shot the works" in town as soon as they were paid off. The town welcomed them with crooked gamblers, bad whisky, and bad women.

The costume of the cowboy, at least a glamorized version of it, is as familiar to an American as the clothes he wears himself. Until Buffalo Bill Cody advertised the glamour with his Wild West Show—the "Bill Show," the range called it—the simple cowhand didn't realize he was picturesque. His clothes were those best suited to his work, though undoubtedly they owed something to the Mexicans. The "cow crowd" in Texas in the late sixties wore felt hats with flat crowns, much like the Mexican *poblano*. John B. Stetson didn't make his first "ten gallon John B." until 1865, and it took a couple of years to get from Philadelphia to the Plains. Texans wore tough jackets to protect them from brush. Who ever saw a cowboy in a coat?

Leather chaps were necessary, too, in that thorn thicket; the boys wore them over levis tucked into boots. Levi Strauss started making "choke bar-

relled," copper-riveted, blue canvas pants in San Francisco in 1849. The Mexican vaquero put leather flaps on his saddle to throw over his legs; he called them *armas*. Sometimes he wore *armitas*, separate leather aprons of boot-top length for each leg. Chaps (pronounced shaps) may have come from these as has been claimed, but the fact remains that chaps were almost identical to the long leather leggings of the American Indians; some were even fringed down the outside edges. Like the leggings, the two legs were entirely separate,

Stetson

covering the fronts and outsides of the legs but leaving the seat of the levis and the backs of the thighs exposed. "Shotgun" chaps were seamed into tubes from lower thigh to ankle, but buckles or snap hooks served better than sewing. Either way, a flap hung free down the outside of the leg; it might be only an inch or so wide and orna-

Batwing and shotgun chaps; levis

the heels started when cowhands still rode with the ball of the foot on the stirrup. Texas spurs, too, were chiefly ornamental; their rowels, though large, were blunt. The cow horse seldom felt them, but his rider always wore them, even for dancing. He wore horsehide or buckskin gauntlets, too, when he was working, to protect his hands from his rope, but he stuffed them into his belt on social occasions.

SADDLES AND EQUIPMENT

The cowhand's most important possession was his saddle; it was his workbench and his home, so he bought the best one he could possibly afford. The early Mexican Texans used a version of the Spanish civilian saddle for punching cattle, and Americans developed a further modification of it. This saddle had a high, slender horn, but the cantle was almost as low as that of an English saddle. They rode it with short stirrup leathers that kept their knees bent. The later California vaqueros followed the style of the Spanish war saddle that came to America with the conquistadors and had for a grandfather the saddle of a medieval knight. It was a heavy affair, but it provided both warrior and cowhand with a solid working platform on which to stay put under stress. The knight found he could best handle his weapons if he rode with his legs straight and his feet thrust far into his stirrups, and when the cowboy took over the California saddle, as he did in time from border to border, he came to ride the same way for

mented with a row of washers or it might be a flaring "bat wing." Most cowhands wore chaps made of cowhide with the hair removed; but up north a good many made themselves comfortable with calf skin, sheep skin, even bear skin, worn hairy-side out. A man needed no chaps at all on the open grassland in good weather; he contented himself with leather patches on the seat of his levis and on the horse-side of the knees where they would do the most good.

The cowboy's neck bandanna, knotted in front or behind, could keep his chin warm on a cold night or strain dust out of the air when the cows were on the move, but chiefly he wore it for a collar. Shirts with attached collars didn't exist, though they had years before, and a long neck looked gawky sticking up above a low shirtband. His inevitable vest may have been a survival of the Mexican's short jacket, but it *was* short, which was desirable in the saddle, and it could be bought ready-made; it also left the arms free and provided something to carry pockets, then unheard-of in a shirt. The tight, ornamented boots with underslung high heels that all but crippled an early cowboy on the ground had no excuse but vanity. The tightness made the foot look trim, and the high heel made the man a little taller. Cutting the heel under, however, did nothing but interfere with walking. The story of the heel preventing the foot from slipping through the stirrup won't wash;

Texas saddle with two cinches

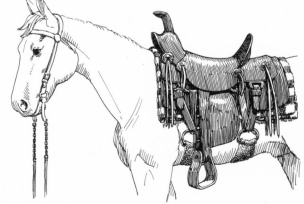
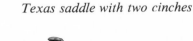

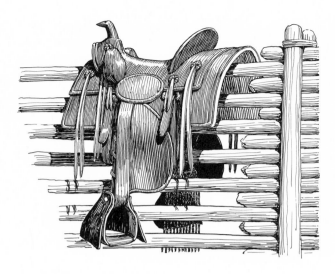

Standard Western saddle

the same reason. He also found it more comfortable, though it countered the theory and practice of all other horsemen of his time.

Different sections and times varied details, but there came to be a typical Western saddle. Its leather covering was stretched over a shaped wood frame and it weighed almost forty pounds. Its seat was wide and comfortable and often ventilated by a slot; its cantle was high and strong to provide back support; its wooden "fork" gave purchase to the rider's legs and was surmounted by a steel horn that acted as a snubbing post for a cow or a towing bit for helping a stuck wagon. Two skirts surrounded the saddle proper, the upper one a continuation of the saddle covering, the lower and larger one lined with wool to add to the padding of the folded blanket that lay between saddle and horse. Just under the edge of the upper skirt, on each side, there were two rings (sometimes only one) for the straps (*latigos*) with which the wide bellyband, or cinch, was tightened and secured with a knot that looked somewhat like that of a four-in-hand tie. The stirrup leathers had wide wings attached to them to take the rub of the rider's legs. The stirrups of the original California saddle were housed in big leather *tapideros;* when standard Western stirrups were housed at all, the hoods seldom had any extra projections.

The various tie-strings on the saddle looked at a glance like ornaments, but they had practical uses. One pair held the coiled lariat on the fork; those on the back of the upper skirt secured a slicker

151

and sometimes a blanket and a tarpaulin as well. The slicker was a loose coat, with appropriate slits, that covered man and saddle together. It and the tarp were made of cotton cloth soaked in linseed oil. They were either soft and sticky or stiff and brittle, depending on temperature, but they shed water.

In times of trouble a cowhand tied a scabbard to his saddle, under his right leg, and put into it the kind of short-barreled rifle that is called a carbine. At nearly all times he carried a big revolver in a holster hung from a cartridge belt, but not because he wanted to shoot anybody. There was little gun fighting on the range, for the killers stayed in towns. The cowhand's gun was a toy to him, but it was useful, too. He shot at everything: flies on the bunkhouse ceiling, wolves, coyotes, prairie dogs, rattlesnakes, and above all, skunks. Western skunks were prone to rabies and made trouble for cows and horses. A cowboy lived in horror of an infected one crawling into his blankets on a cold night. It happened, with tragic results.

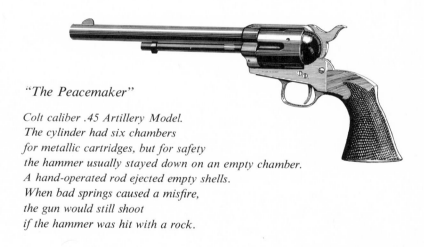

"The Peacemaker"

Colt caliber .45 Artillery Model.
The cylinder had six chambers
for metallic cartridges, but for safety
the hammer usually stayed down on an empty chamber.
A hand-operated rod ejected empty shells.
When bad springs caused a misfire,
the gun would still shoot
if the hammer was hit with a rock.

Normally, shooting near a bunch of cattle was a bad idea, but sometimes a shot fired behind a balked herd would start them moving, or a shot might turn a stampede and start the animals milling. The range hand was seldom an expert marksman. He did snap shooting, without sighting the gun, by placing his forefinger along the barrel and squeezing the trigger with his middle finger. His gun wasn't always a Colt, but a good many times it was; at first, one of the .44 caliber, chamber-loading percussion models—like the Texas or the Walker—later, the 1873 Single-action Army .45—the famous "Peacemaker"—firing metallic cartridges.

Cowhands at work tended to be careless about personal cleanliness and neatness. Most faces were permanently bearded in early days, and shaving was an infrequent ritual later on. A man might not do any noticeable bathing, but he would, now and again, spread his clothes on an anthill to have the "pants rats" removed from them. There was a bunkhouse at the ranch, but many nights the cowboy slept on the ground, removing his gun belt and his boots and rolling up in a blanket or quilt, with his tarp spread underneath and his saddle or his "war bag" for a pillow. The war bag was a canvas sack for his personal belongings. In the morning he threw it and his bedroll into the chuck wagon and ambled around to the tailgate for a tin cup of hot coffee and a hunk each of bread and steak which he sat on the ground to eat. As he rode along to work, he dreamed of a bellyful of green garden "sass."

Colonel Charles Goodnight invented the chuck wagon in Texas. Like most great inventions it was simple. Into the back of an ordinary wagon body, the colonel built a tall box with a drop door which he provided with two hinged legs to make it a worktable when it was lowered. This traveling pantry had on its shelves flour, corn meal, brown sugar, coffee in the bean, bacon, lard, salt fatback, and a firkin of sourdough for raising biscuits. The coffeepot stood in the cooking fire embers twenty-four hours a day. In the body of the wagon along with the branding irons and the bedrolls and war bags of the outfit, the cook stowed his pothooks, skillet, stewpot, Dutch oven (bake kettle, just like the one in the log cabin), and the tin cups and plates and iron knives, forks, and spoons his customers used. Water rode in a cask on the side of the wagon. The cook collected fuel wherever he could find any, in a cowhide slung under the vehicle and known as the possum belly. The cook was usually elderly; to the hands he was "coosie," "old woman," "pot wrangler," "gut robber," or any of a dozen other unflattering names; but he was a respected autocrat and father confessor to the outfit.

Chuck wagon

"BLEEDING KANSAS" AND HOMESTEADING

With the Kansas-Nebraska Act of 1854 Congress established two territories across the whole of the Great Plains from the Missouri River to the Rocky Mountains: Kansas between 37° and 40° north latitude, Nebraska from 40° to the Canadian border. The Act ended the last limp pretense of an Indian frontier and wiped out the Missouri Compromise, replacing it with "popular sovereignty" that allowed each new state to decide the slavery question for itself. Abolutionists and slaveowners at once started campaigns to "save Kansas"—with few holds barred.

New Englanders founded towns, to the ultimate benefit of the state, and the congregation of Dr. Henry Ward Beecher's church in Brooklyn sent them Bibles and rifles. It is said that the rifle boxes were sometimes marked "Bibles." Nebraska was nearly empty, but slaveholders squatted in Kansas before it was a territory; more of the same from Missouri reinforced them. For some years all Kansas elections were rigged, sometimes yielding two votes per voter. Missourians crossed the border to mark an illegal ballot for slavery. A proslavery mob sacked the abolitionist town of Lawrence; John Brown (he of the moldering body) and four of his sons murdered five men in retaliation. In the end, on the second try, Kansas came into the Union as a free state in 1861.

President Lincoln signed the Homestead Act in 1862. Under it, any adult citizen or intended citizen, male or female, could "take up" a quarter-section (160 acres) or an eighth-section (80 acres), depending on the quality and location of the land, by paying a ten-dollar recording fee. Lacking convenient trees to blaze, surveyors marked section corners with four holes, one in each corner, and drove a stake into a mound between them. The homesteader had to live on his land, cultivate it, and make certain minimum improvements; at the end of five years the place was his, free.

18

THE SODBUSTERS AND THE
CATTLE DRIVES

SETTLERS FLOODED into Kansas and Nebraska after the Civil War. The torrent slowed with the panic of 1873 and swelled again in the late seventies and early eighties, spilling over into the Dakotas, Colorado, and even Oklahoma, where it had no legal right to go. Most of the settlers claimed land under the Homestead Act, but some bought it by pre-emption; the more prosperous paid four dollars an acre and up—with ten-year credit—for railroad land, preferred because of its nearness to transportation. The railroads pushed the sale of their vast holdings by advertising and brought in organized groups of Europeans.

SODDIES

Cottonwood trees grew along watercourses; otherwise the Plains grew only grass in age-old sod that was a compact mass of matted roots. A family couldn't live forever in its wagon and the Homestead Act required a house; but there wasn't enough wood for a house. The Mandan and the Pawnee Indians solved the problem with earth lodges and the white men did the same; they cut the sod into blocks and laid up walls with it as bricks are laid—Nebraska marble, they called it. If they could find a bank, they dug the back of the house into it, building only the front and part of the side walls of sod. Poles for roof rafters came from a river bank and on them the builders spread brush, grass, and more sod. The floor was dirt. Canvas or leather made a door, and anything but glass covered a window. A ditch across the bank behind the dugout and down the slope on either side prevented a complete washout, but the roofs of dugouts and of four-walled "soddies," too, leaked so badly that people customarily hung small tents over their beds. Even in dry weather, dirt falling from the roof got over and into everything; women loathed the soddies. Dirt wasn't all that fell; there were also bugs and mice and sometimes a cow wandered onto a dugout roof and suddenly joined the family below.

A soddy was cool in summer, and warm in winter if you could find fuel to create a little heat

154

inside. Wood was out of the question. Buffalo chips at first and later cow chips would do if you could get enough of them, and cornstalks and cobs were fair. But lacking any of these things, you made do with bundles of dry grass laboriously gathered. Grass burned fast, so a great quantity of it had to be stored, which was dangerous because the fuel bin might catch fire. Special grass-burning stoves existed, but few could afford them; you stuffed the fuel into a metal cylinder and a spring pushed it into the firebox; you were forever stuffing and changing cylinders.

WATER

Water was even more a problem than fuel. At first it was hauled long distances from streams; then people began to dig wells. A forty-foot well was deep in the East; in the Plains region few were shallower than a hundred feet and some went down three hundred feet. When you dig that deep by hand you labor, and aside from the actual

digging and the slow winching out of dirt, you face the danger of cave-ins and of suffocating and even of explosive gases. If digging looked hopeless, the settler could try boring from the surface with a post-hole auger, lengthening its shaft in sections as the hole deepened. Or he could drive a well with a heavy maul, banging on the end of a specially hardened pipe armed with a steel point. Pipe and point stayed in the ground, so a section near the bottom had holes in it to admit water once it reached any. A well could also be drilled.

If he decided to drill and couldn't afford to hire a man with a steam rig, the sodbuster could "jig" one down with a weighted drill bit hung by a rope from a springy pole, just as the pestle of the old hominy block was hung. The pole raised the bit, and the driller brought it down by stepping up into a stirrup that also hung from the pole tip. He had to jig many a time and stop many a time, too, to hawl up his drill with a windlass and fish out the earth he loosened with a gadget called a sand pump.

When, one way or another, the homesteader

Dugout soddy

struck water, he had still to bring it to the surface. He could use a bucket in a dug well on the same windlass that had brought up the excavated dirt, but with a driven or drilled well he *had* to have a pump, even though a good iron pump cost money. He could pump by hand, but there was one thing the Plains had in plenty—wind. And wind could pump water. Everybody had a windmill as soon as he could buy one or make one. Any man of a slight mechanical turn could build a windmill. He needed a tower, not a very high one on the flat Plains, with a fan four to ten feet in diameter mounted on it, and a vane behind the fan to keep it headed into the wind. The fan blades might be many and narrow or few and wide, so long as they were angled to the wind; in short, it worked like an electric fan in reverse. A crank on the fan shaft raised and lowered a long rod to work the pump. The windmill creaked, squeaked, and thumped, but nobody minded—it was bringing up water.

The eastern half of both Kansas and Nebraska can count on an average of twenty inches of rain a year. This was enough for hard winter wheat, and the homesteaders in those sections prospered. The miraculous McCormick reaper came into Kansas as early as 1854; it could harvest more grain in a day than could ten men with cradles. At first the grain had to be raked from it by hand, but by 1880 its successor delivered neat bundles ready

for the new "thrashing machine" that was powered by five teams of horses pulling at the arms of a merry-go-round sweep mounted on a staked-down wagon. In another five years, steam traction engines began to replace the sweeps.

The western half of both Kansas and Nebraska can count on an average of no more than fifteen inches of rain a year. This is enough for grass but for little else without irrigation. Some optimist announced that "rainfall follows the plow," that is, once the sod was broken, the ground would absorb moisture and create rain. He was exactly wrong, but hundreds swallowed his idea and took up land in the seventies beyond and way beyond the fifteen-inch line. They struck a series of wet years and wrote letters to relatives in the East and in Europe urging them to come to this Eden they had found. Then in 1876, and again in '77, grasshoppers arrived by millions, ate every green thing, and started on the people's clothes. Dry years followed dry years, with far less than fifteen inches of rain. Fields, broken from sod with such labor, blew away as dust. Wells dried up. A slow, tragic procession of the beaten dragged eastward. But some stayed and survived, and as people move back to the slope of a volcano after an eruption, new settlers came in and the whole thing was repeated. This wasn't farm land until it could be irrigated, and it was too soon for that; but it was good cattle country just as it was.

THE CATTLE TRAILS

The eastern half of the United States was almost entirely occupied by 1865, and its growing cities offered profitable markets for food. A steer worth five dollars in Texas brought twenty-five, even forty dollars at times, in Chicago. No railroad ran into Texas, but in 1867 the Kansas and Pacific (which never made it to the Coast) reached Abilene, Kansas, and the first cattle came north over the Chisholm Trail to meet it. Abilene built stock pens, loading ramps, and hotels and boomed four years as the first "cow town." Lurid entertainment enticed the human escorts of the cows, and a floating population moved in to take a cut of the profits. Hard-eyed characters packed hair-trigger six guns in their holsters; slick-fingered gamblers in fancy vests wore their derringers up their sleeves in wrist holsters; damsels who were "not all they should be" wore little knives under ruffled garters. They made a sharp distinction in Abilene between killing in a fight and murder from ambush. The town hired a marshal to enforce some semblance of order. As a young man, a grotesque upper lip earned him the nickname of Duck Bill, but a sweeping mustache and a cool and deadly gun changed it to Wild Bill Hickok.

Longhorns carried ticks infected with Texas fever and the Kansas farmers wanted none of them. They drew a quarantine line and Abilene was east of it; so as the railroad pushed west, the cow town moved too and reached Dodge City, bringing Wild Bill along. Dodge City was almost directly north of San Antonio by the Western Trail which later ran on through to Ogallala, Nebraska, on the Union Pacific. Dodge City was the real cow capital; it flourished from 1875 to 1885.

THE LONG DRIVE

A venturer sending a herd north from Texas on the "long drive," bought up steers and cows from a number of ranchers, getting a bill of sale from each to make sure he could answer questions. As

Springpole drilling rig

The steel bit, welded to a six-foot iron shaft,
hung from the bottom of a long pole made up from jointed sections.
The crossed handles served to rotate the drill from time to time.
The derrick and windlass pulled the rod up for adding a new section,
for sharpening the drill bit, or for clearing the hole.
A sand pump lies in the foreground.

they collected the animals, his men "road branded" them for quick identification in case some rustler made off with a bunch. The stockman might meet the herd at the cow town to attend to the business of shipping them, but he rarely traveled with them. He hired a trail boss to see them through, with six or eight cowhands, a horse wrangler, and a cook. The hands were specialists and made better wages than ranch hands, thirty or forty dollars a month.

The ox-drawn chuck wagon, driven by the cook, led the procession, followed by the *remuda,* or "cavvy" (*caballada*), that is, the spare horses in the charge of the horse wrangler, who did twenty-four-hour duty. Back of the *remuda* trudged the lead steer, often trained to *gee, haw,* and *whoa,* with two or three thousand of his kind strung out behind him. Near the head of the cow column the two point riders ambled along, one on each side; halfway back were the two, sometimes four, swing riders; and in the dust astern, the drag riders kept stragglers up with the herd. The most useful weapons of all these men were long whips. The trail boss ranged free, riding wherever it seemed to him that he could do the most good.

They pushed the herd fast for the first three or four days, twenty-five or thirty miles a day, to tire the animals and get them off their own range so

On the town

they'd be easier to handle. After that, progress was slow, ten or fifteen miles a day. The cattle grazed early in the morning, inching north; then they moved on the trail a few miles and had a drink of water before resting to chew the cud two or three hours at midday. Another two or three miles in the afternoon brought them to the bed ground where they grazed for the night, lulled, it was hoped, by the singing of their guardians who stood regular watches. Calves born on the bed ground had to be given away or killed; they couldn't keep up and the herd couldn't wait for them. Men sometimes started herds of their own by cosseting calves they picked up from passing drives.

There was always the dangerous possibility of stampede, which once started was hard to stop, and a good many men died trying. A river bank was a sensitive spot; the vanguard of cattle might balk at the water and turn aside; a little excitement, created by the effort to head them in, could start them running with the whole herd behind them in crazy flight. Once the first animals started across a stream, the rest would follow, but if they had to swim, some might be lost. If any cows strayed even a little at night, meat-hungry Indians would make off with them. The Indians in Oklahoma exacted a toll for the privilege of passing through their land; it was payable in cattle, though sometimes it was the white Government agent who demanded ten cents a head and pocketed the cash. North of Oklahoma the trail met the "bob-warr" fences of homesteaders. Those who lacked wire would plow a furrow and line up behind it with rifles, defying the herd to cross. They could be pacified with money or with an offer to use their land as bed ground for the night; this they welcomed for the precious fuel that would be left behind.

At the railroad the trail boss delivered the cattle to his employer or to an agent and paid off his hands. They went immediately to a barber who trimmed them into the shape of civilization and perfumed them like the lilies of the field; then they bought complete new outfits of store clothes, even to derbies and paper or enameled tin collars, sought the nearest gin mill, and "turn't loose." One way or another most of them got back to Texas—broke.

Cow punchers

SHEEP

Great herds of sheep survived from Spanish days in New Mexico and California and they spread gradually north to Oregon. As wool yielders they could stay where they were, but as meat the only market for them was in the East. So since sheep can stand long journeys at slow speed and can go waterless for considerable stretches, men with dogs drove great herds, some-times numbering in the thousands, eastward across the mountains and the Great Plains. When they crossed the cattle trails they met hostility and when they came to the homesteads they met more of it.

Sheep crop grass close to the ground; if the grass is short, they sometimes pull the roots. Their great numbers muddied the water holes. Cowhands and farmers alike cherished the fiction that cattle wouldn't eat or drink where sheep had been before them. They defended their own animals by shooting at sheepherders, who shot back. Many sheep died from being stampeded over cliffs and into rivers, or even, sometimes, from poison.

Night riders

"Bobwarr"

BARBED WIRE

A great many cows driven up from Texas went to stock northern ranches. Once shipped, cattle had to be sold for what they would bring. If the market was known to be off, it made sense to hold them on ranges near the railroad until prospects improved. The next step was raising cattle on those ranges. Between 1870 and 1880 the number of beef animals in the five states of Kansas, Nebraska, Wyoming, Montana, and Colorado increased from about 600,000 to over 4 million.

Barbed wire was introduced in 1874 and rapidly dropped in price. At first homesteaders used it to keep range cattle off their claims; then cattlemen used it to fence the range and keep cattle in. Much of the land they fenced wasn't theirs; it was the public domain, but they felt it belonged to them. They ran their wire across public roads and often completely enclosed some poor sodbuster; they also cut off vital water holes so that the cows of small ranchers couldn't reach them. Abused and abusers masked their faces with bandannas, loaded their guns, and as "night riders," cut the fences with long-handled wire cutters. An ugly shooting war went on over wire for years. A national law did little to stop it, because the big ranchers controlled the courts which smugly convicted them and imposed fines of small change. This outrage couldn't last, and when the big outfits finally had to buy range land, they used any and all means to get it: Cowhands registered claims and assigned them to the boss without bothering about resi-dence and improvement formalities; Civil War widows, to whom the Government made special concessions, received small sums for registering claims they never saw.

The dust all settled eventually and neighbors lived peaceably together. A man used his wire cutter only on his own fences, and the ranchers turned to improving the quality of their stock by crossing imported bulls with longhorn cows. They saw the cash advantage of protecting cattle in winter, and cowhands who in old days scorned "ground work" found themselves mowing grass and stacking hay on frames to make storm shelters which the cattle could eat from the inside. Stiff quarantine laws accomplished their real purpose of ending the cattle drives, but by that time the railroads had reached Texas and the concept of ranching had changed there, too. Then the price of beef fell to $2.50 a hundred pounds; and after 1900 many of the northern ranchers raised the sheep that a few years before they had scorned and detested.

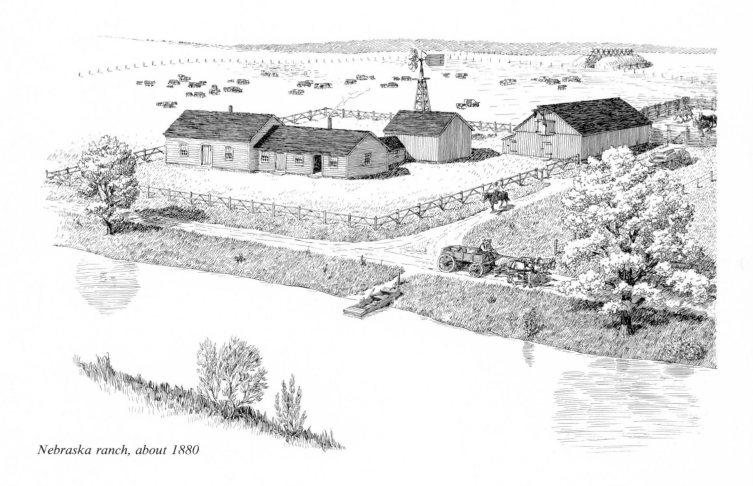

Nebraska ranch, about 1880

19

THE RUN

WHEN THE Indian Territory was parceled out to the tribes that had been forced to go there, some was left over in the Cherokee Strip. It was the last public land worth homesteading. White "boomers" made repeated attempts to squat on it, and the army ejected them year after year. Presently the pressure was too great and a date was established for opening the land to settlement. A hundred thousand people on foot, on horseback, in buckboards and wagons, and even on special railroad trains lined up at the border on April 22, 1889, and at the firing of a noon gun they raced to grab the best they could get. Naturally they found that enterprising "sooners" had sneaked in the back way and staked the prize claims; some of the racers got nothing at all. It took only eight years after that to make a state out of Oklahoma.

The run didn't end frontier living, but the only change in it after that was in the direction of improvement. Men and women still build log cabins on homesteads in Alaska and live rugged lives in them; but if the going gets too bad, they can take a job in town, and when they go into the wilderness the law goes with them.

INDEX

(Asterisks after page numbers refer to illustrations)

Abbott and Downing, 140
Abilene, Kan., 157
Achomawi Indians, 137
Adams, John Quincy, 95
Alabama, 88
Albany, N.Y., 93
Algonquian Indians, 32
Allegheny River, 61
Alta California, 124–29
alum salt, made from wood ash, 36
American Fur Company, 110, 117
    posts of, 111–12
Apache Indians, 139
Appalachian Mountains, 13, 14, 15, 39, 41, 61, 88
Arizona, 136, 142
ark, 63, 64
Arkansas, 98, 142
Articles of Confederation, 60
ash hopper, 80
Ashley, William, 112
Astor, John Jacob, 110, 111
Audubon, John J., 63
Austin, Stephen, 98

Baltimore, Md., 37, 70, 73
Baltimore and Ohio Rail Road, 95, 96
bandanna, 150
Bank of United States, 85, 86
Baptists, in Kentucky, 57
barbed wire, and cattle, 159*, 160
barn, settler's 76–77
barrel, assembling, 55*, 55–56
bear grease, as frontier product, 36
bear meat, 20, 28
beaver hat, 110
beaver meat, 28
beaver trap, 113, 113*
Becknell, William, 103
beef cattle, 52, 159–60
bees, 51
Bell, Tom, 137, 138
bend, river, rounding upstream, 66–67, 67*
Benton, Jessie, 120
Bible, 56
"big wheel," 47, 47*
binding, and cradling, 78, 78*
Birch, Jim, 135, 137, 139
Black Hawk Purchase, 99
Black Hawk War, 68, 99
blacksmith, frontier, 37, 55, 85
Blainville, Céloron de, 41
"block cheer," 22*, 23
blockhouse, 39
bluegrass, Kentucky, 44
bonnet, 82
Book of Mormon, 121
books, in general store, 56
Boone, Daniel, 16, 40, 42, 43, 44, 98
Boone's Trace, 43, 44, 47
Boonesboro, 43
boots, cowhand's, 150
    worn in Old Northwest Territory, 81
Bowie knife, 104*

Braddock, Edward, 41
Braddock's Road, 61, 62
branding iron, for cattle, 146, 146*
bread, 80
breeches, settler's, 29
Bridger, Jim, 113, 120
    fort built by, 117, 118*, 123
broadax, 74, 74*, 75
broom, splint, 48–49, 49*
Brown, John, 153
Buchanan, James, 139
buffalo, 43, 44, 119–20
    slaughter of, 144
Buffalo, N.Y., 91
bullboat, 109, 110*
Bunting, Redding, 73
Bureau of Indian Affairs, 144
bushwhacking, 66, 66*
Butterfield, John, 139, 140, 141

cabbage, 80
cabin, log, 16*, 20–24
cabin door, inside of, 23, 23*
"cabin right," 39
California, 14, 60, 124–29, 142
    gold rush in, 131–35
    and railroads, 142
    stagecoaches in, 137–38
Californios, 125–28
Calk, William, 43
"camp, half-faced," 19, 20*
camps of forty-niners, 134–35
Canada, 14
canal lock, 89*, 92
Cane Ridge, Ky., 83
carbine, 105
Carlisle, Pa., 37
Carolinas, 14, 88. *See also* North Carolina;
    South Carolina.
carpenter, frontier, 55
Carroll, Charles, 95
Carson, Kit, 113, 120
Carson City, Nev., 138, 141
"casa de campo," 126*
Catholics, Roman, in Kentucky, 57
cattle, beef, 52, 159–60. *See also* cowhunt; long-
    horn.
cattle trails, 157
Cave in Rock, 65, 65*
Central Pacific Railroad, 142, 143
Chagres River, 132*
chair, Texas, 98, 98*
chaps, cowhand's 149, 150*
Cherokee Indians, 14, 39, 42, 43, 44
Cherokee Strip, 161
childhood, on frontier, 34–35
Chisholm Trail, 157
chocolate, 80
chopping blade, 50*
Christian Advocate, 114
chuck wagon, 152, 152*, 158
church, log, 40
churn, coopered, 50*
cimarrón cattle, 98, 98*

Cincinnati, Ohio, 93, 96
Cincinnati *Centinal,* 66
Civil War, 105, 141, 142, 145
claims clubs, 101
clapboards, rived, 20, 21, 21*
Clark, George Rogers, 43, 44, 61
Clark, William, 68, 87, 98, 109
Clay, Henry, 73
clearing, in "fur back," 15*
    Kentucky, daily life in, 46ff.
Clermont, 90
Cleveland, Ohio, 69, 91, 93
Clinton, DeWitt, 92
clothes, of *Californios,* 127
    of Eastern settlers, 28–30, 57
    of mountain men, 113
    in Old Northwest Territory, 81–82
    of Western cowhand, 149–50
coach lines, in California, 137–38
    in Old Northwest Territory, 72–73
    for overland mail, 139–40
cobbler, frontier, 55
cockfight, 56
Cody, Buffalo Bill, 149
coffee, 80
Colorado, 136, 142
Colorado River, 132
Colt gun, 104*, 105, 151, 151*
Columbia River, 110, 113, 118
Columbus, Ohio, 71
Comanche Indians, 105
compass, surveyor's, 69*
Comstock Lode, 135, 136*
Concord coach, 140*, 140–41
Conestoga wagon, 70, 71*, 71–72, 103–04
Congregationalists, 114
Connecticut, 60, 62, 69
Continental Divide, 112, 113
conveyor, spiral, 80, 80*
cooking on hearth, 80
cooper, frontier, 55, 56, 85
Cooper, Peter, 95
copperhead, 33
coppersmith, frontier, 85
cordelle, 66, 66*
corn, 25–27, 53, 77
corn bread, 80
corn grater, 25, 25*
cotton, 80
cotton frontier, 88
cotton gin, 88, 88*
cottonwood dugout, 109, 110*
cougar, 44
cowhand, Western, 145, 148–50, 159*
cowhunt, in Texas, 146–47
cows, owned by settlers, 28, 49
cradle, grain, 78, 78*
    log, for baby, 24, 24*
    panning, 133, 133*
cradling, 78, 78*
Cresap, Michael, 35
Cumberland, Md., 70, 95
Cumberland Gap, 41*, 42, 44
Cumberland Road, 62

Custer, George A., 144
cutting horse, 147*, 148

Declaration of Independence, 17, 45, 95
deer, 18, 28, 31, 44
deer hide, as frontier product, 36
Deere, John, 100
Delaware Indians, 32, 43
Delaware River, 15, 32
Demming, Montgomery, 73
Denver, Colo., 136, 141
derringer, 104*
Deseret, State of, 123
Detroit, Mich., 91
Dinwiddie, Robert, 41
Doddridge, Rev., 33
Dodge City, Kan., 157
dogfight, 56
dough trough, 80, 80*
Dow, Crazy, 84
Dragging Canoe, Chief, 43
dragoon, 87*
Drake, Daniel, 45, 47, 49, 58
drilling rig, 155, 157*
Dubuque, Julien, 100
dugout, cottonwood, 109, 110*
Duquesne, Fort, 41
dyeing, 48

Enterprise, 90
Erie, Lake, 41, 62, 91, 92, 93
Erie Canal, 91–93, 92*
erysipelas, early treatment of, 33

Fairfax, Lord, 39
Fall Line, 41
Fallen Timbers, Indians defeated at, 64
farming, in Kentucky, 52–54
    in Old Northwest Territory, 74–79
fence, worm, 52, 52*, 78
ferry service, river, 70–71
fireplace, 80, 80*
Five Civilized Tribes, 88
flatboat, 63, 63*, 64, 64*, 66*, 67
Flathead Indians, 114
flax brake, 46, 46*
flintlock rifle, 16–17, 17*, 105
Florida, 14, 41
footwear, 81, 81*
Forbes, John, 41
Forbes Road, 61
foreclosure sale, 85*, 86
Fort Benton, 111
Fort Boise, 117, 119
Fort Cumberland, 62
    as trading point, 37
    and wagon trail cut by Braddock, 41
Fort Greenville, 68
Fort Laramie, 108*, 111, 117, 141
Fort Loudon, 37
Fort Necessity, 41
Fort Pitt, 41
Fort Union, 111
forts, as defense against Indians, 32–33
forty-niners, 131–36
France, possessions of, 14
    loss of, 41
Frederick Town, Md., 37
freight, in West, 138, 139
freight wagon, 71–72
Frémont, John C., 120, 123
French, as allies of Indians, 32
    in Missouri, 97
French and Indian War, 32, 33, 41
fulling, in Kentucky, 48
Fulton, Robert, 90, 94
fur, as frontier product, 36
fur trade, 109–13

Gadsden Purchase, 129
gear, wooden, 80, 80*
general store, 56
Genesee Road, 91
Genesee Valley, 62
George III, 41
Georgia, 60, 88
Germans, Palatine, 13, 15
Gilroy, John, 128
ginseng root, 36
glut, in rail-splitting, 51*, 52
gold rush, California, 131–35
Golden Spike, 143–44
Goodnight, Charles, 152
grain cradle, 78, 78*
granary, 77–78
Great Migration, 70
Greeley, Horace, 132
gridiron, 25, 25*
gum, dugout, 24, 24*
gunpowder, 35
guns, types of, 104*, 104–05, 151, 151*
gunsmith, frontier, 37, 55

hackamore, 148
Hagerstown, Md., 37
"half-faced camp," 19, 20*
Hamilton, Henry, 44
hand mill, 26, 27*
harness maker, frontier, 55
Harris's Ferry, 41
Harrisburg, Pa., 37
    and trail cut by Forbes, 41
Harrison, William Henry, 70
Harrison Land Act, 70
Harrod, James, 43
hat, 30, 82
    beaver, 110
    Stetson, 149, 149*
"hating out," 34, 34*
hay, 54, 77
Henderson, Richard, 42, 43
"hetchel," 46, 46*
hewing dog, 74, 74*
Hickok, Wild Bill, 157
hoe, 53
Holliday, Ben, 140, 141, 142
Hollidaysburg, Pa., 94
Homestead Act, 153, 154
hominy, 26
hominy block, 25, 26*
honey, 51
horse, Western, 147–48
housekeeping, in Kentucky, 48–50
    in Old Northwest Territory, 79–80
Houston, Sam, 99
Hudson River, 32, 92, 93
Hudson's Bay Company, 112
Humboldt River, 132
hunting, by frontiersman, 30–31
hunting shirt, 29, 81
husking pin, 53, 53*
Hutton, Finley, 74

Illinois, 44
Independence, Mo., 102–03*, 104, 115, 117, 121
Indian Territory, 144, 161
Indiana, 68, 93
Indians, 32, 33, 44, 45, 64, 118
    Five Civilized Tribes of, 88
    furs supplied by, 112
    and mission fathers, 125
    stagecoaches attacked by, 141
    treaties with, 68, 87, 99
    See also names of specific tribes.
infare, 59
inns, along National Road, 73–74

Iowa, 101
    squatters in, 100, 101
Iowa River, 99
Iroquois Indians, 14, 32, 62

Jackson, Andrew, 88
James River, 13
Jamestown Island, Va., 13
jeans, 80
Jefferson, Thomas, 68, 92, 98
jerky, 28
johnnycake, 27
Johnstown, Pa., 94
Juniata River, 61
justice, frontier, 34, 57

Kansas, 105, 117, 142, 153, 154, 156
Kansas and Pacific Railroad, 157
Kansas-Nebraska Act of 1854, 153
Kaskaskia, Ill., 44, 97
keelboat, 65*, 65–66
Kelley, Hall J., 115
Kenton, Simon, 45
Kentucke Gazette, 57
Kentucky, 42–43, 44–59
    daily life in clearings, 46ff.
    housekeeping in, 48–50
    outdoor work in, 51–52
    Saturday in villages of, 56–57
    schools in, 57–58
    social occasions in, 58–59
    Sunday in villages of, 57
    trades practiced in, 55
    villages of, 54
    weaving in, 47–48
Kentucky rifle, 16–17, 17*
kettle, bake, 25, 25*
Kirtland, Ohio, 121
Kittanning Path, 61
knives, as weapons, 104*

Labrador, 14
Laclède, Pierre, 97
Lancaster, Pa., 16
    as trading point, 37
land, public, 69–70
lariat, 146
Larkin, Thomas, 129
Lathyrus polymorphus, 44
lead mining, in Missouri, 97
leather-making, 30
LeBoeuf, Fort, 41
Lee, Jason, 114, 115
levis, cowhand's, 149, 150*
Lewis, Meriwether, 68, 87, 98, 109
linen, 46–47, 48, 80
linsey, 29
linsey-woolsey, weaving, 48, 48*
"little wheel," 46*, 47
lock, canal, 89*, 92
log cabin, 16*, 20–24
logs, saddle-notched, for cabin, 21, 21*
Long, Stephen, 87
"long drive," 157–58
longhorn, 145–46
Los Angeles, 14, 139
Louis XV, 41
Louisiana, 14, 98
Louisiana Purchase, 68
Louisville, Ky., 64, 90, 91

McIntire tavern, 73*, 74
mackinaw, 109, 110, 110*
McLoughlin, John, 117
mail, overland, 139–40
Maine, 98
Mandan Indians, 154
"Manifest Destiny," 129

map of United States (1790), 60
maple syrup, 50, 51
Marietta, Ohio, 60, 69
marksmanship, teaching, 35
Marshall, James Wilson, 131, 132
Maryland, 37, 60
mat hook, 54, 54*
maul, in rail-splitting, 51, 51*
Mays Lick, Ky., 54, 56, 57
Maysville, Ky., 70
medicine, 33, 36
melon, 80
Methodists, 57, 84
Mexican War, 129
Mexico, 14, 98, 125
Miami Canal, 92*, 93
Michigan, 98
Migration, Great, 70
mining, gold, 130*, 131–35
        lead, 97
        silver, 136, 136*
Mission of San Luis Rey de Francia, 124–25*
missionaries, in West, 114–20 pass.
missions, in Alta California, 124–25
Mississippi, 88
Mississippi River, 14, 64, 66, 67, 68, 88, 90,
    93, 96, 99, 100, 142
Missouri, 97–98, 142, 153
Missouri Compromise, 98
Missouri River, 14, 98, 109, 111, 122, 138
Mobile, Ala., 88
moccasin, 29, 29*
Mohawk River, 91
molasses, 50, 80
money, in frontier life, 56, 85–86
Monongahela River, 41, 61, 62
Monroe, James, 68
Montana, 136
Monterey, Calif., 126, 128, 129, 131
moonshiner, 78
Mormons, 86, 121–23
mountain men, 112, 113
mud wagon, 137*
musket, 105
Muskingum River, 69, 70
mustang, 127, 147

Natchez, 80, 90
Natchez Trace, 64
National Road, 70, 71, 71*, 72, 74, 93
Nauvoo, 121, 121*, 122, 123
navigation, 63–64
        steam, 90–96
        upstream, 66–67
Nebraska, 117, 153, 154, 156
        ranch in, 160*
Nevada, 129, 132, 135, 136, 137, 139, 141
New Harmony, 86, 86*
New Mexico, 142
New Orleans, 14, 50, 64, 68, 80, 88, 90, 91
New Orleans (steamboat), 90
New York, 62, 93
New York Herald, 142
New York State Barge Canal, 93
Newfoundland, 14, 41
Nez Percé Indians, 114, 115, 144
Niagara River, 91
night rider, 159, 160*
North Carolina, 39, 40, 42
Northwest Ordinance, 60, 97
Northwest Territory, Old. See Old Northwest
    Territory.

oats, 77
Ohio, 68, 69, 70, 74, 93, 95
Ohio Canal, 93
Ohio Company of Associates, 69

Ohio River, 32, 41, 44, 50, 60, 63, 64, 66, 67,
    69, 70, 90, 91
    Falls of, 64
    Forks of, 41, 62
Oklahoma, 144, 158, 161
Old Northwest Territory, 44, 60, 68, 69–86,
    110
        clothes worn in, 81–82
        coach lines in, 72–73
        farming in, 74–79
        housekeeping in, 79–80
        inns in, 73–74
        money used in, 85–86
        National Road in, 70, 71, 71*, 72, 74
        people of, 82*, 82–83
        public land in, 69–70
        religion in, 83–84
        towns of, 84–85
Oldtown, Md., 37
Omaha, Neb., 142, 143
Omaha Indians, 122
onion, 80
Ordinance of 1785, 60
Oregon, 110, 113, 114, 115, 118, 120, 129
Oregon Trail, 116–18, 123
Orleans, 90, 90*
oven, 80, 80*
overland mail, 139–40
Owen, Robert, 86
oxen, 100–01

pack train, 36–37, 138
packet boat, 92*, 93
packsaddle, 35*, 36
pail, dugout, 24, 24*
Palatine Germans, 13, 15
panning, for gold, 133, 133*
panther meat, 28
Parker, Samuel, 114, 115, 120
Parkersburg, W. Va., 95
passenger pigeon, 28
patrón, 106–07, 107*
Pawnee Indians, 154
"Peacemaker," 151, 151*
"peavine," 44
peddler, 55
Penn, William, 13
Pennsylvania, 15, 37, 69
Pennsylvania Dutch, 15, 72
Pennsylvania Road, 61
Pennsylvania System, 93–94
peon, 107, 107*
percussion rifle, 105, 106
pewter, 37, 50
Philadelphia, 15, 16, 93, 94
Piedmont plateau, 15–16
pig, as food animal, 27
Pike, Zebulon, 103
Pike's Peak, 136
Pilgrim's Progress, 56
Pioneer Fast Line, 93, 94*
Pioneer Stage Line, 137
piracy, 65
pirogue, 67, 67*
pistol, Colt, 104*, 105, 151, 151*
Pittsburgh, 37, 41, 61–65 pass., 70, 73, 80, 90,
    93, 94
placer mining with "long tom," 130*
Plains Indians, 144
Platte River, 112, 113, 117, 136, 138
    fording, 117, 117*
plow, 52*, 53, 77
Polk, James K., 129
Pony Express, 139, 141–42
porcupine, 28
Portage Railway, 94
Portolá, Gaspar de, 124
Portsmouth, Ohio, 93

possum, 28
potash, made from wood ash, 36
potato, 80
Potawatomi Indians, 122
pothook, wooden, 24*, 25
Potomac River, 94
potpie, 28
potter, frontier, 85
powder horn, 29*, 30
prairie schooner, 116, 116*
prairie vetchling, 44
Preemption Act, 101
Presbyterians, 57, 84, 114
Presque Isle, 80
public land, 69–70
pueblo of Nuestra Señora la Reina de los An-
    geles, 126*
pumpkin, 50
Putnam, Rufus, 69

Quakers, 15
Quebec, 41
quern, 26, 27*
quilting party, 58

railroads, early, 94–96, 142–44, 157
rail-splitting, 51
rake, wooden flop, 77, 77*
Rappists, German, 86
rattlesnake, 33
reaper, McCormick, 156
Redstone Old Fort, 62
religion, in Kentucky, 57
    in Old Northwest Territory, 83–84
Revolutionary War, 15, 28
revolver, 104*
rifle, flintlock, 16–17, 17*, 105
    percussion, 105, 106
Ring-tailed Roarer, 45, 58, 67, 113
Rio Grande River, 103, 129
rivermen, 67
rivers, trade on, 64
Robertson, James, 42
Rocky Mountain Fur Company, 111, 112
rodeo, 127
rolling up, of cabin walls, 20–21, 22*
Roman Catholics, in Kentucky, 57
Roosevelt, Nicholas, 90
rope hobble, 118, 118*
Rush, Benjamin, 17
Russell, Majors & Waddell, 139, 141
rye, 54, 77

saddle, cowhand's, 150, 150*, 151, 151*
St. Clair, Arthur, 60
St. Louis, 71, 97, 98, 110, 111, 112, 140
    Through Line to, 95*, 96
sala, of patrón's house, 106, 106*
Salt Lake City, 122*, 123, 138, 139, 141
salt licks, Kentucky, 44
    Missouri, 98
San Antonio, Tex., 98, 139
San Diego, Calif., 126, 128, 139
San Francisco, Calif., 140, 141
Sandusky, Ohio, 95
Santa Anna, Antonio López de, 99
Sante Fe, 103–06 pass., 106*, 107, 132
Santa Fe Trail, 105
sausage gun, 50*
sawmill, 75*, 76, 85
schools, Kentucky, 57–58
Scioto Company, 69
Scotch-Irish immigrants, 13, 15
Scott, Winfield, 99, 129
scythe, 53*, 54, 77
seft, 54, 54*
Serra, Junípero, 124, 125
Seven Years' War, 32, 33, 41

165

Sevier, John, 42
Shakers, 86
Shaw, Joshua, 104
Shawnee Indians, 32, 43
sheep, 47, 159
Shippensburg, Pa., 37
shirt, hunting, 29, 81
shivaree, 59*, 83
shoemaker, frontier, 81
shoepack, 29*, 30
shoes, 81
shooting match, 35
shot pouch, 29*, 30
Shreve, Henry, 91
sickle, 54, 54*
silver mining, 136, 136*
Sioux Indians, 144
Sitting Bull, 144
skillet, iron, 25, 25*
Smith, Joseph, 121, 122
smokehouse, 79, 80
snag, as danger to navigation, 63–64, 65
snakebite, remedy for, 33
Snake River, 114, 118
snake root, 36
snakes, menace of, 33
snow shed, in mountains, 144*
soap, made by housewife, 49
soddy, 154–55, 156*
South Carolina, 95
South Pass, 113, 117, 120, 123, 132, 138
Spain, possessions of, 14
    loss of, 96
Spalding, Henry and Eliza, 114
spice, 80
spinning wheel, 30, 47
spoon, wooden, 24, 25*
squared-log house, 74, 75*
squash, 80
squatter, 69, 70, 91
    Iowa, 100, 101
squirrel, shooting, 28
Stanford, Leland, 143
stationery, 56
steam navigation, 90–96
Stearns, Abel, 129
Stetson, John B., 149
stewpot, 25, 25*
still, 78–79, 79*
stirrup, 35*, 151
store, general, 56
Stourbridge Lion, 95
Strauss, Levi, 149
straw hat, of frontiersman, 30, 82

Studebaker, John, 138
sugar, 80
"sunfishing," 148, 148*
Susquehanna River, 15, 16, 61, 94
Sutter, John, 129, 131
Sutter's Fort, 131*
Swedish settlers, 15
Sweetwater River, 112, 113, 117, 120, 123

tanner, frontier, 55, 85
Taylor, Zachary, 129
tea, 50
Tennessee, 42, 88
Texas, 60, 98–99, 139, 142, 145, 146, 157, 160
theft, punishment for, 34
Thompson, Snowshoe, 138, 144
threshing, 54
Through Line to St. Louis, 95*, 96
tinker, frontier, 54*, 55
Tippecanoe, Battle of, 68
Tirador, Chino, 131
Toledo, Ohio, 93
Tom Thumb locomotive, 95
tomahawk, 35
tomahawk claims, 44
trade, fur, 109–13
    and ranchos, 127–28
    on rivers, 64
    in Santa Fe, 107
Transylvania Company, 42
trap, beaver, 113, 113*
    wolf, 31, 31*
Treaty of 1819, 96
Treaty of Paris, (1763), 41
trencher, wooden, 24, 25*
truck patch, 80
tub mill, 40, 40*
turkey, wild, 20, 28
turnip, 49, 80

Union Pacific Railroad, 142, 143, 157
United States, map of (1790), 60
Utah, 23

Vandalia, Ill., 71
vaquero, 127, 150
Venango, Fort, 41
venison, 20
Vera Cruz, 103, 106, 129
Vincennes, Ind., 44, 61
Virginia, 39, 42, 43, 60

Wabash and Erie Canal, 93
wagon train, organization of, 115–16

Walk-in-the-Water, 91, 91*
Walla Walla River, 115, 118
walnut bark, as medicine, 33
War of 1812, 70, 82, 86, 110
warping, in upstream navigation, 66, 67*
Warriors' Path, 43
Washington, George, 41
Washington (steamboat), 91
Washoe, 135, 138
Watauga River, 42
water supply, in Old Northwest Territory, 78–79
    of sodbusters, 155–56
Watson, Elkanah, 92
Wayne, Mad Anthony, 64, 68
weaving, 47–48, 48*
wedding, 58–59, 83
wedge, in rail-splitting, 51, 51*
Wells, Fargo & Company, 141
Western Reserve, of Connecticut, 60, 62, 69
Western Trail, 157
wheat, 54, 77, 80
wheat bread, 80
"wheel, big," 47, 47*
    "little," 46*, 47
Wheeling, W. Va., 70, 73, 74
wheelwright, frontier, 55
whetstone, 54, 54*
whisky, 28, 37, 57, 59, 78
Whitman, Marcus, 114–18 pass.
Whitney, Eli, 46, 88
Wilderness Trail, 43, 61
Willamette River, 114, 118
windlass, cooper's, 55, 55*
Wisconsin, 110
witchcraft, 33–34
wolf trap, 31, 31*
woodcraft, learning, 34
wooding up, for river steamers, 91, 91*
woodpecker, 18
woodshed, 79
wool, 47, 80
wool card, 47, 47*
worm fence, 52, 52*, 78
Wounded Knee Creek massacre, 144
Wyoming, 112, 117

Yellowstone River, 111
Yellowstone (steamboat), 111, 112*
Young, Brigham, 122, 123

Zane, Ebenezer, 70
Zane's Trace, 70
Zanesville, Ohio, 70, 74

A floating gristmill on the Ohio River, about 1830

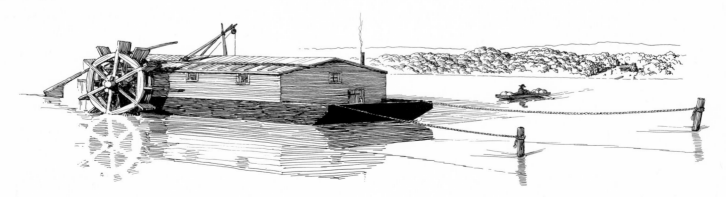

ABOUT THE AUTHOR

Edwin Tunis has a distinguished reputation as an artist, illustrator, and muralist. His articles have appeared in various magazines and he has exhibited at the Baltimore Museum of Art, Society of American Etchers, National Academy of Design, Victoria and Albert Museum, and many other galleries. His most ambitious art project was a mural depicting the History of Spices, which is 145 feet long and took two and a half years to paint.

The study of American history was always one of Mr. Tunis' passions, and it was natural for him to combine this interest with his art to produce the superb books of American social history for which he is famous. Among these are *Frontier Living,* which was first runner-up for the Newbery Medal; *Colonial Living,* which won the Thomas A. Edison Award; *Oars, Sails and Steam,* which was chosen by the A.I.G.A. as one of the "Fifty Books of the Year"; *Wheels,* which won the Gold Medal of the Boy's Clubs of America; and *The Young United States: 1783-1830,* which was nominated for the National Book Award in 1970.